WHAT FOLKLORISTS DO

WHAT FOLKLORISTS DO

Professional Possibilities in Folklore Studies

Edited by
TIMOTHY LLOYD

INDIANA UNIVERSITY PRESS

This book is a publication of

Indiana University Press
Office of Scholarly Publishing
Herman B Wells Library 350
1320 East 10th Street
Bloomington, Indiana 47405 USA

iupress.org

An earlier version of part of the Introduction was published in Timothy Lloyd's essay about the American Folklore Society and the field of folklore studies in *Learned Societies Beyond the Numbers*, a 2016 publication he edited for the American Council of Learned Societies (http://www.acls.org/uploadedFiles /InfoBoxes/Learned_Societies/Learned_Societies_Beyond_web.pdf), and is included here with the permission of the Council.

Manufactured in the United States of America

Library of Congress Cataloging-in-Publication Data

Names: Lloyd, Timothy Charles, editor.
Title: What folklorists do : professional possibilities in folklore studies
    / edited by Timothy Lloyd.
Description: Bloomington, Indiana : Indiana University Press, [2021]
Identifiers: LCCN 2021012952 (print) | LCCN 2021012953 (ebook) | ISBN
    9780253058430 (hardback) | ISBN 9780253058423 (paperback) | ISBN
    9780253058416 (ebook)
Subjects: LCSH: Folklore—Vocational guidance. | Folklore—Study and
    teaching. | Folklorists—Professional relationships.
Classification: LCC GR50 .W43 2021 (print) | LCC GR50 (ebook) | DDC
    398.023—dc23
LC record available at https://lccn.loc.gov/2021012952
LC ebook record available at https://lccn.loc.gov/2021012953

First printing 2021

CONTENTS

ACKNOWLEDGMENTS

I first want to thank those who helped create *Time and Temperature*, the ancestor of this book (see the introduction for details), in 1989: its editor, Charley Camp; its sixteen contributors; and the American Folklore Society's Centennial Coordinating Council, led by Roger Abrahams and Marta Weigle, which commissioned *Time and Temperature* in the first place.

Second, I owe deep gratitude to my teachers Pat Mullen, Francis Lee Utley, John Rheinfrank, John Vlach, Dan Barnes, Bob Byington, Archie Green, Bess Lomax Hawes, D. K. Wilgus, and Joe Wilson, and to the members of the American Folklore Society, past and present, for their generosity in sharing their learning and insight.

Third, I thank my friends and colleagues Ray Cashman, Diane Goldstein, Bill Ivey, Jason Baird Jackson, and Michael Ann Williams (all contributors to this book) for their good counsel on parts of the manuscript and its organization. I'll also cite contributors Ian Brodie and Dorry Noyes, and keen-eyed designer and editor Judy Sacks, each of whom gave me much-needed pieces of advice at just the right time.

Mostly, though, I am in debt to the seventy-seven contributors to this volume for their belief in and commitment to this project, for their willingness to undertake a different sort of thinking and writing assignment, and for sticking with their commitment through an especially difficult year for all of us and for the entire world.

Finally, my thanks go to my wife, Barbara, for her love, wisdom, and support.

INTRODUCTION

Timothy Lloyd

WHY THIS BOOK?

It's hard to go for long these days without being faced with yet another news article or op-ed about the perilous state of the humanities. Enrollments in humanities majors and classes, and job prospects for those with humanities BAs, are trending downward. Jokes and other narratives about humanities PhDs waiting tables or needing to learn how to write code to be seriously employed are never in short supply, but the situation of humanities PhDs who can only find piecemeal academic work without benefits or security is no joke. Within universities there has been much thinking and talking about what an undergraduate or graduate liberal arts degree is good for in the present world: committees and task forces have been created, conferences and symposia held, and reports issued, but the same thorny issues seem to persist.

At the same time, a new narrative has also begun appearing in reports and op-eds in which writers question the data—or the interpretations of the data—of humanities doomsayers. Those writers propose, on the contrary, that the abilities to think critically and pursue qualitative research, listen with openness and interpret with empathy, and deal with complexity and ambiguity—abilities that are at the core of humanities education—are exactly what are most needed in the world today and in the foreseeable future. In the last decade or so, the learned societies that represent fields in the humanities and the humanistic side of the social sciences have been focusing considerable attention on preparing graduate students and early-career professionals in their fields for what are called "alt-ac" positions, which draw upon the core competencies that education in a humanities field provides to offer alternatives to the diminished number of tenure-track faculty positions in the academy.

But I will let you in on a secret: there is a field that has been at this work, quietly but nevertheless successfully, for quite some time—folklore studies. This book, composed of seventy-six essays by folklorists writing personally and informally about their work, is intended to demonstrate many of the present-day outcomes of our field's fifty-year history of engagement with these issues of purpose, usefulness, and public service: in other words, to show what folklorists do, to suggest what you can do in our field, and to evidence what other fields can learn from our experience.

None of this is to say that folklore studies has solved the problems of the diminishing number of tenure-track faculty positions or how to provide support for those who struggle in the academic or public workforces; far from it. These problems are a result of fundamental changes in the last half century across our economy, politics, and society and require comprehensive, sustained attention from many partners, including but not limited to the organizations that serve academic disciplines. People and institutions in our field have achieved some success at carving out new opportunities for productive folklore work and in advocating—as this book does—for the deep relevance of the perspectives of our field across society. But more remains to be done.

The Field of Folklore Studies

In the United States, the field of folklore studies straddles the humanities and the social sciences and is among the earliest organized of the seventy or so fields that exist in one or both of those universes. Members of three groups made common cause by simultaneously creating the American Folklore Society (AFS, the learned society and professional association for folklore studies) and establishing the American version of folklore studies in January 1888: scholars in then-developing humanities departments at colleges and universities, museum anthropologists, and private citizens with an interest in the subject and the financial means to pursue that interest.

The fifty years following the Civil War was not just the era when US folklore studies was born: it was the period when the modern American university, and the humanities and social science fields that live there, were created. We may think that the US university as we know it today—with multiple fields and departments; faculty who teach within those departments, conduct specialized research, and publish; and both undergraduate and graduate education in various departments and majors—has existed for many centuries. The fact is that this sort of university, based on German models, did not exist in the United States until the 1870s and 1880s, when it began to replace a world of undergraduate-only colleges, which instead of separate departments offered a single curriculum for all (in most US colleges at the time, "all" primarily meant well-off young White men), intended to create cultured citizens and leaders through the study of Latin and Greek grammar and literature, mathematics, ancient history, theology, and a few other subjects.[1] During this same fifty-year period, new fields in the humanities and social sciences—many of the ones we know today—started to take shape, become professionalized, and occupy newly created disciplinary territory, as evidenced by the birth years of some of the learned societies that represent these fields: the Modern Language Association (English and modern foreign languages), 1883; the American Historical Association, 1884; the American Economic Association, 1885; the American Folklore Society, 1888; the American Philosophical Association, 1900; the American Anthropological Association, 1902; the American Political Science Association, 1903; and the American Sociological Association, 1905.

During its history, our field has advanced several core ideas, among them that folklore—learned, practiced, and transmitted largely outside official settings and channels—constitutes a significant proportion of all cultural expression, not just a minor corner of it; that vernacular narratives, objects, beliefs, and performances offer especially productive routes toward understanding the identities and values people and communities create, and the extent and operations of human imagination; and that folklore shapes and is shaped by everyday life in our own (or any) time and place, not just in the past or somewhere else. Since its founding, the field of folklore studies has built an inclusive view of culture and creativity in communities by examining expressive life across boundaries of time and distance. Folklorists, using the core concepts of our field—including art, context, folk, genre, group, identity, performance, text, and tradition—work within the shared intellectual and social culture of what I have called a "listening discipline" to understand the intersections of artfulness and the social world, community-based creativity in a global economy, and both communication and conflict within and across religious, geographic, and ethnic divides.[2] Folklore studies describes the relations of lay and expert knowledge, advocates for mutual understanding and respect within the world's diverse cultural commons, and has contributed unique intellectual insights to the creation, analysis, and evaluation of public policy.

In the United States, our field is organized somewhat differently than most of our sister disciplines in the humanities and social sciences. A number of universities support departments, centers, and programs in folklore studies that offer undergraduate majors and minors, graduate degrees, or both, whose faculty and students energize the field by creating their own approaches to scholarship, teaching, public service, and professional preparation. (For links to more information, please visit "Where to Study Folklore" on the AFS website, https://whatisfolklore.org/where-to-study-folklore/.) But most US universities do not have folklore departments; accordingly, the majority of folklorists in academic life work alone or in small teams across the full range of humanities, social science, and arts departments at hundreds of US universities, engaging in undergraduate and graduate teaching, research and publication, and service in our field and the fields of their departmental homes.

In the last fifty years, US folklorists—building upon a long history of strong public interest in our subject and extensive public engagement by our field since its founding—have also built homes for their work in arts and humanities agencies at all levels of government, in nonprofit organizations devoted entirely or in part to public education about folklore, and in private consulting practice. For the last twenty years, almost half of US folklorists—including an increasing number based at universities, where they train newer folklorists—have been working in this "public sector," engaging with audiences of all ages and descriptions through public programs, including performances, museum exhibitions, media and other documentary works, and the development of curricula and teaching strategies for K–12 school programs.

A note: Although this book focuses on our field as it is practiced in the United States—just five of our authors work in other countries— folklore studies, since its nineteenth-century creation in Europe, is active around the world, as evidenced, for example, by the research and teaching of scholars abroad and by the robust activities (including conferences, collaborative projects, and communications in all media) of the national, regional, and international societies and associations that serve our international colleagues. (For links to more information, please visit the International Organizations page of the What Folklorists Do section of the AFS's "What Is Folklore" webpage, https://whatisfolklore.org/ what-folklorists-do/.)

FIELDWORK

Folklore lives at the multiform intersections of artfulness and everyday life—or, as Henry Glassie put it, "the center [of the folklorist's subject] is the merger of individual creativity and social order."[3] Thus, to engage with folklore requires fieldwork: immersive research in the social world. Ethnographic fieldwork—presence in and engagement with a community and its people to observe, document, and come to understand their traditional cultural expressions as enacted in the course and context of everyday life—is the fundamental research activity of the field of folklore studies. If folklore is a listening discipline, most of the engaged listening and looking we do is done in the field: in the widest imaginable range of homes, workplaces, and gathering places, from our own familiar locations to those a dozen time zones and cultures away.

Although library- and archive-based research are necessary complements to fieldwork—since to be properly situated, knowledge of the ethnographic present also requires deep historical and social understanding—even those folklorists who do most of their research in libraries and archives are in many instances working with scholarly publications based on, and documentary records created in the course of, fieldwork done by others.

There are many forms and kinds of fieldwork, including—to name just a few—basic collecting and documentation of traditional materials, long-term participant observation to address questions of change over time, quick surveys of the most visible traditions that characterize a community at a given moment, in-depth studies of particular individuals, and "salvage" field-work to document traditions rapidly evolving because of social, economic, or geographical change. Folklorists' approaches to fieldwork, and the fieldwork activities they plan and carry out, often depend upon the desired outcomes of their project—film, exhibition, scholarly publication, public performance, cultural resource survey report, middle school social studies curriculum, or historic preservation plan. You will encounter stories of these and other sorts of fieldwork in this book, but underlying this diversity is the reality that fieldwork of some sort is central to what folklorists do. As Jim Leary, an author in this book, put it in his response to the essays in a 2020 special issue of the *Journal of American Folklore*: "If we really want to figure out what it all means . . . we need to do fieldwork with a lot of individuals and cultural groups over extended periods in particular places; listen deeply to what they have to say; share our findings with them; learn as much as we can about his-torical forces bearing upon their lives and traditional practices; and ponder meanings with comparativist circumspection."[4]

This book begins with an essay about becoming a fieldworker, and throughout the book you will find evidence of the critical importance of field-work to folklorists. Regardless of the work they do, the great majority of our authors note the key importance of their ethnographic training—including their capacity for deep and engaged listening—to their professional lives.

Where This Book Comes From

As I noted previously, folklore studies as a field has been exploring profes-sional alternatives for many years; accordingly, this book has its origins in another that was published more than thirty years ago. In 1987, Charley Camp, my longtime friend and folklore colleague who was then the Mary-land state folklorist and had served as American Folklore Society executive secretary-treasurer from 1981 to 1986, was commissioned to edit one of the two volumes to be published by the society in celebration of its centennial in 1988 and 1989. (The AFS was founded on January 4, 1888, in Cambridge, Massachusetts, and held its first annual meeting in Philadelphia in 1889.) The first of these two volumes, a history of the field, was published in AFS's first centennial year (*100 Years of American Folklore Studies: A Conceptual History*, edited by William M. Clements). The second volume Charley named *Time and Temperature*. Published in AFS's second centennial year, it included lists of the society's members in 1889 and 1989 and both visual and written essays on a variety of topics by contemporary folklorists, all illustrating the present and possible future states of our field and the organization that served it.[5]

Time and Temperature's fourth section, though, is the one that concerns us here. Called "Faces," it was composed of sixteen brief personal essays collectively describing some of the "ways in which folklorists apply and exercise their abilities" in a variety of professional roles common for folklorists to have occupied at the time. The essays' titles all began "The Folklorist As . . ." and concluded with Academic Administrator (authored by Polly Stewart), Archivist (Jay Orr), Bibliographer (James R. Dow), Biographer (Edward D. Ives), Community Organizer (Lydia Fish), Cultural Critic (Archie Green), Curator (Marsha MacDowell), Dramatist (Robert McCarl), Editor (Judith McCulloh), Filmmaker (Tom Rankin, also an author in this book), Performer (Carol Silverman), Public Servant (Robert T. Teske), Publicist (Elaine Eff), Publisher (Marta Weigle), Record Producer (Neil Rosenberg), and Teacher (Ellen J. Stekert).

Collectively, these essays—informative, inspirational, and written by a "who's who" of beginning to mid-career folklorists at the time—provide a valuable inventory of the state and repertoire of the field of folklore studies in the mid-1980s, and they remain valuable today on that score. Many folklore colleagues and I have found these essays to be of continual interest and use as a snapshot of the range of work folklorists do. However, since *Time and Temperature* was published, much has changed: the range of work folklorists do has greatly expanded in the past thirty years, and the ways even the original 1989 roles are now carried out have been altered, as the surrounding contexts of the academy and public-sector work—and our culture, technology, economy, and society in general—have been transformed, sometimes several times over. So for some time I have believed it would be worthwhile to create a new version of this part of *Time and Temperature* that would speak to the state and prospects of our field today.

What Folklorists Do is the tangible outcome of that belief—shared, happily, by more than six dozen of my colleagues in folklore studies whom you are about to meet. Like the original publication, this book focuses attention on the ways the perspectives of folklore studies inform the professional orientation and activities of those trained in it, regardless of what they do as folklorists and where they do it. Like its predecessor, it evidences the range of good work today's folklorists actually do so folklorists-to-be (and the people who are in positions to hire folklorists) know the range of professional roles folklorists can and do fill, and how they do that work.

WHAT FOLKLORISTS DO

The seventy-six essays in this book are not intended to illustrate all the non-folklore things you can "do" with a folklore degree; they are intended to illustrate many of the ways you can work in the world *as a folklorist.*

I have organized these essays into four categories—researching and teaching, leading and managing, communicating and curating, and advocating and partnering—but I encourage you not to take those categories too definitively. At some time in their careers, each of the contributors to this book could have been appropriately placed in any of these categories because each has done work in most or all of them, often at the same time— and more than occasionally they evidence this in their essays. All folklorists share a body of academic training, all create scholarship in some form and teach audiences in some educational context, all are called upon to provide leadership at some level, most of their professional activities are communicative and involve curatorial selection of what to talk about and how, and all have served as advocates and partners. Although a great many folklorists work in "alt-ac" occupations, many in the academy also carry out a range of activities extending far beyond teaching and research. And folklorists working outside the academy, like their sisters and brothers holding faculty positions, have a range of teaching responsibilities; they simply carry them out through different means for different audiences. Finally, please remember that each of the authors in this book represents many others doing similar work in our field.

That the range of folklorists' work is this wide is in part a testimony to the creativity, the initiative, and (as one of this book's essays notes) the scrappiness of those in our field, but it has other, more institutional sources as well. As I noted previously, the robust development of public-sector work in the 1970s brought folklore studies into a richer and more diverse version of today's "alt-ac" business quite some time ago, and both educational curricula and professional development efforts in our field for many years have reflected this commitment to opening more doors to folklorists' professional orientation and practice. The American Academy of Arts and Sciences' report on its 2017 survey of humanities departments, to cite just one example, found that academic programs in folklore studies ranked highest among those in all humanities disciplines in offering presentations, workshops, and course-work on occupationally oriented subjects and that folklore studies also has the "highest rates of overall engagement with the digital humanities."[6] The American Folklore Society has assisted in these efforts by managing a series of annual meeting preconferences and special sessions on many occupational issues and a year-round professional development funding program.

That's how our field works. Our authors and I encourage you to read and engage with all the essays here; it's our belief that each of them offers something for you to think with and learn from. Welcome to *What Folklorists Do*.

NOTES

1. Veysey, *The Emergence*; Veysey, "The Plural Organized Worlds."
2. Ivey, "Values and Value," 16; Feintuch, *Eight Words*.
3. Glassie, *Turkish Traditional Art*, 9.
4. Leary, "Old Thoughts," 478.
5. Camp, *Time and Temperature*; Clements, *100 Years*.
6. American Academy of Arts and Sciences, *State of the Humanities*, 47, 51, 87.

BIBLIOGRAPHY

American Academy of Arts and Sciences. *The State of the Humanities in Four-Year Colleges and Universities (2017)*. Humanities Indicators Project, n.d. https://www.amacad.org/sites /default/files/media/document/2020-05/hds3_the_state_of_the_humanities_in _colleges_and_universities.pdf.

Camp, Charles, ed. *Time and Temperature*. Washington, DC: American Folklore Society, 1989. https://scholarworks.iu.edu/dspace/handle/2022/9008.

Clements, William, ed. *100 Years of American Folklore Studies: A Conceptual History*. Washington, DC: American Folklore Society, 1988. https://scholarworks.iu.edu /dspace/handle/2022/9008.

Feintuch, Burt, ed. *Eight Words for the Study of Expressive Culture*. Urbana: University of Illinois Press, 2003.

Glassie, Henry. *Turkish Traditional Art Today*. Bloomington: Indiana University Press, 1993.

Ivey, Bill. "Values and Value in Folklore (2007 American Folklore Society Presidential Address)." *Journal of American Folklore* 124, no. 491 (Winter 2011): 6–18. https://doi.org /10.5406/jamerfolk.124.491.0006.

Leary, James P. "Old Thoughts on (A)New Critical Folklore Studies: A Partisan's Response to the Special Issue." *Journal of American Folklore* 133, no. 530 (Fall 2020): 471–488. https://doi.org/10.5406/jamerfolk.133.530.0471.

Veysey, Lawrence R. *The Emergence of the American University*. Chicago: University of Chicago Press, 1965.

———. "The Plural Organized Worlds of the Humanities." In *The Organization of Knowledge in Modern America, 1860–1920*, edited by Alexandra Oleson and John Voss, 51–106. Baltimore, MD: Johns Hopkins University Press, 1979.

WHAT FOLKLORISTS DO

CHAPTER 1
Researching and Teaching

DOING FIELDWORK: TOM MOULD

Tom Mould earned his PhD in folklore at Indiana University and is Professor of Folklore and Anthropology at Butler University.

Humans have been fieldworkers since the beginning of time. We watched, we learned. We joined in, we learned. Eventually, we began to ask questions to learn even more. Fieldwork is embedded in our species' DNA. For the vast majority of the population, the process stops there—life recorded in memory and embodied in practice at the boundaries of our own cultures. The work is often invisible even to ourselves. Only when we engage in this work consciously and record it to share with others do we call it Fieldwork with a symbolic capital *F*. Observing, participating, and interviewing— these are the cornerstones of ethnographic fieldwork that are foundational to the study of folklore.

I remember my own transformation from fieldworker to Fieldworker as a rite of passage.

First, separation: Christmas Day, 1995. With a belly full of ham, mashed potatoes, and lupini beans, I borrow a car from my parents and set out—as a folklore grad student and novice fieldworker—for the tribal lands of the Mississippi Band of Choctaw Indians. I am a White, southern, male, single, cisgender, Italian American, second-generation college student. All these identities will play roles—some positive, some negative—in how I enter the Choctaw community. Then, transition: I struggle over the next six years, making missteps and breakthroughs in roughly equal measure. In no particular order, I come to learn about individual tribal members, ethnographic

1

fieldwork, Choctaw culture, folklore, narrative, and myself. Finally, reintegration: I return a folklorist and a Fieldworker. Black robes and a blisteringly hot and humid graduation day formally proclaim my new identity. But the real confirmation happens before I leave Mississippi, at a farewell backyard barbecue where my relationships with tribal members are cemented. I am given a handmade Choctaw stickball shirt. Eventually I realize the most important integration achieved through the rite of passage of fieldwork is not into academia but into the community where I have worked.

Separation, transition, reintegration. Repeat. Simple and not so simple. The transition period of doing fieldwork is dynamic, exciting, exhausting, and, above all else, unique: what works in one community may not work in another. Among the Choctaw, where the interests of White men have rarely resulted in favorable outcomes for the tribe, I was most often met with suspicion. I worked hard to convince people I had no ulterior motives and that any money made from the books I wrote would go back to the tribe. Among members of the Church of Jesus Christ of Latter-day Saints, on the other hand, I was greeted most often with open arms, with members often assuming I *did* have an ulterior motive: that of joining the Church. In both, there were exceptions. There were individuals among the Choctaw who befriended me far sooner than I should have expected, and among the Latter-day Saints were those who worried I might be one more academic from outside the Church whose goal was to expose rather than shed light. Honesty, sincerity, and transparency underlay my approach in both communities but emerged in response to very different expectations each group had about outside researchers.

The politics of identity, complex and unique histories, dynamic performance contexts, and the vast diversity of individuals ensure fieldwork can never be as objective, systematic, and uniform as books on methodology tempt us to believe. Social, cultural, and political norms change; so too must fieldwork. In the twenty-five years between my first visit to the Mississippi Choctaw and my most recent, the landscape has changed dramatically. Tired of research guided by exoteric interests, false assumptions, stereotypes, and misguided charity, indigenous groups the world over have been instituting formal procedures for determining what research can be conducted within their communities. And so it was with some trepidation that I found myself standing at a podium in the tribal council hall in early 2020, answering questions from the newly elected chief and the seventeen-member council of the Mississippi Band of Choctaw Indians. Thoughtful and insightful, the council members seemed interested, even encouraging. And then: "Why isn't a Choctaw person doing this work?" The question was pointed but not unexpected. After all, the pros and cons of insider versus outsider research have been debated for years. I offered an answer that clearly did not satisfy the councilwoman, who directed her follow-up question to Jay Wesley, the head of the Chahta Immi Cultural Center.

Jay was there as a coresearcher, one of seven leaders in the community with whom I had spent the last year developing a research project. Within the proliferation of models for collaboration that attempt to recenter power and agency within the local community, I have most often used a community-based research model that attempts to play to the strengths of each member. I used this model a few years earlier with research on narratives about public assistance undertaken with a group of ten community partners in North Carolina spread across a range of social service agencies. The model served us well that day. Jay answered questions with an understanding of local politics I could not hope to navigate so well or so quickly. The council voted to approve our work.

In recent years, community-based research has become common in the social sciences and humanities, particularly with indigenous communities. If this sounds bureaucratic and impersonal, it is and it isn't. The tribal process of formal approval surely is formal, with its committees, resolutions, precouncil meetings, and official voting, and it would be easy for the work to suffer a similar fate. But the friendship model of fieldwork I learned from Henry Glassie provides a blueprint for nurturing rapport and fostering relationships built on trust that can run parallel to formal procedures.

This model is not without its critics, who believe such an approach imposes interpersonal obligations that lead to flattery rather than honesty. Henry's response, offered in a footnote in his book *The Stars of Ballymenone*, provides a defense of the friendship model, suggesting that fieldwork done without rapport and trust may yield an understanding of 20 percent of a tradition while friendship can lead to 80 percent. Because our work is fundamentally humanistic, our shared respect of people's privacy and dignity leads us to avoid reporting on perhaps 10 percent of that knowledge, which still leaves 70 percent to be made public (see fig. 1.1).

To be sure, these numbers are imagined and impossible to prove, but many of us have had experiences like the one I had talking with a Latter-day Saint family. One hot June evening in 2006, I was enveloped in an overstuffed sofa in Tim and Meredith Sampers's apartment, where they lived with their two children. (These names are pseudonyms; the reason will become clear in a moment.) I had gotten to know the whole family through my weekly Church attendance, Sunday school classes, and Priesthood meetings. An hour into our conversation, Tim paused and asked me to turn off the audio

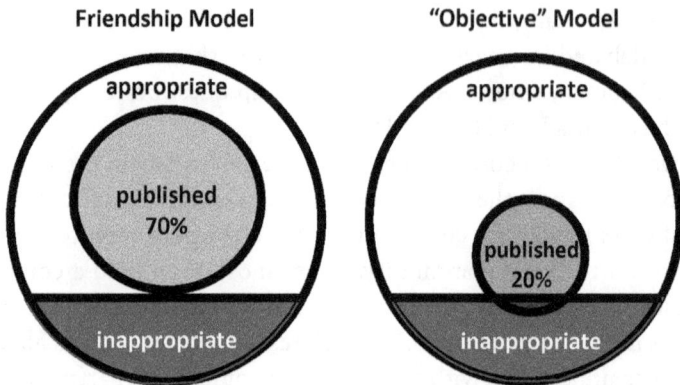

Fig. 1.1 The friendship model of fieldwork contrasted with an "objective" approach. Note: it is not by accident that the first looks like a rising sun while the second looks like the Death Star from *Star Wars*. Image courtesy of the author.

recorder. He and Meredith wanted to share two stories with me. "These are for you, not for the book," he said. They were deeply personal, spiritual stories he wanted me to understand even though he didn't want them shared more widely. Knowing these stories helped ensure that what I wrote was accurate, even if those particular stories could not be part of the written record. Tim understood what critics of the friendship model of fieldwork do not: that accurate and nuanced research in the humanities and social sciences is good because of our bonds of trust and respect, not despite them.

In the end, the binaries we construct to define our work fall apart. The clinical objectivity of the fieldworker who avoids friendship is as artificial as the accusations of utter subjectivity made about the work of the fieldworker who embraces it. Fieldwork versus archival research, qualitative versus quantitative research, insider versus outsider, lone researcher versus collaborative team, natural versus artificial performance contexts, face-to-face versus online: for many of us, these binaries either erode into a continuum or orient us toward both/and solutions rather than either/or ones. I have found synthesis and integration far more productive than working in absolutes. Coupling my ethnographic fieldwork with collaborative data collection, archival research, and online data has allowed me to ask quantitative as well as qualitative questions, exponentially expanding my interpretive lens.

The variations are as numerous as the research projects we develop, but at the heart of it all are the people we are privileged to learn from. The names of these people are also too numerous to mention, although early in my drafting, I imagined this essay filled solely with their names. Unable to list them all, I list none, save one: Gladys Willis. Her photo has been on my desk for twenty-five years. Many have followed, but Grandma Willis was the first to show me the power of fieldwork to introduce us to people, wise in ways we cannot imagine, who effortlessly reveal the astounding depths of our shared humanity.

Integrating Fieldwork and Library Research: Elissa R. Henken

Elissa R. Henken earned her PhD in folklore at Indiana University and is Professor Emerita at the University of Georgia.

Many things fascinate and delight me about studying folklore: its patterns and their variations, the way folklore both reflects and shapes people's attitudes and behavior, the way it continually changes in accordance with the sociocultural context, and the fact that one can study it with any group, in any place, at any time. I'm continually in the field, taking notice and collecting—whether in a library, classroom, or community—combining research spheres of folklore studies. Sometimes I go in search of a specific topic; sometimes a topic just leaps out at me, which sounds haphazard but is very exciting.

My first major project was on folklore of the Welsh saints: men and women who were hermits and ecclesiastics in the fifth through seventh centuries. Narratives about them eventually appeared in a variety of sources, mostly in Welsh or Latin, beginning in the eleventh century. My study entailed culling all these sources, scanning them by eye, page by page, in those days before digitized texts and electronic searches—indeed, probably the most useful aspect of my work was providing a resource guide to the narrative traditions of these saints—and then trying to examine them as folklore. Researching folklore in written texts is always complicated by uncertainties about the original context and sources of the materials; these complexities only increase when dealing with medieval texts. Descriptions of saints' lives, for example, were political—created in a clash of Celtic and Anglo-Norman churches and cultures—and copied other texts, shared motifs, and recorded local lore. Very often, working with medieval materials becomes a balancing act between figuring out what's going on and not imposing one's own sense of a satisfying narrative or seeing patterns where none exist. Nonetheless, one of my proudest moments was when I recognized a biblical and Norwegian folktale motif and was able to emend one letter in an otherwise unintelligible line of poetry to reveal a saint's staff blossoming in divine proof.

Beyond the pleasure of gathering materials and contemplating sources and lines of transmission was the satisfaction of recognizing broader patterns: the male saints, who were local heroes, followed the same biographical pattern as secular heroes, starting with wondrous births, precocious childhoods, and marvelous feats, while the pattern for the female saints did not begin until they were confronted with male sexuality. Male sanctity was predetermined at conception, while female sanctity was accomplished only when the woman "won" her virginity or became the mother of a saint. Although lore about the saints is still shared in many places, this project remained mainly library focused due to problems with travel, language skills, and shyness.

My next major project, however, was more evenly divided between library research and fieldwork. Owain Glyndŵr, who led the last major armed rebellion of the Welsh against the English (1400–1415), was seen in his own time as a redeemer hero, the hero who is prophesied to come—or, never having died, to return—to restore the nation to its former glory. The Welsh, who suffered under the Romans, Anglo-Saxons, and Normans, were in need of a redeemer hero, and Glyndŵr, known as *y mab darogan* (the son of prophecy), was seventh in a line of eight major redeemers (King Arthur is fourth in that line). Again I spent innumerable hours in the library, thumbing my way through manuscripts and printed editions of poetry, histories, antiquarian reports, nationalist journals, and political writings as I traced the pattern leading up to Glyndŵr, saw how he used the traditions to present himself as the prophesied redeemer, and examined how, after his disappearance, he became the subject of legend and eventually a symbol of modern Welsh nationalism.

But I also spoke with people from all over Wales about Glyndŵr. Again, shyness was a problem—fieldwork for me is like wading into cold water: agony to make that first move but glorious once you're in—but an even greater problem was that Glyndŵr, a nationalist symbol, remains politically fraught. One woman, who had been willing to talk with me and wasn't even put off by my tape recorder, ran from me in the street when I mentioned Glyndŵr, and another woman kept repeating that she couldn't talk to me and that her boss was English. And these occurred in Machynlleth, where Glyndŵr had set up his parliament, and they could have simply (and safely) pointed out the building. These less-than-successful encounters were instructive in themselves, but it was more exciting to hear people tell stories connected to local sites—the place from which Glyndŵr threw his sword, which left its imprint in a stone that is now part of the church; the field in which he dressed wooden poles as soldiers and tricked the enemy into not attacking; the cave where he sleeps while waiting for the right moment to return—all perfect demonstrations of the link between place and lore. While the overall study covered many centuries, fieldwork also permitted comparative study in a single time period, revealing how different people used the same legend. Take, for example, one legend (dating at least to the sixteenth century) in which Glyndŵr, having emerged from his cave, meets an abbot and remarks on him being up early. The abbot replies, "No, it is you who is up early, a hundred years too early." And by that, Glyndŵr knows it is not time, and he goes back to his cave. With wistfulness for unaccomplished dreams, one older man, who had been describing Glyndŵr as a man of vision, told me this story and then explained that Glyndŵr was a man before his time. A younger man, a member of a group that teaches Welsh people more about their history so they can better appreciate their right to independence, ended his rendition of the story with the abbot by saying that Glyndŵr had come sooner than he should have; he suggested that the Welsh hadn't been ready to fight but might have been had Glyndŵr waited two centuries, in which case Wales would be a free nation today.

Glyndŵr was noted for his destructiveness, but even when he burned whole towns, he left the homes of his supporters standing. During my first semester at the University of Georgia, my students, sharing their own local legends, told me how Civil War Union general William Sherman razed everything in his path but left their town—and only their town—unharmed. This was said of at least a dozen towns for reasons such as a former classmate or an old girlfriend living there, the women of the town making him and his men a fried chicken dinner, or the town being simply too beautiful to destroy. These and other stories showed the ravaging monster—that devil Sherman— tamed by southern civility to civilized, gentlemanly behavior. I continued to collect these and other stories from my students but also in the field.

I felt very strange as a New York Jew wandering around Georgia saying, "Tell me about Sherman." One of my most difficult times was attending the annual conference of Georgian Sons of the Confederacy. I was fortunate that after an awkward start, a couple decided I was all right and took me under their wing, calling people over to talk with me. However, I found it confusing to work with people with whom I disagreed on almost everything politically and socially (the opposite of my experience in Wales) and at the same time to find myself tearing up alongside them as they told their family stories of wartime hardship. I wondered whether my own convictions were so malleable, but then I thought about shared humanity and the reality of suffering no matter the cause. When one man challenged me that I would misrepresent them, I could only promise that I would present his views as accurately as possible and that my job was to let each person's voice be heard. Although it is sometimes painfully difficult, I still believe that. I have found myself constantly shifting between library research (Welsh legends of hidden treasure; Arthurian folklore) and fieldwork, often inspired by my students (legends about famous people sacrificing to join or leave the Illuminati; legends told by gamers versus nongamers about the dangers of video games; legends and beliefs about human sexuality) and sometimes requiring archival or online research, but the excitement of discovery is always the same. Very different discoveries—finding a previously undiscussed narrative genre (origin stories for proverbs) in medieval Welsh and Irish texts and recognizing in contemporary lore a pattern by which women of a distant enemy appear in jokes as dirty and ugly, while the women of a nearby enemy appear in legends as especially beautiful, luring men to death or disease—each left me high on excitement. No matter where a project starts—in the library, in the classroom, or from a casual bit of conversation, often with my tripping over one thing while looking for another—it generally requires research through the other spheres, and in each place I have observed and learned more I can share.

Collaborating across Disciplines: Sheila Bock

Sheila Bock earned her PhD in English and folklore at The Ohio State University and is Associate Professor in the Department of Interdisciplinary, Gender, and Ethnic Studies at the University of Nevada, Las Vegas.

During a campus visit to interview for a faculty position in interdisciplinary studies at the University of Nevada, Las Vegas (UNLV) soon after I defended my dissertation, the search committee asked me how my academic training and professional experience made me a strong applicant for that position. In all honesty, I don't recall exactly what I said in response, but I remember I did not have a difficult time answering the question.

Throughout my graduate training in the field of folklore studies at The Ohio State University (OSU), I was incredibly lucky to have advisers and faculty mentors who so adeptly navigated the interdisciplinary landscape of that institution while also modeling engagement in research that straddled the boundaries of folklore and other disciplines, including political science, disability studies, Middle Eastern studies, and dance, among others. As is the case at many graduate programs in our field, at OSU students receive training in folklore studies while occupying different disciplinary homes within the institution: in my case, the Department of Comparative Studies for my MA and the Department of English for my PhD. As we came in contact with people from varying disciplinary backgrounds in our courses and attended different professional conferences to network and present our research, my fellow folklore graduate students and I had many opportunities to practice articulating for different audiences what folklorists study, how they do it, and how folklore as a discipline both overlaps with and differs from closely related fields that also lay claim to the study of informal knowledge, creative communication, and the complex dynamics of culture.

I am grateful for having acquired this ability from my graduate school experiences to cross disciplinary borders that were not heavily policed, to use a geopolitical metaphor. The interdisciplinary nature of my folklore training has not only enriched my scholarly work but has helped me envision and articulate the relevance of my work to different audiences and has also very directly informed my teaching in the Department of Interdisciplinary, Gender, and Ethnic Studies at UNLV, particularly in classes that guide undergraduate students through the process of conceptualizing and carrying out research-based projects that explicitly integrate at least two different disciplinary perspectives. In addition, it has helped me develop the confidence to converse with people in different disciplines about the value of folklore studies and its approaches, which became particularly beneficial when I found myself as the only folklorist on campus when I started my first year as a faculty member in 2011.

I still feel lucky to be in this departmental home, which appreciates my disciplinary grounding in folklore studies and encourages interdisciplinary connections. On multiple occasions during my time at UNLV, informal conversations across disciplinary boundaries (after lectures on campus, during faculty "meet and greets," or at social events at colleagues' houses) have developed into cross-disciplinary collaborations.

When I teach my students about doing research that crosses disciplinary boundaries, I distinguish between *multi*disciplinary and *inter*disciplinary research, and my collaborations have fallen at different positions on this spectrum. At one end of the spectrum, multidisciplinary research brings together the perspectives of two or more disciplines with the goal of gaining a more comprehensive perspective on a given research topic. In multidisciplinary research, the contribution of each disciplinary perspective is clearly defined from the beginning. For example, when I worked with colleagues in health-care administration and nursing to study patient perspectives on the Patient Centered Medical Home Care delivery model, especially among patients with type 2 diabetes, I was the only one on the research team with experience using in-depth open-ended interviews as a method. Within this project, my collaborators deferred to my expertise with qualitative methods as well as my disciplinary training in attending to people's perspectives and experiences. Although we worked together to create the research design and analyze the interview data we collected—so the process was not just assembling the pieces of a premade jigsaw puzzle—each participant's domain of expertise was clearly demarcated throughout the collaboration.

At the other end of the spectrum, interdisciplinary research also involves bringing different disciplinary perspectives together to more completely understand a given topic, but it also leaves open space for dialogue across the boundaries of the disciplines, creating opportunities for articulating new relationships between different domains of expertise and for thinking critically about the assumptions embedded within them. For example, I collaborated with a historian colleague to tell the story of an unpublished tale collection her father documented in the Sonora region of Mexico in the 1970s. While the demarcation of disciplinary expertise at first glance appeared pretty clearly defined, our project ultimately developed into an examination of the generative and at times uneasy interactions that emerged at the borderlands of our disciplinary affiliations within the academy. These dialogues at the borders of our disciplines led to a critical rethinking of the "archive" of materials we were working with and the hierarchies of interpretation that were grounding our analyses, both individually and collaboratively.

If we carry the borderlands metaphor farther, it is perhaps not surprising that my training as a folklorist has heavily informed the cross-disciplinary collaborations I've participated in at various points on the multidisciplinary-interdisciplinary spectrum I previously described. The foundational elements of folklore studies include a sincere desire to understand the perspectives of others and a willingness to think critically and reflexively about how our own background, perspectives, and biases inform the work we do. Folklorists, especially although certainly not exclusively those doing ethnographic work with communities in the present, recognize that the best and most fulfilling work grows out of sustained relationships with people and the respect, trust, vulnerability, reciprocity, and friendship those relationships can engender (although, of course, the intimacy of friendship can create its own challenges in scholarly enterprises). Finally, my folkloristic training, particularly in ethnographic methods, has helped me see value in the experiences of "failure" in those moments of uneasiness, and here I use the term *failure* not as the opposite of success but rather as the destabilization of our initial expectations through our encounters with the people with whom we work. In cross-disciplinary collaborations, such destabilizations can be incredibly generative, although, as with doing fieldwork, they require us to reflect on the messiness that emerges through a sincere commitment to dialogue. This is not always possible—given the institutional expectations and constraints of the university, among other factors—but I have found it to be an ideal worth working toward that reaffirms what I love most about the field of folklore studies.

Practicing Internationalism: Dorothy Noyes

Dorothy Noyes earned her PhD in folklore and folklife at the University of Pennsylvania and is Professor in the Departments of English and Comparative Studies at The Ohio State University and a past president of the American Folklore Society.

My father, a corporate executive in an aging rustbelt industry, once explained to me that management consultants command such outrageous fees because they are free to say what cannot be said by employees: they are simply ventriloquists who provide a safe channel for internal critique. I wasn't convinced. Were all those *Harvard Business Review* buzzwords pure camouflage, then? Were the consultants actually listening to people like him or just peddling their formulas? Wasn't his company bamboozled by the magical name of the prominent firm that promised to sweep in and set them right?

As an American folklorist working frequently in international settings, I have found myself playing both the ventriloquist and the mystifier. My nationality and, in due course, my professional position have called me to play both parts. But being a folklorist makes a difference. Practicing what Tim Lloyd has called a "listening discipline," folklorists inevitably end up being transformed by what they hear. Associated with the study of practices deemed marginal, backward, minoritarian, or trivial, folklorists are forced into egalitarian, even deferential relations with others who can offer a useful counterweight to our national and professional identities. Both our working methods and our substantive focus on the local and vernacular can help us practice an internationalism less fraught than the kind tied to power politics and national interests.

When I first went to the struggling industrial town of Berga in the foothills of the Catalan Pyrenees for my dissertation fieldwork, I was at once sized up for any value I could offer. Americans were infrequent visitors, meriting attention, but a timid graduate student hardly fit local preconceptions; at one point I heard, "*That's* not an American! It's too short!" Still, as the only American handy, I was available to hear critiques of US foreign policy and answer questions about Michael Jordan and English grammar. As a future academic who planned to write a book, I was found somewhat worthy of cultivation by local elites seeking international amplification for Berguedan tourist attractions and Catalan nationalist claims. Most important, as someone talking across social boundaries within the town—partly by intention, partly out of ignorance—I became a conduit for indirect local communication. In short, I was recruited to play the ventriloquist at more than one level. Idiosyncratic social theories, personal grudges, political analyses, transgressive jokes, and inadmissible longings were all expressed to me insofar as it was my job to pay attention to anyone who approached me. The opportunity was of special interest to marginal individuals of every kind. Having had ample leisure to contemplate the grounds of their marginalization, they were always worth hearing, even though they were hardly objective observers. Over time, as I kept showing up, more central actors began to talk to me freely, blowing off steam about local irritants or formulating ideas they had no reason to articulate to their neighbors. In festive settings, my presence often prompted heightened performance and the acting out of small social scenarios, with a glance or a call to ensure I was attending and sometimes an explicit command: "Put this in your book!"

In the short term, as I published small pieces in the local press, my ventriloquism lent some legitimacy to the minority report of the festival I had come to study: a less reverential, more present-based, more experiential, and more contested account than the one articulated in the established channels but that still endorsed, even flattered, local convictions of the festival's importance. As an ethnographer I was, of course, pulling together fragmented communications and making tacit understandings more explicit, and in the matter of the dancing mule's orgasm, this provided much public glee. Occasionally I was able to offer an affirming mirror in which some actors could recognize their best individual and collective selves. I believe a few of them found this useful in imagining their next steps forward.

Still, the power of the ventriloquist is ephemeral; it does not always work for good, it does not work for everybody, and even the most illuminating ethnographic dialogue counts for nothing in relation to sustained economic forces, political struggles, and institutional frameworks. Conversely, I lost my perceived innocence and became aligned with certain views only; I went back to the United States and did other things. After thirty years the dialogue is only intermittent, now and then sparking interest or proving useful to someone there.

The greater impact was, of course, felt on my side. The folklorist's modus operandi of learning to participate in shared social forms and taking insider views seriously poses inevitable challenges to the self. Many of my habits were altered; others were made visible. My assumptions were challenged, tacitly and explicitly. Some I revised or abandoned; others I came to acknowledge and value more carefully. Most important, as a late baby boomer White suburban American interacting intensely for the first time with people formed in a hardscrabble town under an authoritarian regime, I was forced into a radically different understanding of personal agency and freedom. Indeed, I learned to recognize my freedom as a constraint of its own: in the words of a Finnish immigrant proverb, once you've crossed the Atlantic, you're always on the wrong side.

I was hired into a folklore job in an English department and did not remain a Catalan specialist. Instead, because my students came from around the world and because the network of folklore scholars is relatively small but global, I learned to think my way into a range of international situations, and I traveled a lot. Along with other folklore scholars at Ohio State, I was recruited into the interdisciplinary conversations of the university's Mershon Center for International Security Studies because we were perceived as offering expertise into foreign cultures or, more subtly, the ability to ventriloquize other voices that would not otherwise enter into policy debates. What we really offered was the ability to knock the United States off its pedestal and enter into international conversations on a more equal footing. Because we were full of self-doubt, because we were accustomed to synthesizing other positions and imagining rationales for them, because as a discipline we were associated with localized low-status endeavors that pointed to inequities and imperfections in the achievement of the modern—because, in short, we did not intimidate anybody—we were able to go where respectable social science could not. Accustomed to making the most of accidental juxtapositions rather than having the resources to design our activities from the top down, we organized conversations among people who would not have thought to talk to one another. For example, take the 2010 "Making Sense in Afghanistan: Interaction and Uncertainty" conference my OSU folklore colleague Margaret Mills and I organized, in which high-ranking US military officers and low-level recruits, Afghan intellectuals, anthropologists critical of the US counterinsurgency strategy, folklorists listening to the gossip in the bazaars, NGO workers, and political scientists all managed to speak frankly to one another about the impact of confusion on all sides of a highly asymmetrical international conflict.

Now a professor of a certain age, I am frequently invited to speak to students and scholars in other countries, which is facilitated by the still potent mystique of US academia even as the nation's prestige is in free fall and its state capacity has come into serious question. Sometimes I hear my words quoted and feel as bogus as the management consultants who used to plague my father.

More often, however, PhD students, academics, policy makers, and cultural professionals receive me with friendliness, hear me politely, and then feel free to argue. They know my knowledge of their circumstances is incomplete, even when I fail to acknowledge it. They know my analytical frameworks are formed out of particular experiences, just as theirs are. Formed outside the insulation of a superpower, they are accomplished practical comparativists in multiple directions, well aware that I need their mirroring insights more than they need mine. As a certain kind of American, I am still learning to listen. But as a folklorist, I've got a lot of opportunities to do so.

CONNECTING FOLKLORE STUDIES TO DIGITAL HUMANITIES: JOHN LAUDUN

John Laudun earned his PhD in folklore at Indiana University and is Professor in the Department of English at the University of Louisiana.

As a researcher and teacher, what drives me is making connections, sometimes between ideas and sometimes between people. At its best, folklore studies connects people and ideas, making it clear how all of us—no matter who we are or where we live—think our ways through the world with the resources we have at hand. Those things "ready to hand," which we sometimes call vernacular, are the foundation for folklore studies, which sees the warp and weft of the ordinary as the only way to answer big questions. In collecting tale after tale to assemble archives of humanistic "big data," early folklorists contributed to our understanding of human history as well as human psychology.

The strength of folklore studies as a domain has always been in the possibility of larger syntheses based on its diverse, and sometimes diffuse, data. Our focus at the local level is a strength, a commitment to understanding people as people and not as something other than that, and continuing to work with them as they seek their own place within a world where we all are reduced to so many numbers. If numbers are the lingua franca of our time, folklorists must be conversant.

The first time I realized there was a larger dialogue waiting to be had was when I was overseeing efforts to digitize the contents of the Archives of Cajun and Creole Folklore. We had won a grant from the GRAMMY Foundation and were steadily digitizing fragile recordings and entering information into a database that acted as a catalog. When it became apparent that not everyone understood the opportunity of making such material accessible to anyone with an internet connection, I wrote a grant to create a digital humanities lab so scholars and students alike could create their own "born-digital" materials: both original documentary materials and productions based on those materials.

This desire to reach both within and without more broadly, as well as to do it in a fashion that makes the data, the methods, and the outcomes of the work more accessible to any and all interested others, has been the nexus of the digital humanities: an umbrella term that brings together archivists, media creators, and computation specialists as well as scholars and, increasingly, scientists interested in exploring the synthetic possibilities of the information age. In folklore studies, our work has largely focused on building better, more accessible archives and on exploring new kinds of scholarly outputs and new forms of public outreach that include the possibility of interaction among curators, objects, and their many audiences.

As an Americanist interested in vernacular texts, I was frustrated by how all these high-quality texts, documented by colleagues near and far, were not readily available for comparison. We were the discipline that invented big data textual databases in the form of the tale type and motif indices, and yet these were useless when seeking out contemporary texts. (Because relatively little of the contents of folklore archives has been digitized, these texts remain off-line to this day, which boggles the imagination.)

Adding to my interest in finding comparative texts, as I pored over the recordings and photographs I made as part of the fieldwork that led to my book, *The Amazing Crawfish Boat*, and pinned things to both a time line and a map, I realized I was seeing networks of people and ideas and the groups within which they trafficked. When Tim Tangherlini invited me to join the National Endowment for the Humanities–funded seminar he had organized on network studies, I jumped at the opportunity. Later, Tangherlini also organized a National Science Foundation–funded long program that explored how the math behind networks, and other statistical methods, could both enhance traditional humanities theories and methods but also be enhanced by them.

That is, there is room *in* the field to get involved in these broader discussions and in the process to create more room *for* the field: dismissing the quantitative turn in scholarship of the current moment is as counterproductive as dismissing the turn toward performance that occurred in the last generation. What I find in the ideas and methods of the quantitative turn are realizations and extensions of ideas, and even methods, central to folklore studies. After all, the last third of Vladimir Propp's *Morphology of the Folktale* is nothing but tables he compiled into a formula for a body of Russian folktales in the same way Claude Lévi-Strauss used his encyclopedic memory to compile the formulas at the heart of his *Mythologiques*. The more I look, in fact, the more I uncover startlingly prescient work, like that by Benjamin Colby and Pierre Maranda: work that was inhibited by the technology of the moment but overcame those inhibitions through powerful imaginations.

Inspired by the possibilities, I have found myself part of a larger set of conversations taking place in and between the humanities and the data and information sciences. Much of the groundwork for how texts are processed computationally in the current moment was achieved by computational linguistics and is focused at the level of the sentence. At the same time, the humanities remain dominated by the large texts that are the objects of literary studies. The result, when it comes to something like the study of narrative, is that the debates leap from texts of a few sentences to those of hundreds of pages. Meanwhile, all those mostly middle-sized texts—like folktales, legends, and personal-experience narratives—collected by folklorists across space and time are left out of attempts to build a computational model of narrative. This is my current work: combining advances in discourse analysis with advances in statistical modeling to build programs that come closer to seeing narrative the way humans do. As part of this work, I find myself not only attending the meetings of the American Folklore Society but also the Society for Data Science and Statistics and giving talks to rooms filled with as many computer scientists and mathematicians as literature scholars. The questions are different, but the answers are increasingly the same.

Perhaps most important, in my work as a digital humanist, I have experienced the power and rewards of collaboration. There is so much work to be done, and it requires not only many hands but also many minds. The things I have learned working with librarians and archivists to deposit digital materials and describe them with the correct metadata, and with data scientists to get the algorithms right, have been far more than what I have learned working on my own.

Using Big Data in Folklore Scholarship: Timothy R. Tangherlini

Timothy R. Tangherlini earned his PhD in Scandinavian at the University of California, Berkeley, where he is a professor in the Department of Scandinavian.

The COVID-19 pandemic started its march across the globe in the early weeks of February 2020, gained steam through March, and forced huge numbers of Americans into their houses by April. While the mainstream media presented a sobering yet informative view of the crisis, the internet exploded with everything from quite reasonable suggestions on how best to wash one's hands to the most convoluted conspiracy theories that managed to link the pandemic to bioweapons research, chemtrails, a globalist Jewish elite, pangolins, and the 5G cellular phone network. The pandemic engendered an overwhelming outpouring of stories that spoke to the widespread anxieties caused by the poorly understood virus and the lack of accessible, authoritative, and trustworthy information. As any folklorist will tell you, rumor loves an information void, and the one caused by the pandemic was an almost perfect vacuum. Rips in the fabric of trustworthy news sources created by the vortex of social media and the current political environment allowed all sorts of stories to rush in to fill that vacuum.

When the COVID-19 pandemic hit, and the internet blew up with memes, videos, and conspiracy theories, our team at UCLA had already been heavily focused on computational modeling of conspiracies (actual) and conspiracy theories (fictional) from social media data (see our article "Conspiracy in the Time of Corona: Automatic Detection of COVID-19 Conspiracy Theories in Social Media and the News" at https://arxiv.org/abs/2004.13783). In early March we had pivoted our research away from the QAnon conspiracy theory to the emergence and dynamics of conspiracy theories about the virus that were spreading across social media. Our goal was to track the formation of these stories and the real-world actions they endorsed, providing the basis for a system to assist analysts tasked with identifying potentially dangerous ideas while supporting positive responses. We had started this work several years earlier by exploring the narrative frameworks of vaccine hesitancy and the anti-vaccination communities. By automatically analyzing thousands of conversations on "mommy blogs," we showed that communities of belief on social media are remarkably stable, even if there is enormous turnover in the people who make up those communities, and that the narrative framework undergirding the tens of thousands of posts was endorsing exemption seeking, an overlooked activity that had greatly eroded herd immunity across the nation.

Since my earliest training, I have focused on storytelling and, in particular, the interrelated narrative genres of personal experience narrative, rumor, legend, and conspiracy theory. The current age of ubiquitous internet access and easily accessible social media is a golden opportunity for almost real-time collecting from a wide range of groups. Working at a very large scale—that of tens of thousands, if not millions, of stories and story fragments, expressed by individuals in very large groups—creates challenges that the philologically anchored close-reading methods of the humanities are not well equipped to handle. At the same time, this enormous scale, already present to some degree in the historical archives of tradition found across the globe, is something folklorists have long been trained to work with directly or at least to consider; see, for example, examples as widely spread in time as the *Types of the Folktale* (1910), the *Motif-Index of Folk Literature* (1932), and the 2016 "Big Folklore: A Special Issue on Computational Folkloristics" special issue of the *Journal of American Folklore*. Experts in data sciences—including machine learning, natural language processing, and geographic information systems (GIS)—can bridge that gap.

This "macroscopic" approach requires computer-based methods since the scale of the data is well beyond the cognitive limits of a single individual. It would be impossible, for instance, for a single person to read and remember the entire 4chan site, let alone to extract a meaningful understanding of the interrelationships and interdependencies of threads on that site. Yet by working with big data resources, we were able to develop a dynamic picture of the ongoing negotiation of belief organizing the conversations preserved there and potentially understand the implications of those discussions for real-world behaviors in the context of crises such as the COVID-19 pandemic, from the positive (people coming together to sew face masks for neighbors and friends) to the very negative (demonstrators encouraging armed action against statewide stay-at-home orders).

In this project, our problem was a classic one in folkloristics: while we recognize that we can only observe and record performances that are often incomplete, we also recognize that there must be something driving those performances to make them recognizable and, on some level, acceptable to the group. Much of our work over the past decade has been on understanding the relationship between narrative's deep structures—the limits that a domain of discourse places on "what one can talk about"—and the surface-level, observable phenomena that comprise actual performances, and then on figuring out a way to create a model of those interdependencies. In short, our goal has been to devise a useful model of storytelling at internet scale. Although ethnographic fieldwork is rightfully the gold standard in folkloristics, it is necessarily constrained by problems of sampling, access, and time; the internet provides us with a form of self-archiving folklore: noisy, biased, and chaotic but still the product of collaborative, negotiated performances of informal cultural expressive forms circulating on and across social networks. So we used the internet as our data source and set our sights on developing a formal model for internet-scale storytelling.

Inspired by the work of Algirda Greimas—published in 1966 in French in the journal *Communications*—on the interpretation of myth, coupled with the narrative analysis of William Labov and Joshua Waletzky published in *Essays on the Verbal and Visual Arts* in 1967, we think of a narrative framework as a network graph: stories or parts of stories, which we capture as social

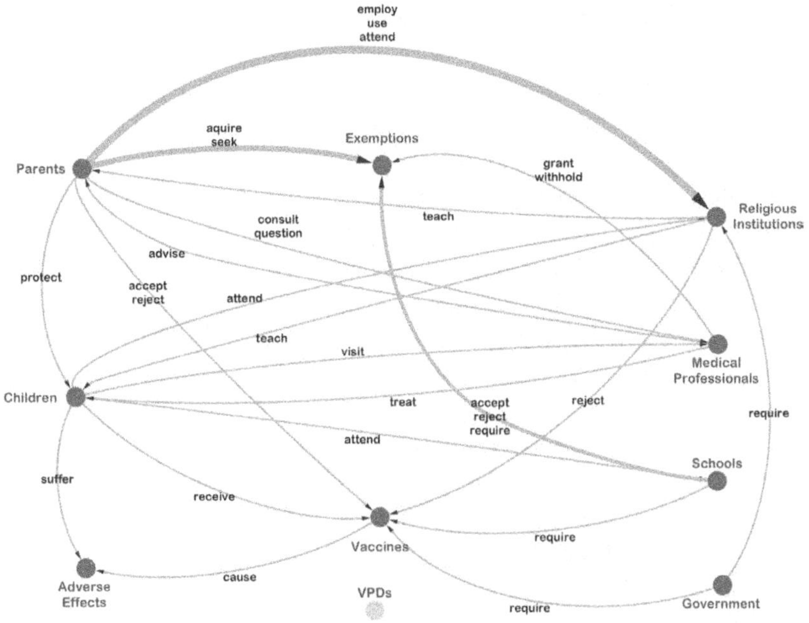

Fig. 1.2 The generative narrative framework undergirding vaccination discussions on a "mommy blog." Image courtesy of the author.

media posts or newspaper articles and then activate part of the graph. Over time the activated parts of the graph become more important, making it harder for new terms or relationships to be considered "part" of the narrative. Although the resulting narrative graph can be fairly simple, it provides clear information about not only what people are discussing but also how they are discussing it, even though individual posts can at times seem utterly unconnected (see fig. 1.2). It is worth noting that in the studied conversations, the vaccine preventable diseases (VPDs) are not connected to the graph: the real threat agent is the vaccine. Consequently, seeking an exemption is an understandable strategy for combating that threat.

Since we were already monitoring a set of social media forums on Reddit and 4chan, it was immediately clear to us that the pandemic was a factory for conspiracy theory and rumor. After an early March meeting, we focused our scrapers and narrative framework pipeline on the pandemic, which gave us daily views onto what was happening. We also developed "crawls" of other social media sites and news sites, resulting in amounts of data so large that our crawlers were barely finished with one day before they needed to start crawling the next day's data. By turning what we now were calling our "pipeline"—a set of interlocking computational modules developed for our two previous projects—we were able to rapidly derive the narrative framework graphs for large parts of the social forum space. These graphs let us explore the germination of new narrative material (which appears as disconnected components in the overall narrative space graph) and witness the process by which, over even very short periods of time measured in days, some narratives fade away while others connect up.

In the midst of the COVID-19 pandemic, we continue to monitor, discuss, and refine our methods; catch up on other research, such as work on Twitter bots or Facebook groups; and address ways to approach new problems. One part of the team ensures the crawls are successful while I, as the lone folklorist on the team, scour the dark web to see if there are other places we should scrape. We keep in touch with various computing support groups to make sure our pipeline can keep up with the significant computational demands of processing tens of thousands of posts and news stories daily, and we spend evening meetings talking about the day's pipeline output, designing the observatory website, and watching to see how the graphs evolve. We also look at the time lines derived from various metadata we collect, figuring out how to model the constant feedback between the discussions on the internet and the reporting of those discussions in the news media. We also keep an eye out for narrative frameworks that seem to have a clear real-world action associated with them: for example, "film your hospital" or "resist social distancing." We're building a website that will allow users to track these narrative networks daily so it can act as a narrative observatory. We don't know where the pandemic is headed, but it is clear that in crises such as this, having big data folklorists involved will keep folkloric thinking at the forefront, allowing us to develop culturally informed and theoretically sound models while potentially developing strategies for averting disruptive activities and supporting positive community-centered action.

Understanding the Information Technology World Ethnographically: Meghan McGrath

Meghan McGrath earned her MA in folklore and her MIS at Indiana University and is the design lead for IBM Pervasive Encryption and the IBM Future Demands Initiative.

"Everyone ends up writing theirs on Post-its," the woman seated next to me is saying. She is a Londoner and works on cybersecurity at one of the biggest banks in the world.

The bank's security policy, she explains, has always been on the stricter side. Employee passwords must be whole sentences with numbers, special characters, and both upper- and lowercase letters, and they need to be changed every four weeks. This is an excellent security strategy—it makes passwords labor-intensive to crack and useless not long after they are discovered—but the bank's employees struggled to remember, then forget, and then remember again their latest passwords. Most people just wrote them down.

"The real problem," she admits, "is that this happens even on the ground floor. Where all the desks are facing the windows. And all the windows are visible from the street—one of the busiest in London. Anyone could look in and see the passwords written there."

Many people struggle to remember login information, but what happens when their passwords are meant to protect things like a home address, a bank account, or a political affiliation? What if that data's vulnerability could result in real, embodied vulnerability for the people it describes? These are more than strings of numbers and characters in a database. Sexual orientation, membership in a religious or philosophical group, membership in a trade union, pregnancy status, and genetic data are considered sensitive by the European General Data Protection Regulation because their exposure "is likely to result in a high risk to the rights and freedoms of individuals." When systems holding that sensitive information are imagined and built without acknowledging the way humans really work, they can be used accidentally or on purpose to cause harm. That's where ethnographers come in.

I joined IBM Z, the company's mainframe branch, after graduating from Indiana University in 2015. Having come across endangered languages in graduate school, I was fascinated by the chance to work with what I still think of as "endangered programming languages"—COBOL, FORTRAN, Assembly—things that "first-generation" programmers learned at college fifty years ago but newer programmers tend to overlook in favor of more approachable languages like Python and Ruby. The paradox is that these languages are becoming as rare as they are ubiquitous—70 percent of universities no longer teach COBOL, but it is used in 70–80 percent of business transactions worldwide. These languages are also used for processing the majority of citizen data, hospital records, airline transactions, mortgage information, and financial data, and not just between people but between nation-states. They are as much a part of the global infrastructure as concrete, shipping containers, or hydroelectricity. In this way, they are disappearing and present at once. It is like a haunted house in which the ghosts are very, very busy.

My role at IBM is officially "design research"—more specifically, cyberse-curity ethnography. I spend time with security professionals around the world to better understand what they love about their jobs and the systems they use, what is frustrating, and what surprises them. One security architect shared the science fiction piece he'd written to navigate the stress of managing a sys-tem that, if breached, could crumble his country's financial infrastructure in minutes. Another talked about the cryptographic key ceremony and the dif-ferent roles participants played on her team. A group of database administra-tors in another country shared joke after joke about the audit process and the pieces most likely to go wrong. That field visit led my team to look more into workplace humor, creating a wall of jokes, riddles, comics, and memes about security—almost a temperature gauge of which topics we may need to dig into more. These jokes often targeted the heart of a problem and articulated how it affected our users in incredibly succinct ways. At one point, we hosted an extremely lively open-mic comedy session for security engineers at IBM's worldwide conference, inviting participants to share their stories about the complexity of their work and the audit compliance process. They killed.

Working with the people using IBM's machines is only half the job. We then take those stories back to IBM hardware teams in a process the com-pany calls "empathy-building." We don't just share statistics about the tasks a mainframe customer does or how fast; we share a multifaceted view of the culture that includes both users and machines. Often a technical team member will come back to ask more about the challenges our users have, the things they care about, or what will make their lives easier, after recognizing a better or different way to design the system with those people in mind. It's here that a joke at a data center in Turkey is turned into a laser-thin change in silicon or copper in Poughkeepsie, New York.

This is the work Dorothy Noyes calls "humble": it is informed by theo-retical frameworks in the abstract but grounded in the practicalities of every-day lived experience. It occupies a middle space, and that in-betweenness, Noyes suggests, is a strength. That we move happily between applied spaces and the loftier edges of capital-T theory—"it's more significant than we think."

Technological infrastructure tends to be built in laboratory conditions. There is often an assumption that everything will run as expected, all the features included will be used, and users will always read the manual. Out in the wild, however, human behavior can get a bit messier. Shortcuts, work-arounds, and roadblocks are a part of our relationships with machines and the increasingly complex, increasingly cyborg networks of which they are a part. I spend a lot of time looking at what *didn't* go as expected or what hap-pened that was surprising or strange. Often, these incidents point to a place where reality strays from the original blueprint of a system's architecture and becomes a whole lot more interesting. The role of the technological folklorist in part is to better understand how humans and computers relate and what that means for the way a system's architecture has explicitly imagined that relationship in code.

The skills and academic heritage of folklorists are incredibly useful in this space. Folklorists are trained to see a world that is nuanced and rich and full of interconnected meaning—which is not necessarily the default among IT disciplines. Approaches that guide us in examining a song tradition that tells a story about displacement, a work of pottery that indicates a relationship between people and land, or the urban legends intertwined with a set of community expectations about the world are no less useful when we approach the relationship between humans and machines.

For those interested in applying folkloristics in this way, finding opportunities to do fieldwork and conduct interviews can be invaluable. Someone who knows how to observe and ask thoughtful questions, who has developed the muscle memory to *listen*, who thinks about structural implications, and who can communicate that to others is someone who can help technological infrastructure itself to be more thoughtfully built on a global scale.

There are many ways to bring technological perspectives into fieldwork and to use your fieldwork to influence technology. The work of tech ethnographers like Genevieve Bell (Intel), Melissa Cefkin (Nissan), and danah boyd (Microsoft) are great examples. The Ethnographic Praxis in Industry Conference (EPIC) community is another amazing introduction to the work being done today, and there is a wealth of materials available online. (I recommend IDEO's design zines and IBM's *Design Thinking Field Guide*.) For those looking into an industry career, creating an online portfolio that shows your process—how you gather data, make sense of it, and share it back with a larger community—can be a powerful way to make visible the value of folkloristics in this context.

Living in what has sometimes been called the Fourth Industrial Revolution, where humans and machines not only work together in deeply networked ways but increasingly share responsibility for autonomy and decision-making, the future and the number of shapes that revolution could take feel incredibly diverse. Some versions of that future may be worrisome or problematic—furthering, for example, systems of oppression—so we hope to anticipate their warning signs and take steps to minimize harm. Some versions might be so delightful and promising that we might ask ourselves what steps we can take this year, next year, and the following to make them even more likely to come about.

Of the many futures toward which our current moment might evolve, I would most like to live in one that folklorists have taken an active part in creating—one that has the fingerprints of the discipline (including a willingness to see informal expression as valid, a hyperawareness of the many forms communication can take, and a fundamental respect for the people who share their stories and skills with us) mottled all over its surface. And possibly one in which the central paradigm for data protection doesn't involve Post-its.

Doing Public Humanities: Danille Christensen

Danille Christensen earned her PhD in folklore at Indiana University and is Professor of Public Humanities in the Department of Religion and Culture at Virginia Tech.

Well into her eighties, my father's mother's mother made scrap quilts, sewing random widths of stripes, plaids, florals, and paisleys across paper diamonds cut from magazines. After trimming these unruly rays, Mary Verona Cox Smyth pieced them into pulsing eight-pointed stars connected by buffering stretches of plain cotton. The one thrown over the back of my couch is backed with flannels; the wide strips she basted over the top and bottom edges to protect against hair pomade and hand oils are still tacked in place.

My favorite bedspread as a teenager was a peach variation of this quilt, one more carefully constructed as a wedding gift for my parents. But it still contained action and mystery. Like the speaker in Teresa Palomo Acosta's poem "My Mother Pieced Quilts," "every morning I awoke to these/october ripened canvases . . . armed/ready/shouting/celebrating," and wondered how my great-grandmother had staked out her plan, what "separate testimonies" were caught in the fragments of poplin and seersucker and flour sack. These quilts—and other storied everyday objects I encountered at interpretive sites during family meanderings—eventually led me to study folklore.

I am drawn to what bell hooks called "humanizing survival strategies," embodied theory and critique, the everyday "habits of being, forms of artistic expression, and aesthetics" that stiffen weary backbones and make space for seeing and speaking. The interplay of private and public has especially intrigued me, and my scholarship has centered on moments when steady, un(re)marked practices like *kī hoʻalu* (slack key guitar) or home canning have become the focus of broader participation and commentary.

In 2015, I was hired at Virginia Tech. My folklore PhD is unique in our unit; my colleagues' degrees come from anthropology, history, religious studies, literature, art history, and linguistics. Together we exemplify the humanities as a field of allied disciplines that explores how people process experience and how we deliberate about conduct and value by means of debate, story, music, and material culture.

Early in the twentieth century, humanities instruction largely bulwarked a cultural canon grounded in classical antiquity, aesthetic analysis, and a presumption of historical objectivity. Since the 1960s, several critical turns have emphasized instead the sociopolitical circumstances (including policings of difference) that shape and are shaped by expressive culture. The field of folklore—at the crossroads of art and anthropology, rhetoric and sociology—has contributed to humanities-based conversations about meaning, identity, performance, and power in part because folklorists have long been focused on the nuances of speaking from (and about) positions of otherness. We have attended to contexts—situational, historical, ideological, economic, communicative—and the ways that savvy individuals adapt to and shift them. We also know that scholars rise on layers of cultural brokerage, including an absolute reliance on local fieldworkers, conservators, and artists.

Public humanities is often framed as a bridging endeavor—an effort to link the institutional to the everyday—or as a mediating impulse that translates the academic into the vernacular. In this usage, the word *public* names a mass audience sometimes imagined in terms of deficits (e.g., non-academics). *Public-facing* is another descriptor, suggesting an outward orientation: the opposite of navel-gazing. What is at stake, in any case, is knowledge production and transmission, realized in verbs (*document, display, inform, disseminate, preserve, revitalize*) that assert various relations of power. One model of public humanities assumes that academics generate specialized ideas that are then packaged for the public in festivals, films, exhibitions, lectures, and mediated discussions.

But the town/gown divide is more complicated than that rhyme suggests. Sitting at my desk in the mountains of southwest Virginia, in a subdivision abutting an R1 university known for its "Invent the Future" tagline, I can hear a fiddler practicing across the back fence, ornaments and refrains sliding over the steady drone of a lower string and the engines from a nearby highway. A young raccoon is holed up in the shade under my neighbor's solar panels, waiting until nightfall to make its escape. The folklorist in me recognizes divides constructed through speech and symbol but also sees the complexities of real-time interactions. Here in Blacksburg, wildlife companionably coexists with cutting-edge technology; Appalachia has always been a space of performed traditions and the exchange and transformation of new ideas;

and engineers share knowledge in academic journals, but also via informal practices shot through with pattern and play.

Although the practice of public humanities is often located in museums, libraries, arts councils, and historical societies, as a professor I seek to bring experts framed as vernacular into the academy and its discussions. My aim is to host and amplify rather than to bridge or translate. A public humanities mindset can encompass diverse publics (including constituents internal to the academy), and it influences what I study, where I publish, and how I teach.

For instance, I try to disrupt dichotomies that bracket laypeople. What can seventeenth-century gooseberry recipes reveal about innovation's capacity to exceed the bounds of laboratories? How do fan behaviors affect the ideological messages encoded in American football? What can scrapbook makers teach credentialed ethnographers about the risks of reflexive documentation? What will surprise, delight, and inform graduate students when they visit a one-room museum maintained by curators with no formal training? As I explore these questions, I prefer writing styles that feel familiar and publications that are accessible to broad readerships, including social media conversations, poetry links in email signatures, podcast recommendations, and blogged encounters.

I also work to welcome local experts to campus. R&B artist Doris Fields, who grew up in West Virginia's coalfields, recently asked my students why academic conferences about the blues are so often dominated by White commentators while Black performers hold private discussions at side tables as they wait to take the stage. At a panel about apple cultures in Appalachia, Monacan elder Sue Elliott shared powerful testimony about her family's orchard knowledge and labor in segregated Virginia. And students are regularly surprised by how much they enjoy square dance workshops, experiences that help them attend to gender dynamics, recognize the string band's skilled event management, and discuss conflicting framings of the genre's history.

My teaching does facilitate the technical skills important to public humanities practice: budgeting, media production, label writing, metadata design, and so forth. As students learn to gather, process, and present primary data, we also consider how grant writing, fieldwork, transcription, and description demand analytical acuity and ethical attention. What does it mean to "show"? How do asymmetries of power determine what gets documented, conserved, and displayed? What community-identified needs will this programming address? Who is excluded and why? What technologies will enable source-community input on object contextualization and care? How will you reciprocate?

In short, a folklorist's public humanities involves decentering the academy as the site of knowledge production. Field schools like those organized by the American Folklife Center share techniques broadly in order to enable self-documentation, and field surveys can be an exercise in "asset mapping," honoring the expertise all around us. Mini-apprenticeships with beekeepers, welders, bakers, farmers, and quilters offer students opportunities to consider how people teach, comment, and create and then to bring their conclusions back to campus as exhibits, poster sessions, or reflections of smaller scope. For instance, during the first stressful weeks of the COVID-19 quarantine, my spring 2020 undergraduates pivoted to a "maker" project. They asked relatives for cooking tips, learned elaborate braiding techniques from websites, admired peers' newly embroidered high-tops, and offered each other advice on perfecting guitar licks or preparing potato beds. In the process, they experienced the achievement of innovation, the complexities of knowledge transfer, and the meanings and markers of expertise.

Experiential learning of the kind intrinsic to public humanities work is gaining traction in the academy. Administrative models that privilege revenue production mean that departments increasingly compete for enrollments; facing uncertain job markets, students want evidence that coursework delivers marketable skills. Stung by populist critiques, arts councils and universities seek out new audiences and experiences, making perspective taking central to programming and degree progression. Sometimes this holistic "purpose-driven" approach is valorized as "authentic learning"—an idea I push back against on grant panels or advisory boards. The point is not to reify difference but to envision publics (and their knowledges) as coextensive with historically elite spaces, as bodies always created through engagement.

I was in high school when I first read Acosta's resonant poem quoted on page 24 about scrap quilts (and spinach fields, illness, and courtship). It turns out that her poem was part of a groundbreaking 1973 gathering of Chicano writers at USC, a three-day public event named after the Náhuatl term for poetry. I am grateful for this attention to the imbrications of personal and political, material and verbal, creative labor and intellectual inquiry—work that reframed the makings of my own foremothers and set me on a path through the humanities that keeps the daily ever in mind.

SERVING A CAMPUS AS AN INTERNATIONAL SCHOLAR: ZIYING YOU

Ziying You earned her PhD in East Asian languages and literatures at The Ohio State University and is Assistant Professor of Chinese Studies at the College of Wooster.

In 2015 I came to the College of Wooster (COW) as a visiting scholar, and my position there became permanent in fall 2020. I chose to work at

COW because of the college's commitment to cultural diversity, equity, and inclusion and its strong support system for the well-being and success of its students and faculty members. My COW faculty colleagues and I work to prepare students, as the college says, to "become leaders of character and influence in an interdependent global community." As a COW faculty member and a scholar from another country, I have tried to find opportunities to contribute to the well-being of this community: this orientation is also a core value of the folklore studies field.

Saturday, February 8, 2020, the fifteenth day of the first month in the lunisolar Chinese calendar, marked the traditional Lantern Festival and the end of the Chinese New Year celebration. I organized a special party for Chinese scholars and students to celebrate the festival at the college. The COVID-19 pandemic broke out in Wuhan, China, in January 2020, and as of early February, the World Health Organization had not yet officially recognized it as a global pandemic. COW faculty, staff, and students were still living a peaceful life on campus, as the pandemic had not yet affected people's lives in the United States. However, I sensed Chinese students' internalized trauma in my Food and Religion in China course in late January and decided to cancel the class field trip to a Chinese restaurant and grocery stores since no Chinese students signed up for the event. In addition, I worked with administrators and staff to support Chinese students during the outbreak of COVID-19. As a scholar from China and also a female faculty member of color, I devoted myself to building a diverse, inclusive, equal, and just community at Wooster and beyond. I understood Chinese students' pain to read the heartbreaking news from China, their deep concerns about their families and loved ones, and their anger at racial discrimination toward Chinese people during the outbreak of COVID-19.

On January 30, the US State Department issued a travel advisory telling Americans not to travel to China because of the public health threat posed by COVID-19. Under complicated circumstances, Chinese students had no choice but to stay on campus to finish their schoolwork, which made some of them feel helpless and desperate. Representing the Chinese Studies Department, I reached out to Chinese students and asked them what we could do to support them at that moment. I was touched to know that some of them wanted to be together and eat *tangyuan* rice balls to celebrate the Lantern Festival, something that had never been done before at COW. *Tangyuan* is an important food to serve for the Lantern Festival, the Winter Solstice Festival, and other important occasions, such as weddings and family reunions, because it symbolizes union and happiness. Our department chair kindly approved the budget quickly, and I ordered 140 *tangyuan*, 140 dumplings, and fried rice noodles from the China Garden restaurant for the Lantern Festival celebration. China Garden did not sell *tangyuan*, but Xiufang—the restaurant owner, a native Chinese—asked her mother to make *tangyuan* for us as a special case. The celebration was scheduled three days before the Lantern Festival, and the restaurant workers quickly bought ingredients and prepared for our order. On the day of the festival, Xiufang's mother made 70 *tangyuan* with sweet fillings and 70 *tangyuan* with salted meat fillings. She boiled them with hot water right before our party started on the evening of February 8.

Many people showed up at the Lantern Festival party, including COW chief communications and marketing officer Melissa Anderson, who kindly helped me promote the event in public. I invited participants to bring their own bowls and chopsticks in order to save trees and protect the environment. Melissa brought a bowl made of coconut, and we started to chat over our bowls filled with these delicious foods. Our students had a great time eating *tangyuan* and celebrating the Lantern Festival together. Because of the strict quarantine policies in China, for the first time, most Chinese people did not get the chance to reunite with their big families to celebrate the Chinese New Year and Lantern Festival together. It was a luxury for Chinese scholars and students to share the celebration overseas. As the celebration came to an end, some friends suggested I organize the Lantern Festival celebration every year at Wooster with *tangyuan* and lanterns. I was very happy that I was able to integrate my folklore scholarship and practice through this event.

Four days later, Sarah Bolton, the president of the College of Wooster, kindly invited Chinese scholars and students to an open house at her home for a casual gathering of fellowship, food, and conversation. Particularly at a time when COVID-19 was affecting so many Chinese people in different ways, we all were very touched by President Bolton's kindness and compassion, and we felt strongly connected and united when dealing with this unprecedented challenge. Later, when COVID-19 spread in the United States, President Bolton led the whole COW community as we worked together to keep everyone safe, healthy, and supported.

As an international scholar, my training, teaching, and research in China and the United States have broadened my perspectives and strengthened my faith in social justice and equality. Concern with diversity, equity, and inclusion has been central to my research, teaching, and service. My folklore research broadly focuses on grassroots work and authority in cultural protection and heritage management and the role of ordinary people in cultural transmission, reproduction, and transformation. My book *Folk Literati, Contested Tradition, and Heritage in Contemporary China: Incense Is Kept Burning* (Indiana University Press, 2020) addresses the role of folk literati in transmitting, producing, and reproducing local traditions, as well as controversies and conflicts over tradition reconstruction and the safeguarding of intangible cultural heritage (ICH) within local contexts in contemporary China. I coined the term *folk literati* to refer to people trained in classical Chinese literature; knowledgeable about local history, legends, and beliefs; and capable of representing those traditions in oral communication and writing. Although the elite literati have been widely studied as a significant social group in cultural production in premodern Chinese history and literature, little attention has been paid to the living conditions of folk literati and their important role in remaking and representing local traditions in contemporary China. I draw on my ethnographic research to present their important role in reproducing local traditions and continuing stigmatized but persistent beliefs in a community context.

My international perspectives also contributed to the completion of my other work, including *Chinese Folklore Studies Today: Discourse and Practice* (coedited with Lijun Zhang, Indiana University Press, 2019) and "Intangible Cultural Heritage in Asia: Traditions in Transition" (a special issue of the journal *Asian Ethnology*, coedited with Patricia Ann Hardwick).

As a folklorist, I strive to be a good member of the communities with whom I work and identify professionally and personally. In 2009–2011, I served as the junior convener of the Transnational Asia/Pacific Section of the American Folklore Society (AFS), and I organized several panels at AFS annual conferences. After a flood devastated the villages where I had done fieldwork in China, I organized a silent auction at OSU in spring 2013 that raised $2,500 for disaster relief, after which I returned to my fieldwork site and worked with local community members to distribute the funds to support thirty-one households, fourteen of which had lost their homes to the flood. I also used the funds to purchase educational supplies for students at three elementary schools and to sponsor a performance of regional opera at the village temple fair.

My interests in disaster narrative led me to collaborate with faculty member Wang Xiaokui of the Southern University of Science and Technology in Shenzhen, Guangdong Province, China. In February 2020 he created an interdisciplinary collaborative research team to study the memories of the COVID-19 pandemic, and I was very honored to be part of the team. My original plan was to collect survivor-centered narratives about the outbreak of COVID-19 in Wuhan and propose better strategies to deal with public health crisis in the future, but as the pandemic spread globally, I started to collect oral histories and personal experience narratives of Chinese people in the United States about the COVID-19 pandemic. This research aims to convey the voice of Chinese people in the United States when they have been marginalized to some extent in both the United States and China during the pandemic and to help us build a diverse, inclusive, and equal global society.

WORKING AS AN INDEPENDENT SCHOLAR: LUISA DEL GIUDICE

Luisa Del Giudice earned her PhD in Italian studies at the University of California, Los Angeles, and is an independent scholar in Los Angeles.

The term by which I now call myself, *independent scholar*, covers a wide range of roles: university professor, public educator, advocate, community organizer, local historian, cultural mediator, public intellectual, community leader, cultural programmer, and public-relations person—all of which I have filled, along with a host of other as-needed roles, including Knight of the Italian Republic (as recognition for this work)! The fact is, from the moment I discovered the field of folklore rather late in the game (just as I was to choose a dissertation topic), I felt a compelling, all-consuming need to reconnect broken cultural identity lines. The professional and the personal fused as I sought to recompose an oral history and oral culture that were also my own and learn where I belonged in the Italian diaspora and within Italian history and migration. Therefore, the topics I chose to pursue, despite not much interest from or long-term support in academia, led me to a broad spectrum of communities, organizations, and international and political arenas. But, upon reflection, it may have been precisely because of the lack of institutional affiliation that I had no one to censor me and few paradigms into which I needed to fit, and thus I was free to speak, act, organize, and advocate as my head and heart guided me. When I saw a need, I tried to fill it; where there was no one speaking for Italian oral culture and history, for example, I created an Italian Oral History Institute to express a very specific vision of cultural work. And because I enjoyed wide horizons and a fairly unhampered life, I gravitated toward an international arena and became a world wanderer. I especially enjoy this aspect—being free to say yes to the widest sorts of opportunities and interests: collecting ballads in the mountains of Lombardy for the regional Italian government, conducting Veterans History Project workshops in the Northern Mariana Islands for the Library of Congress, lecturing in the University of Aberdeen's Elphinstone Institute field school, delivering a keynote at an Island Dynamics conference in China, accepting a visiting professorship of oral history in the Department of Ethiopian Folklore at Addis Ababa University, and serving on past and present editorial boards of Slovenian, French Canadian, American, and Italian journals.

While turning away from more conventional medieval and Renaissance Italian literature and toward Italian folk song began my journey, as the daughter of peasant Italians, it was the deeply self-ethnographic project of orality that engaged and sustained all I pursued. My dialectologist husband encouraged this path of oral research, but it soon became self-propelled, and this discovery of the highly personal and the highly local led me into ever-widening global arenas. Throughout all those years as a "wandering" independent scholar, organizations such as the American Folklore Society (on whose Executive Board I currently sit, chairing its International Committee), the KfV (the Kommission für Volksdichtung, or International Ballad Commission, where I have served as vice president and president), and the SIEF (la Société internationale d'ethnologie et de folklore) kept me focused, publishing, and connected to my field. I assumed leadership roles within these organizations to express my professional identity as an academic and public-sector folklorist.

Having had a good grounding within the academy, I continued to address many of its guideposts: teaching, publishing, attending conferences, and lecturing. But it was the growing conviction that what I was discovering through research was important to a wider segment of the Italian diaspora that led me to seek out ways to share and present and advocate more broadly. My goal was to benefit the public *outside* the academy, as well as insiders, both Italians and non-Italians. I added "public sector folklorist" to my list of roles, seeking to link and network as widely as possible with city administrations, cultural and arts institutions, universities, faith traditions, and local Italian government authorities—without whose support not much could have been accomplished. I sought to speak to wider and more diverse audiences and learned to become an advocate. Such mainstream attention seemed to increase the value of historical traditions for diaspora Italians themselves. My "formula" was simply this: program both a conference and a festival so scholars could share their expertise with other scholars as well as with a wider and more general audience and thereby present that art or cultural form in its fullest three-dimensionality through exhibitions, concerts, workshops, food events, and tours. Many of our programs crossed cultural and even faith boundaries, attempting to model global citizenship and more expansive dialogue for Italians themselves.

Such work helped me evolve as a scholar and a public intellectual, from the work of cultural equity and advocacy, toward what most deeply motivates me today: social justice. I intentionally use many of our own traditions and cultural figures to focus scholarship and public attention on current (and recurring) issues such as food justice (e.g., St. Joseph's Day Tables; the *Paese di Cuccagna*, or Land of Cockaigne), migration and belonging (the Watts Towers), and even indigenous rights (in the No Columbus Day campaign), often in collaboration with other scholars. That is, we can see Sabato Rodia's Towers in Watts (which he named *Nuestro Pueblo*) as a single immigrant artist's monumental expression of cultural memory, a gathering place, and a site of migration history and communal art. The towers may also be the greatest work of "outsider" art in the world. Through international conferences and festivals, we refocused local and global on this artwork for a new generation of activist scholars, including those who support Black Lives Matter and immigration reform. As a result, I have been invited to sit on the mayor's Watts Towers task force: an opportunity to help advocate for the monument and its communities from a local, cross-cultural, and international perspective, all while still speaking about the Watts Towers from an Italian perspective. Similar plural values are manifest in the mid-Lenten Sicilian St. Joseph's Day tradition, which serves as a way of welcoming the stranger and feeding the poor and has also evolved in a multicultural context as it has been pressed into service to address current crises, such as food insecurity and immigration policies. Even the No Columbus Day campaign was our way, as scholars of Italian descent, to become allies for indigenous peoples and advocate for righting historic wrongs.

This evolving and heightened sense of purpose was intertwined with my growing sense of who I wanted to be in the world and the ethical stance I wished to defend as a scholar. I honed my listening skills to better discern what was needed for individuals, communities, and those beyond and how I might respond. Along the way, I trained as a spiritual director, adding that dimension to a listening folklorist and oral historian's tool kit, deepening the practice of listening from the heart that I think so important to become scholars of head *and* heart. It is the sort of listening, discerning, and sharing from the heart that I encouraged other scholarly women to engage with in a collection of essays I edited, *On Second Thought: Learned Women Reflect on Profession, Community, and Purpose*. It was an exercise in life review (as is this short essay itself), an experience in self-reflection and self-expression (something academics are not always encouraged to do), and ultimately also an act of political advocacy from deep within the War Against Women, the #MeToo movement, and the regressively patriarchal world being defended by the current administration, for which it seems to be nostalgic.

And here I am, writing in the time of the coronavirus. As someone who has personally faced and survived many professional hurdles as a folklorist and experienced others in the range of work folklorists engage with, I feel freer to reflect, speak, and advocate on our own behalf as well as on behalf of those we "serve"—besides being a vocal protestor, joining every march, signing every petition, and writing letters to politicians and voters—such that my own research and public programs seemed to have momentarily taken a back seat, and yet not really, because we continue to defend the folklorist's favored worldview and the values folklorists care so much about and over which they have gone to battle for generations: diversity and inclusion, human rights, cultural equity, and the common good of the people.

So, while only a small portion of my professional work has ever been remunerated, my life's work has been richly rewarding. I've acquired skills, knowledge, and insights on this path, for which I am immensely grateful. And you can't pay for that.

TEACHING AT A COMMUNITY COLLEGE: DAVID J. PUGLIA

David J. Puglia earned his PhD in American studies at Penn State Harrisburg and is Associate Professor and Deputy Chairperson in the Department of English Language and Literature at Bronx Community College of the City University of New York (CUNY).

Community college—thirteenth grade, halfway college, high school with ashtrays—is often seen as a second-rate school for slacker students and amateur professors. Facing such grim, albeit flawed, public perception, why would any academic risk community college stigma? While not for everyone, I've found community college life not only adequate but ideal for a folklorist wishing to teach introductory folklore and study local folkways.

A community college is, in brief, an undergraduate institution where students can earn a two-year technical degree or complete the first two years of a bachelor's degree. Community colleges do not seek prestige; they are access oriented, shun exclusive admissions standards, and exude the same democratic, populist, and community-centered ethos folklorists champion. Slacker students? Many do come underprepared and in need of remediation. More common, though, are students of modest means who wish or need to remain close to home while working less-than-desirable jobs, raising children, caring for elders, or striving for upgraded careers. Busy? Yes. Distracted? At times. Lazy? Certainly not. How about these so-called professors? While I can speak only for our discipline, notable folklorists teach or have taught at two-year, junior, vocational, technical, and community colleges.

As to credentials, community colleges do rely heavily on part-time faculty, but these instructors do not lack credentials—many hold PhDs or their equivalent in other fields. The plight of contingent academic labor resides in their negligible status, stability, and compensation, not their classroom readiness.

In my own case, I learned of Bronx Community College the semester I defended my dissertation when I stumbled upon a job advertisement hours before the deadline while sitting in rural Pennsylvania. The posting sought a prospective assistant professor with a specialty in folklore who could also teach writing courses. I'd visited New York City only a few times, but I did have a *Style Wars* poster hanging in my study. And for the past five years, I'd taught folklore and writing at Penn State Harrisburg. I was intrigued. It wasn't the hollers of Kentucky or the rolling hills of Pennsylvania that I'd envisioned for my folklore career, but the urban adventure appealed to me. Full-time, tenure-track, teaching folklore, in Gotham . . . and salaried? I finished my application a minute before midnight.

Half a decade later, my experience, simply stated, comes down to this: being a folklorist at a community college resembles being a folklorist at any other school but with an added emphasis on teaching. If a research university emphasizes research, teaching, and service, in that order, a community college emphasizes teaching, service, and research, in that order. By added emphasis, I don't mean to imply community college professors' teaching is superior in skill or gravity. We simply do it more, fret over it more, discuss it more. I'm not convinced community college faculty, at least at CUNY, haunt the classroom *that* much more than faculty at regional or directional four-year colleges; after accounting for reassigned time, supplemental hours for special courses, and various university release programs, my average colleague teaches a few courses per semester a few days per week, with a couple preps per semester. That is to say, emphasis on teaching encompasses more than a heavy teaching load—it denotes an incessant striving for novel ways to reach a hyperchallenging but ultrarewarding student population. To that end, professional seminars, campus conferences, professional development opportunities, institutional assessments, presidential grants, and conversations in the hallway address teaching. Research on the mind, perhaps, but teaching on the lips.

As a folklorist teaching at a community college, I teach Introduction to Folklore *a lot* (lower level by definition, two-year college catalogs lack the cornucopia of upper-level and special-topic seminars to choose from). I consider myself fortunate, as Introduction to Folklore provides endless stimulation and satisfaction. In my role, I teach folklore and folklore methods primarily to nonspecialists. Besides occasional English majors (who, even then, in my experience, consider themselves literati, not folklorists), students take my course to fulfill an elective graduation requirement. And how lucky am I? For these students, the course amounts to a literal once-in-a-lifetime opportunity to study and appreciate folklore. My students don't wish to upend the discipline or even contribute to it in any formal sense, but, as neophytes, they sharpen my folkloristic acumen by keeping me on my toes, challenging my lazy disciplinarian assumptions, and demanding practical explanations for how theoretical concepts apply to significant real-world settings. My modest goal: encourage these students to carry on as amateur folklorists for the rest of their lives.

Community colleges foreground teaching; their faculty teach frequently and, by necessity, also teach *broadly*. While I'm fortunate at CUNY, elsewhere twelve to fifteen hours (or four to five courses) per semester is the norm. Since most humble two-year campuses cannot sustain four to five sections per semester of Introduction to Folklore, folklorists at community colleges must diversify, offering either kindred courses (e.g., children's, ethnic, or regional literature), bread-and-butter service courses (e.g., English composition, cultural diversity, or a first-year seminar), or cross-listed courses (e.g., art or music surveys). Fortunately, folklorists are enthusiastic transdisciplinarians and talented curricular magicians. We can transform any teaching assignment. *Abracadabra!* Poof, a folklore course appears. In the same spell of transmogrification, folklorists make for excellent shapeshifters, deftly melding into any department—an essential skill in a two-year institution. Community colleges bankroll no folklore departments, nor am I aware of any student earning an Associate of Arts in folklore. Folklorists at community colleges teach in other disciplines' departments, where they thrive at coexistence, perhaps even animating their colleagues with the vernacular spirit.

Some denigrate community college careers because of the perception that these jobs do not afford the time or resources to conduct research. While strenuous course loads and needy students lead to prioritizing teaching, tenure-track community college professors are active scholars. (At CUNY they must be if they aspire to reappointment, tenure, and promotion.) I can sympathize with scientists who might rue their lot at community colleges. A small teaching-oriented campus often lacks adequate facilities for complex chemical or biological laboratory research. Not so for folklorists, who can think of themselves as living and working in their laboratory. In fact, most community college folklorists, whether by predisposition or necessity, wisely ground at least some of their research in the local community, as opposed to interest exclusively in distant lands or abstract theoretical concepts. Rather than bemoaning the teaching load or intellectual isolation, I laud the opportunity to study a community in an institution devoted to the same. The community college jells with the community to a degree that four-year colleges cannot: the mere idea of a town/gown divide repulses community colleges. For inroads into the community, the staggering diversity notwithstanding, one trait students share is being from "around here." Despite my degrees and supposed expertise, every semester students in my folklore classroom demonstrate mastery of city folkways I've never even heard of. For a folklorist seeking community-based research, these students make for willing guides and brilliant mentors, always eager to tutor the teacher. Community colleges also excel in exhibiting folklore and folklife research, with their campuses constituting potential public programming outposts in every state, province, and territory. With or without folklorists' input, community college campuses host exhibits, lectures, and performances of local history, heritage, and culture. As prominent and practical places to present and display the fruits of folklorists' fieldwork, community colleges offer plentiful possibilities for programming and presentation.

In my opening, I speculated that community college, on closer inspection, might form the ideal job setting for a folklorist. The reverse may prove equally true: folklorists are the ideal community college faculty members. In collegiality, in teaching, in research, and in service, the folklorist's raison d'être shines at the community college: embracing community, spurning elitism, extoling diversity, and championing democracy. As a community-based home for scholars interested in communities, community colleges are a perfect match for folklorists: a mutually beneficial symbiotic relationship to encourage, nurture, and increase. I urge more academic folklorists to seek out full-time careers at community colleges, and I suggest that public, applied, and independent folklorists across North America pursue abundant part-time teaching opportunities at their local community colleges, where thousands of two-year schools give rise to favorable conditions for introducing the local community to the study of emergent and living traditions.

Teaching Undergraduate Students: David Todd Lawrence

David Todd Lawrence earned his PhD in English at the University of Missouri and is Associate Professor in the Department of English at the University of St. Thomas.

I teach at a medium-sized university in St. Paul, Minnesota. It is primarily an undergraduate institution, so while our faculty and students certainly engage in research, our emphasis is on undergraduate teaching. I am housed in an English department where there are no folklore courses on the books. Judging from their titles, most of the courses I teach might seem to have no connection whatsoever to folklore . But the truth is that I am actually teaching folklore all the time, and there are two very important ways folklore influences the work I do as a faculty member teaching mostly undergraduate students. The first has to do with *what* I teach and the second with *how* I teach.

I was hired into my department to teach African American literature and culture, but like a lot of college faculty who don't teach at research institutions or are members of smaller departments, this is not the only area I teach: I also teach courses in introductory writing, American literature, and cultural studies. Once in a while, I am able to teach a dedicated folklore course, but with my other teaching responsibilities, this doesn't happen too often. As a result, when I teach folklore, it is usually within a course on one of these other subjects. This is often because the kinds of texts I choose to teach and the way I think about any particular subject are always influenced by folklore studies.

For example, my training was in both folklore *and* African American literature and culture. These two areas have always been inextricably connected. African American culture is rooted in an oral tradition of storytelling, music making, foodways, belief, and customs. Black people who were brought to the United States as slaves carried their culture along with them. Kidnapped and enslaved Africans came from peoples with highly developed cultures, and Wolof, Akan, Mande, Igbo, and other African people did not leave their culture behind them in Africa. It traveled with them embedded in their minds, emerging in their everyday lives as they struggled to survive in the New World. Learning about African American literature, then, requires that you learn about and engage with the traditional culture and practices of the African diaspora before, during, and after slavery, and elements of that culture still manifest in contemporary African American culture today. So, whenever I teach African American literature and culture, I am always teaching folklore.

The other way my teaching is influenced by folklore comes from my training as an ethnographer. I am a folklorist, but I am not an expert on any specific aspect of folklore. I am not a specialist in any particular genre or group. I do teach these things, but my research isn't focused on any one area of folklore. I think of myself primarily as an ethnographer. My expertise is in a research methodology. I write and think about and theorize ethnography as much or even more than I actually do it. While I tend to work on projects that focus on the experiences of Black people in some way, I have also worked on other projects with groups whose members' connections to each other haven't been defined by race at all. The one connecting factor in my work is ethnography.

When we do ethnography, we attempt to learn about, understand, and represent the "groupness" of people—the features of their everyday lives that tie them together. When we do ethnography, we attempt to do something that is both fascinating and impossible. I think it is fair to say that most folklorists who have done ethnographic studies would admit that their efforts to understand and convey significant understanding of the groups they have worked with have inevitably come up short. For the ethnographer there is always something missing, always something that evades her grasp. Even if we practice the most careful and conscientious brand of ethnographic observation, we will be unable to fully represent the aspects of the group we hoped to convey to our readers or viewers or listeners. In this way ethnography is a failed endeavor, and the ethnographer must learn to accept that reality. In so doing—in embracing the vulnerability of failure—the ethnographer makes herself even more perceptive and enables herself to practice a more radical form of listening.

Early ethnographers saw themselves and the research they did as objective. They thought of themselves as coming to their research as completely neutral observers who would, if patient and skilled enough, capture a comprehensive picture of a group (usually "exotic" and "other") and represent it in its entirety to their Western audience. Ethnographers today have largely rejected this way of thinking about our work. We now recognize that ethnography is as much about understanding ourselves and our own position in the world as it is about representing other people. Ethnographers acknowledge that they bring much to the encounter with others—not all of it good—and that rather than an endeavor in which we conquer the unknown, ethnographic work is a constant struggle to surrender to it. As ethnographers we must work to accept inevitable failure in trying to fully comprehend and present the experience of people who are not ourselves. In positioning ourselves this way, we enter into the space of encounter as novices rather than experts, as listeners rather than speakers. As one of my former teachers told me recently, as an ethnographer the most important thing you bring to the encounter is "the gift of your presence." If we are willing to be completely present with the folks we work with, if we are willing to accept the probability that what we think will happen is not what will happen, if we expect and embrace the reality that what we hope to achieve will probably not be achieved, if we open ourselves up to the inevitable failure of ethnography, we open ourselves up to so much more than we might ever have expected to encounter. In doing all this, we open ourselves up to more readily receive from our collaborators that which resists our expectations of them. For me, learning that this kind of failure can actually be productive is another way folklore has profoundly influenced my work as an undergraduate teacher on a daily basis.

This approach is mirrored in my teaching pedagogy. As an undergraduate teacher, my job is not to disseminate information or "fill students' minds." My job is to help them understand themselves as members of a community. As teachers in the liberal arts, we do more than simply make sure students have read certain books or know certain ideas. We help them become critical subjects able to clearly see the world as it is and as it can be. To that end, I have found that I must utilize many of the same attributes that make a good ethnographer. There is certainly something to be said for the college professor who can hold a room of three hundred students enraptured for an hour-long lecture. Most of us, however, ply our trade in the presence of far fewer students, and in those more intimate settings, it is far more important to be a good listener than it is to be a rapturous speaker. To listen fully and radically, we must consider our own position in the world and how our history and experience color how we show up in any particular moment in time. To facilitate the collaborative production of knowledge, a teacher must create an environment of safety in which each student feels she has the ability to try to take a first step toward becoming who she will eventually be as a thinking person. Like the ethnographer, the teacher cannot go in believing she has all the knowledge; we must be open, flexible, perceptive, and nimble, able to respond to whatever unpredictable thing might happen. We need to decenter power as much as possible, and, most important, we need to be vulnerable and willing to have it all fail and fall apart.

The work faculty do with graduate students is important to the continuation of knowledge and research production, but I believe the work of undergraduate teachers is just as important, if not more so. We help prepare students for the lives they will live in the academy or elsewhere. While *what* we teach our students is certainly important, *how* we teach and *who we are when we teach* are equally important. My education and training as a folklorist have helped me teach students in a way that is sensitive to who they are, what they think, what they believe, how they speak, and all the things that make them who they are, even when I'm not teaching folklore . . . which I always am.

TEACHING GRADUATE STUDENTS: RAY CASHMAN

Ray Cashman earned his PhD in folklore at Indiana University, where he serves as Professor of Folklore and Director of the Folklore Institute.

Graduate teaching entails the privilege and duty of replenishing the field of folklore studies in its many forms. More bluntly, I help train our replacements while spreading the folklore gospel to fellow travelers in nearby departments (English, anthropology, history, area studies, etc.).

Familiar with the dynamics of cultural continuity and change, I do not seek disciplinary replication via rote learning or through a selfish-gene model of pointing students only to ideas and methods I like or find useful. I understand my goal to be setting out the merchandise: exposing recent converts and potential new ones to what folklore studies has had to offer over time and then letting students find their own way by trying out those tools and applying them to their own interests. Whether I succeed in doing so is another story, but the guiding principles are clear even when I fall short of the mark.

Let's break down the job into roughly sequential tasks: course design and pedagogy, mentorship, and continuing support through to my eventual (indeed, hoped-for) obsolescence to a fully launched new MA or PhD.

Arguably, a graduate teacher's most crucial task is choosing the readings around which a course revolves and creating assignments that invite students to synthesize those readings and apply them to independent research. In the process, students critique, qualify, and/or extend the methods and ideas in those readings after applying them to new data of their choice and/or reading them against counterarguments, and the circle of thinking life continues. But how do you choose appropriate, productive, and inspiring readings to facilitate the process? It depends, of course, on so many things: which class, which audience, at what level, how the class serves a program's broader curriculum.

For example, take the F516 Folklore Theory in Practice course I teach at Indiana University as a required graduate-level introduction to folklore studies, a course that parallels similar ones elsewhere. My first impulse is to choose those epiphany-provoking readings that led to my own conversion to folklore studies. Equally important are (sometimes less stirring) readings that provide necessary connective tissue in the evolution of thinking in our discipline, ones anyone with a folklore MA, PhD, or PhD minor or concentration needs to have read.

Then comes a mass of equally important concerns, and here we all have to find ways to strike our own balance when cuts have to be made. It's important to me to offer a range of genres, plus beyond-genre categories such as belief; a range of case studies from different periods and places; a range of methods and theories over time (not just the stuff I read in grad school and not just the self-proclaimed cutting-edge stuff published in the last five years); and a fair representation of both male and female scholars and scholars of color, noting that those demographics in earlier eras may be less diverse. In the end, syllabus construction is an exercise in choice; you have only so many reading slots and only so many other courses that can pick up where yours leaves off. Given the impossibility of reconciling all the variables, I believe we should try our best but not allow perfection to become the enemy of the good.

I go on at length about the syllabus not because the class teaches itself thereafter but because even a suboptimal teacher (me on a bad day) or teaching environment (Zoom during the COVID-19 pandemic) cannot compromise the core content if it is well considered. In my experience, teaching is a lifelong process of gradual improvement; it is impossible to completely master but nevertheless is undertaken in the service of others. Here is not the place to elaborate every pedagogical trick of the trade, but there are some I like to reuse across courses. For example, having guest speakers, particularly the authors of readings, join the class is always intellectually productive and offers students inside information into how and why real people like themselves hone their craft. In most seminars, I also like to take advantage of online discussion sections to include a "what I wish I had said" assignment—a chance for people (like me) who may be slow to speak to share in a later class what there wasn't time for or what they hadn't yet fully formulated.

Other moves are better suited to one type of class than another. In an introductory grad course such as F516, I am prepared to lecture more, but I must temper that with the knowledge that (usually) the person having to do the most talking is doing the most learning. I try to talk less, ask more open-ended questions, and have students take more responsibility in advanced theoretical seminars, such as those on performance studies, folklore and memory, and tradition and modernity. Likewise, in methods classes, such as ethnographic fieldwork, the course unfolds more like a workshop and is divided into practical instruction, discussion of fewer readings, and group critiques of hands-on fieldwork exercises that each student completes and that build on each other to culminate in final projects. More and more, my geographically focused courses (such as Irish Folklore or Folklore of the Southern US) have to be offered as hybrid graduate-undergraduate courses, which requires effort to reach different audiences during class and additional time with graduate students for further discussion outside of class.

While syllabi and coursework lay the crucial foundation, they are only the beginning for the teacher-student relationship. Possibly the greater amount of time and energy goes into everything that develops outside the classroom. Apart from what happens around seminar tables, other important work continues: modeling best practices for teaching, research, and editorial assistants; brainstorming approaches to research; discussing comments on term papers and the possibilities for publication after revision; tutoring first-time conference presenters; and coaching students through their qualifying exams and eventually through their dissertation research and writing. Along the way, I find myself forwarding new research, funding notices, calls for papers, and job announcements that fit individual students' interests. Writing letters of recommendation for students and helping them craft grant and job search materials stretches from their early searches for travel funding through their job searches and promotion reviews. The process is not always fun or easy for students, so the mentor role can involve a fair amount of care, including empathetic listening and advice and more material help when appropriate.

I could make the case that the chief value of folklore graduate school is the opportunity to become self-aware about values, refine habits of mind and practice, and gather perspectives (of all sorts, positive and negative) about humanity. Granted, becoming a better citizen of the world alone doesn't pay the rent, and college administrators will always judge graduate programs by the percentage of gainfully employed graduates. So mentors and students should be aware of trends in the world and in the job market. Furthermore, no folklorist should take only folklore courses. Our cousins in nearby disciplines have valuable perspectives on parallel concerns, and being able to meaningfully communicate and collaborate across disciplines has always been essential for the evolution of our field.

The general advice I give to graduate students is that you should pursue the topics, methods, and ideas that most engage you, rather than choose a minor, MA project, or dissertation topic based largely on often incorrect or incomplete perceptions of being hirable. From the short-term perspective of individual progress, ideally your capstone project will be of enough personal interest to help you push through the inevitable doldrums and roadblocks. More broadly, job market trends change rapidly and continually (at least at the surface), making it difficult to pull off the strategy of choosing a topic based on what's hot now but may not be after the years it takes to finish the degree. Following your interests and passions—while taking care to articulate how they matter to the rest of us beyond a given case study—simply makes you a better folklorist and, by extension, a more compelling candidate for jobs, not all (maybe not most) of which we can predict.

If I can get that perspective across, nurture a student's interests, and coach that student across the finish line of a terminal higher degree and into employment that benefits from folkloristic perspectives—whether or not "folklore" is anywhere in the job description—that student is launched, and my job (that part of my job for that student) is done. The parallels with parenting are many, but at least with graduate training there is never an empty nest, just one that keeps refilling until such time as I retire or expire. But no worries there: I'm happy to have already met and, to some extent, shaped those who will take my place. Handing on the responsibility, knowledge, practices, resources, and overall competence necessary to get the job done is not a bad way of describing tradition—the core subject of our discipline—nor is it a bad way of summing up what the folklorist as graduate teacher endeavors to do.

TEACHING IN AN INTERDISCIPLINARY DEPARTMENT: TOM DUBOIS

Tom DuBois earned his PhD in folklore and folklife at the University of Pennsylvania and is the Halls-Bascom Professor of Scandinavian Folklore, Folklore, and Religious Studies in the Department of German, Nordic, and Slavic at the University of Wisconsin–Madison, which he currently chairs.

For the past thirty-odd years, I have held appointments as a professor of Nordic languages and literature/area studies at the University of Washington, Seattle, and the University of Wisconsin–Madison. I've been involved in every level of academic teaching from elementary language instruction through doctoral dissertation mentoring; I've taught large-enrollment courses and small advanced seminars; and I've led students in research projects linked to local communities, particularly heritage communities with ties to the Nordic countries. I've developed curricula, produced scholarship, served as a program and department chair, conducted national and international evaluations of departments in the United States and abroad, coedited two journals (the *Journal of American Folklore* and *Scandinavian Studies*), and served as the president of a scholarly and professional organization (the Society for the Advancement of Scandinavian Study). And I've done all this work despite being (or, more properly, because I am) a folklorist. I am one of a large number of folklorists and ethnologists internationally who work as folklorists outside the relatively few formal departments or programs of folklore studies: in my case in a department of language, literature, and culture.

When I completed my PhD in 1990, the idea of folklorists being employed as members of departments of "foreign" language was fairly common in US institutions of higher education, although such folklorists were definitely a minority in the membership of the American Folklore Society, where many academic folklorists held positions in departments of English, anthropology, or American studies. In the early 1990s, there were folklorists in departments of African studies, Asian studies, Chinese, classics, French, German, Japanese, Jewish studies, Latin American studies, Slavic studies, South Asian studies, Spanish, Turkish, and other linguistically or regionally defined fields. I was fortunate that, for various historical and cultural reasons, the field of Nordic studies already viewed folklore as a fundamental element of the discipline. Many existing departments offered courses in Nordic folktales, legends, ballads, mythology, and epics; all these courses were (and still are) immensely popular with students and contribute to the bread-and-butter "credit output" of departments that include a folklorist. Folklore has also often been the basis of literary adaptations in and about Nordic societies, and courses on Hans Christian Andersen, Henrik Ibsen, or Disney, for instance, often include discussion of folkloric sources and examine how folklore becomes borrowed or adapted. This has meant I have never had to justify my existence to colleagues in the field of Nordic studies in the way one might need to in some other language fields where the study of folklore is not as familiar. At the same time, being a scholar of Nordic studies has meant I don't always have a lot of colleagues to talk to at AFS meetings, although, in that respect, the Nordic-Baltic Section of the AFS has grown considerably in membership and activities over the past two decades, and many Nordic and Baltic folklorists nowadays come to AFS meetings to share their research and learn about and contribute to trends in the American field.

Working in a language and literature department has meant I often gear my courses to speak to a broader student clientele than just folklorists. For instance, when I teach a course on the Finnish national epic *Kalevala*, I end up including more cultural historical, literary, filmic, and "cultural literacy" materials than a folklorist in Finland might do. I have taught a Scandinavian Children's Literature course that uses folkloric and literary sources to examine the construction of childhood in the Nordic countries (where children are regarded as having the same rights as other people) as compared with the United States (where children are largely defined as the property of their parents until they come of age). The cultural and historical reasons for this contrast are reflected in figures like Pippi Longstocking and Greta Thunberg and form a topic a folklorist is probably better able to handle than a literary scholar. Similarly, when I teach courses on Nordic or Irish films, I can do so with an attention to ethnographic issues that is different from what a person trained only in film studies would do but also different from what a folklorist working on ethnographic film might choose to include. My course on Sámi culture includes lectures on Sámi oral traditions, traditional livelihoods, and material culture, but it also includes topics like Sámi media use and film production and draws parallels with indigenous North American communities. As a folklorist in another field, I can bring folkloristic interests and concerns into Nordic studies, but I also can skirt some of the self-imposed focuses and emphases I see in the teaching of colleagues in more straight-up folklore positions and departments.

What I have noted for my teaching goes for my research as well. I have written books on Finnish folk poetry and the *Kalevala*, Nordic pre-Christian religions, North European lyric songs, shamanism, Nordic and Baltic religious wood carving, and Sámi media production and use. I have edited or coedited anthologies on Finnish folklore, Finnish-American folk song, Nordic saints, Nordic storytellers (broadly conceived), and the representation of place in Nordic literature. I have always found folklore studies to provide a tremendous point of entry to the topics I focused on in my research, but I have never allowed myself to feel hemmed in by the disciplinary boundaries the field of folklore studies has erected over time. When scholars in other fields have read and used my research, they often comment on the interesting details a "folkloristic perspective" brings out on a given topic and the distinctive questions I have been able to pursue in my research without the strictures and norms that limit them in their established fields. My *Introduction to Shamanism*, for instance, was novel to scholars in religious studies and anthropology both for its inclusion of material culture and for its focus on the revitalization and adaptation of shamanic traditions in communities today. On the other hand, I sometimes fear that my research doesn't seem "folkloristic enough" for colleagues working in academic departments of folklore studies. My books have often gotten strong reviews in various journals, but particularly in ones devoted to Nordic studies rather than folklore studies.

Being lucky enough to be a tenured faculty member at an American university, I have been called upon at times to serve as the chair of my department or as the president of a major scholarly society, the Society for the Advancement of Scandinavian Study. I have probably been overly scrupulous in these positions in not wanting to take advantage of the power invested in me as a leader to advocate too directly for folklore positions or initiatives in distinction to ones benefitting other subfields like literary studies or cultural studies. But under my leadership in Madison, a stranded folklore studies program came to find a permanent administrative home in the department I now chair: the Department of German, Nordic, and Slavic, or, as we like to call it, GNS+. And it is a potent factor in my department's decision-making that our folklore courses are the department's best-enrolled offerings. That is crucial, because when you are a folklorist in a language and literature department, you always need to plan for succession once you have moved on. And good enrollments often lead to future hiring authorizations.

Becoming a specialist in the folklore of a culture outside the United States can be challenging. One needs to gain competence in a language other than English and become conversant with the normative subjects in the departments that cover that language and culture (often literature and linguistics). I've done my share of learning about language teaching pedagogy and have also learned to design and deliver online courses on popular culture topics I never thought I would study. Becoming an American folklorist with a specialization in Nordic cultures has also entailed learning about the research traditions and norms of the discipline(s) of folklore studies in Nordic countries. What an American folklorist might cover under the single term *folklore studies* is divided into two or even three different disciplinary categories in the Nordic countries. Different norms on the use and conduct of fieldwork, the use of archival materials, and the nature of analysis have to be internalized and integrated. On a person-to-person level, a folklorist in an interdisciplinary department may have to learn to overcome the "triviality factor" more than other faculty in the department, as colleagues (and, regrettably, also students) raise their highbrow eyebrows and ask, "Really, you study *that*?" But what doesn't kill us makes us stronger, and I know my career as a folklorist has been immensely enriched by the interactions I have had with colleagues specializing in the study of literature, history, political science, geography, medieval studies, and many other disciplines. These contacts have allowed me to train my folklorist advisees in ways that help them become similarly broad-minded and versatile so they, too, can land good jobs in similar departments or related public- or private-sector organizations.

TEACHING MEDICAL PROFESSIONALS: BONNIE BLAIR O'CONNOR

Bonnie Blair O'Connor earned her PhD in folklore and folklife at the University of Pennsylvania and is Professor Emerita in the Department of Pediatrics at the Warren Alpert School of Medicine of Brown University, where she continues to serve on the Ethics Committees of Westerly Hospital and Rhode Island Hospital.

I ended up in this unanticipated occupation through galvanizing encounters with two people who set my sights in new directions. The first was Minnie Hammons, member of a much-studied family of tradition bearers;

the second was David Hufford, a folklorist who changed the way the field looked at folk medicine and folk religion.

In the summer of 1980, before I started my graduate studies in folklore and folklife at Penn, I took a weeklong beginners' fiddling course at the Augusta Heritage Center at Davis and Elkins College in Elkins, West Virginia. One night, I went with some folks to the home of some of the Pocahontas County branch of the Hammons family, from whom so many folklorists over the decades have learned so much.

The jam session was hot—I couldn't keep up—so I wandered into the kitchen, where I met the white-haired, gregarious Minnie Hammons and her friends, who were telling stories about delivering babies up and down the hollers. Minnie's mother had become a midwife because she had a calling. Minnie herself had been pressed into service at the age of fourteen because her mother needed a helper just to keep up with demand, and midwifing became her lifelong work.

She caused a seismic shift in my thinking in that one captivating evening. Minnie and her friends were confident possessors of important knowledge based on decades of experience and peer-to-peer learning. They had helped each other and hundreds of other women in childbirth, they had saved lives, and many of the things of which they spoke so matter-of-factly—like turning breech babies into safer birthing positions or stopping premature labor with herbal teas—were considered dangerous and problematic in "official" medical circles, often provoking surgical intervention.

I immediately followed my new fascination with lay midwifery by spending most of my first year at Penn making contacts and interviewing couples who had experienced home births attended by lay midwives. In 1981 Dave Hufford joined the faculty at Penn, and I was his teaching assistant for his Ethnography of Belief course. I knew right away I had met my mentor. Dave was the first folklorist in the United States to hold a full-time faculty position in a medical school and, with his tutelage and encouragement, I believe I became the second.

Everything about being trained as a folklorist and an ethnographic fieldworker is applicable to working in health-care settings: disciplinary perspective, specific skills, cultural awareness, methodological and analytical frameworks, a broad body of general knowledge of fascinating things about regular people, and depth of knowledge in one's special areas of interest.

Fieldwork training teaches us how to enter into communities and cultures of which we are not ourselves members—essential to the folklorist in academic medicine. We learn to be sensitive questioners and deep listeners, continually using and honing our interactional skills. We learn to establish rapport, identify and evaluate contextual cues, and suit our messages and inquiries to the folks with whom we carry out our work. We listen for and follow up on tacit cues, observe and interpret both stated and enacted values, and reason deductively and inductively to discern patterns of socialization, in- and out-group delineations, and authority structures and stratification.

As ethnographers we become comfortable being—at least partly—professional outsiders in the settings we study, however collegial and welcoming they may become over time. To be any good at what I originally went to academic medicine hoping to accomplish, it was important for me to remain what one physician colleague of mine called "one of medicine's failures of socialization": to be *in* the medical setting and culture but not *of* it. That was the stance I took, and I became an interpreter, to physicians, of patients' perspectives on health, illness, and care.

Expertise in folk and alternative medicine and culturally specific health traditions provided me selling points to med schools when I graduated in 1990. AIDS was still new, conventional medicine had little to offer, and well-organized activists were challenging medical authority. Just-released studies contained stunning news that huge numbers of educated, middle-class people spent billions using alternative medicine. Conventional medicine had finally accepted the need for "cultural competence" and required new resources. Those were issues I could address.

In medicine, as in any cultural setting, it is essential to be conversant with the local language. During graduate school I spent a lot of time in Penn's medical library, read articles in medical journals, and took a part-time job as a medical secretary at the university's hospital, all to start learning the language of the work I had chosen. Over time I developed fluency and got better at seeing how best to fit in. I learned how to frame my talks to medical audiences so the framing itself conveyed the message that "everything you are about to hear is data" in this culture where *anecdote* is a term of scorn and *data* are highly prized. (Never mind that for folklorists, anecdotes and personal narratives *are* data.)

The field of medicine is problem oriented and tells individual stories—called "case presentations"—as the basis for thinking about wider classes (what folklorists would call "genres") of similar problems. This was probably my most important cognitive cue. A twelve-year-old boy once came into the pediatric clinic with stomach pain that had worsened over about a week; the doctor thought it was likely caused by anxiety. The boy had said something to the doctor about "Bloody Mary" and that he was afraid. The doctor had no idea what this referred to and asked me if I knew anything about it. It turned out that the boy had learned the "Bloody Mary" incantation from a friend and on a dare had stood before a mirror and performed it; afterward he became increasingly terrified he might actually have summoned a demon. Going beyond the folklore content to a broader category important to pediatricians, this became the kernel of a *Morning Report* titled "Adolescents with Dangerous Secrets," which addressed such additional concerns as sexual abuse, worries over sexual or gender identity, awareness of domestic violence, and similar causes of severe anxiety among kids who know threatening things they are afraid to talk about and included reassuring ways to encourage young people to talk about what frightens them and why.

Being a folklorist equipped me to help physicians better understand patients' behavior by drawing analogies with conventional medicine. When a little Cambodian girl came for a checkup, trainees saw reddened welts on her back caused by coining, a common cultural practice for dispelling "wind" in the body to prevent sicknesses related to cold states of being. Although savvy enough to know these did not indicate abuse, the trainees were upset that parents would cause this pain and bruising in the name of health. My brief was to note that in medicine, "we" do that, too: we give kids shots that hurt and make them cry and raise welts and maybe cause fevers to prevent worse things from happening. Isn't it great that you and her parents are all thinking preventively? Excellent common ground for talking about immunizations!

Being a folklorist made me an excellent fit for the hospital's Ethics Committee—one of the few areas of medical practice where there is no recognized right answer, where learning about a patient and a family is central to resolving stalemates and setting therapeutic goals, and where answers cannot be represented in numbers but must emerge through discussion in their full detail and complexity. Being trained to understand multiple perspectives and translate among them is an invaluable skill. Having knowledge of varied cultural traditions and practices helps a lot. Knowing how to learn what has meaning and value for *this* person is crucial.

Being a folklorist who studied health belief and behavior made me useful in creating curricula for the so-called soft aspects of being a physician. This led, by steps, to my becoming associate director of the pediatric residency program. After years of soft funding, that transition paid me out of a line of hard money. In academic medicine everyone is expected to raise his/her own salary by generating clinical income or getting grants. Administrators and required-course directors can tap hard money for that portion of their time set aside for these duties.

The jobs a folklorist can do in academic medicine do not have particular titles; they are not listed on a roster waiting for applicants. You start with the job you can get and grow it bit by bit. Primary care specialties are good places to start because they deal most directly and continuously with everybody who comes in the door. They know the essential value of communication, people skills, cultural understanding, and the rest of what folklorists are so well equipped to do. I started as a postdoctoral fellow in medical humanities and retired twenty-five years later as a full professor and emerita faculty member. If your interests point you in that direction, by all means, go there.

Teaching Writing: Martha C. Sims

Martha C. Sims earned her PhD in English and folklore at The Ohio State University, where she is an associated faculty member in the Department of English.

Academics with degrees in English and other humanities disciplines often end up as teachers of composition by default. But I confess: I was immediately excited to be a college composition teacher. I loved working with first-year students who were learning about themselves and about the lives of people they'd never interacted with before. Those young adults often expressed surprise on learning that their peers and classmates experienced life differently than they did. I can't say that was my "Aha, folklore!" moment, but I did find myself, soon after teaching those first several quarters of first-year writing (FYW), starting to develop a syllabus that would bring together my passion for folklore and my students' curiosity about culture.

After reading Bonnie Stone Sunstein and Elizabeth Chiseri-Strater's *FieldWorking*, I was able to develop a writing pedagogy that fit my folklorist self. Students in my FYW courses now study dorm life, bingo halls, and bathroom graffiti. We discuss ethics and positioning and their roles and biases. They learn how to view people and behaviors through new lenses and train themselves to refocus their lenses to better understand what they are observing. We discuss how being intrigued by bathroom graffiti—wondering who wrote it, why, and how people responded to it—is actually taking a scholarly perspective. I explain to them that this critical thinking process—seeing something, being curious about it, and turning it over to look at it from as many perspectives as possible—is at the core of good writing. Once they are familiar with that strategy, we can expand it to other types of ideas and consider how critical thinking can be applied to other writing assignments. Using an ethnographic perspective can move them out of their comfort zone and introduce them to writing as a way of examining ideas without already knowing what they are going to say about them. This is the most important practice a writer can take away from my classroom: to understand how incisive simply looking closely, openly, and with curiosity and respect can be.

Writing as inquiry and discovery is a premise of some composition pedagogies, and the open-ended approach that comes from ethnographic research parallels this philosophy. This approach is one of the strategies the folklorist's lens brings to teaching writing. It is an integral part of the work students perform in my composition classrooms. Regardless of whether they are doing ethnographic research or examining cultural artifacts, my students work with me to examine oral and material texts from a variety of critical perspectives so they can understand and present the ways different thinkers approach analysis.

Being a good writing teacher means helping students understand how to ask, observe, and reflect. Sometimes this leads to analysis, and sometimes it leads only to more questions. But having questions is what ideally drives a writer. What do I want to learn about? What do I want to better understand? What do I want my readers to learn about? Why is that important to them, or why *should* it be? I have carefully considered the bones of my pedagogical approach and have become more explicit, particularly in upper-level composition classes, about the value of researching from a stance of discovery, rather than from a position of a desire for proof.

In the second-level writing class I teach, designated as having a folklore focus, we read what folklorists have written; discuss cultural beliefs, practices, and objects; and examine the world immediately surrounding us. When I introduce the discipline of folklore, I explain what thinking like a folklorist does for writers. It deepens their understanding of research, audience, purpose, and argument. These skills develop naturally when doing folklore. In addition to guiding these students to use new thinking strategies, I work with them to examine the underpinnings of an effective writing practice that can be developed by writing from a folklorist's sensibility. Of course, the content of our readings and discussions feeds into this, and that's invaluable to critical thinking, but it is essential to think about a folklorist's *way* of presenting information as well.

As folklorists, it's not only how we think that informs our writing. The writing strategies we bring to the composition classroom make us effective writing teachers. Our understanding of the performer-audience relationship—that is, of the myriad choices a performer has to make to reach that audience—can be leveraged to accomplish our goals as composition teachers. Yes, other composition teachers deal with audience. But folklorists have a rich store of methods and examples that can show students what it means to adapt to an audience's needs: we can investigate jokes, songs, and both visual and material culture in the composition classroom to illustrate the strategies we already use to shape our presentation of information in everyday expression. Those strategies are available to us, too, as writers. Making clear that very little is written "for everyone," we can help students determine the language, voice, and particular information likely to be most compelling for their reading audience and purpose. Who is the intended audience? What position does the student-author have in relation to the audience? What is the context for the essay, and how does that influence the writer's approach? These rhetorical strategies are especially legible in folklore analysis.

Regardless of what we ask our students to write, our practice as folklorists is instructive in helping them present their ideas. Folklorists want to know about the small-scale response to an idea. Valuing the local and vernacular, folklorists have strategies for helping student writers think about how specific people's perspectives shape a large-scale idea or practice. This idea of scale can be seen clearly when, for example, we compare the ways a close-knit group expresses a belief through practice with the behavior of a larger, less intimately connected group. It doesn't matter what the idea, object, or practice is; being able to help students see the nuances that make the presentation of an idea personal or local rather than mainstream or generic is valuable. Considering scale is especially useful for students working with persuasion and argument: How can they present the information to capture a local, specific perspective on the idea? What details can students present to show the particular elements they have observed and/or discovered in their research? What description can they provide to mark their experience or observation as their own and develop the most compelling essay by relying on their perspective and/or their discoveries? What distinct experiences might influence a reader's attitude about or perspective on the issue? These questions are useful ways to help students make their writing more engaging and more meaningful. Simply by having students practice observing and describing and then comparing their write-ups of the same scene, a folklorist can illustrate the value of incorporating such small-scale, distinctive details within a writing assignment. Our work is grounded in looking at concrete, material examples; expressions of belief; and specific, vernacular language, and we can teach our students how such strategies can work in various contexts to help them become more skilled thinkers and writers.

We folklorists can both employ and share with students the methods we ourselves use in research and writing to devise an effective composition course. Because we are trained to look at and think about ideas and cultural expression in concrete ways, folklorists lay bare the mechanics and methods of critical analysis. Asking students to study cultural texts and group practices gives composition teachers a way to help student-writers see beneath the surface to understand how the ideas for an analysis or argument come together. When students build up from the cultural text or practice, instead of starting with the abstract task of "proving a thesis," they are better able to see critical thinking at work, analyze an audience's expectations, and convey evidence in clear, detailed ways.

Integrating Vernacular and Mainstream Science in Teaching: Sandra Bartlett Atwood

Sandra Bartlett Atwood earned her MA in folklore at Utah State University and is currently teaching third grade at Cardston Elementary School in Cardston, Alberta, and pursuing a MEd in Blackfoot ways of knowing and being.

Before I even knew that folklore existed as a discipline, my own perspectives were deeply informed by the traditions of various folk groups, and I was unwittingly conducting folkloristic research and incorporating folklore into my own science education. I have always bounced between the humanities and the sciences in search of a more complete understanding of the world. When I finished high school, I attended Brigham Young University to study linguistics. After a year, I switched to forestry at Utah State University, eventually earning a Bachelor of Arts in education with a French major and a history minor. Following two years of teaching high school French and English, I missed the sciences and returned to college for a major equivalent in biology and physics for teachers. I taught middle school science for four years but felt troubled by the Eurocentric agenda of the K–12 curriculum at that time, particularly the way STEM subjects were taught in isolation from the humanities.

I had long been exploring the creation narratives of various cultures and considering them alongside Western physics, chemistry, and biology when, one day, I was convinced by Nikola Tesla's bold assertion from 1900 that "of all the frictional resistances, the one that most retards human movement is ignorance. . . . The friction which results from ignorance . . . can be reduced only by the spread of knowledge and the unification of the heterogeneous elements of humanity. No effort could be better spent." I decided to apply for graduate school and formally pursue the topic. After talking to several scientists at Utah State about doing a thesis on comparative etiologies, ontologies, and epistemologies, each of the science departments assured me that although my "little project" was interesting, it was not very scientific. At that point, I was redirected to the departments of history and anthropology. After explaining my proposal to individuals in those departments, I was met with concerns about comparing mythical accounts of creation to those found in the discourses of philosophy and physics. However, classicist Frances Titchener mentioned a philosophy professor—Charlie Huenemann, a Spinoza expert who had served on the committee of a graduate student in the sciences—and recommended that I speak to him. After introducing myself, Charlie said, "You know, my wife is doing a master's in folklore, I think that might be a good fit for what you are proposing." Initially I felt aggrieved. I didn't even know a person could get a degree in fairy tales, the only connection my mind made to folklore. I remember thinking that no one was taking me seriously and, more important, that no one was taking these origin stories seriously, but I agreed to meet with folklore program director Steve Siporin anyway. To my delight, not only did he take my work seriously, he shared with me examples from Jewish lore and language that supported some of my claims.

I distinctly recall the moment I realized that folklore was in fact the ideal and perhaps only discipline with the epistemological parameters necessary to acknowledge and inform my holistic science research. It was my first semester, and we were learning about the theory and methods of folkloristics when I came across the words of Jacob Grimm (recounted by Alan Dundes) imploring that once folklore has been "salvage[d] and collect[ed]," it must be "research[ed] in detail," asserting that modern knowledge can be fully understood only in relation to its "ancient and true origins" and explaining that "despite all the ridicule and derision with which it has been treated, it has survived in secret, unconscious of its own beauty, and carrying its irrepressible essence alone within itself." Similarly, Edward D. Ives's statement that "it all goes to show that the facts—for whatever reason collected—know more than we do at the time, and, if they are properly saved and stored away, they may someday answer questions we never knew enough to ask" seemed to describe my experiences with sacred narratives and further encouraged me to consider Western science through a folkloristic lens. By the time I encountered David Hufford's methodological symmetry and experiential-source hypothesis along with the structuralist methods of Claude Lévi-Strauss and Vladimir Propp, I knew I had found a place to ground my research and experiences. Folklore has given me the language, theory, methods, and academic authority to engage in meaningful transdisciplinary and transcultural conversations with scholars from every domain of science and has positioned me as an effective and welcome ally to my indigenous Blackfoot and Hawai'ian friends as they strive for the social-ecological revitalization of their traditional ways of knowing and being and as we coproduce scientific knowledge together.

Following my master's, I pursued a PhD in human dimensions of eco-system science and management through the Utah State Department of Natural Resources with a focus on sustainability and the management of sacred environments. Although I never completed my PhD, I continue to present my work at the International Symposium for Society and Resource Management, where I have been invited to contribute my perspectives as a folklorist on climate change, water, recreation, place identity, and cultural sustainability. After presenting my research on sacred ecosystems and the decolonization and indigenization of recreation in 2019, I was asked by the United States Forest Service to participate in a think tank in Colorado to restructure the USFS public lands recreational use model to better reflect the diversity of its patrons. Following my presentation, one professor of ecol-ogy expressed her gratitude by saying, "This conference has been missing the poetry, stories and mysterious realities that is folklore. We thank you for coming. We need more conversations where ecologists, hydrologists, soci-ologists, computer modelists, geologists, policy makers, geographers, econo-mists, and folklorists come together with stakeholders to evaluate and solve the complex social-ecological problems that threaten our communities."

As a folk scientist, I have also collaborated with Florida Keys Commu-nity College economist Nicole McCoy to examine the basic tenets of classical economics that don't adequately explain the lived experience and collective identity of many traditional folk groups that don't seem to be motivated by self-interest or the extraction/exploitation of their natural resources for mon-etary gain. She now teaches and refers to these perspectives and methods as *folk economics*, a term we coined together. Likewise, I have engaged in conver-sations with various quantum physicists—from indigenous Dené mathema-tician and string theorist Percy Paul to Nobel Prize–winning MIT quantum physicist Frank Wilczek—regarding symmetry and the relationships among folk and academic etiologies, ontologies, and epistemologies. As a third-grade teacher in an elementary school where roughly a third of my students are Blackfoot, I have used these conversations with scientists to develop a cross-curricular and cross-cultural pedagogy that grants authority to mul-tiple ways of knowing and being by teaching the entire curriculum through the concept of worldview. In third grade we teach water, rock, and life cycles; time; numeracy; literacy; identity; structures and engineering; sound; plant and animal adaptations; chemical reactions; measurement; and wayfinding. We also study countries like Peru, Ukraine, Tunisia, and India and the First Nations, Metis, Inuit, and immigrants of Canada. By considering each of the concepts in the third-grade curriculum through the lens of each world-view, students gain robust nonhierarchical understandings of each concept.

Instead of pitting Western knowledge against traditional knowledge, we explore each knowledge system through multiple lenses, and my students are free to make meaning based on what makes sense and resonates with their own experiences and beliefs. They get to decide whether dichotomies like "living/nonliving" are useful or if an animate world is a more meaningful point of reference for them. For example, one student decided that chemical reactions made more sense if she thought of the elements and atomic particles as animate beings that communicate with and trust each other, a notion that Utah State University quantum physicist Jim Wheeler had also shared with me. I am also currently working with Blackfoot scholars and elders to challenge Western neutrality and normalize indigenous pedagogies and methods as part of my capstone project for an MEd in Niitsitapiisinni and Poo'miikapii (Blackfoot ways of knowing and being).

Finally, perhaps the most important thing I have done as a folklorist and science educator is to conceive of a community where those considering the relationships among folklore and science can share ideas and support one another in the transdisciplinary and transcultural coproduction and application of science knowledge. The new Folklore and Science Section of the American Folklore Society is the realization of many like-minded scholars who shared that dream with me.

CHAPTER 2
Leading and Managing

LEADING AT A UNIVERSITY: PATRICIA A. TURNER

Patricia A. Turner earned her PhD in rhetoric at the University of California, Berkeley, was UCLA's dean and vice provost of undergraduate education from 2012 to 2020 and the senior dean of the college from 2016 to 2020, and is now a professor in two UCLA departments: African American Studies and World Arts and Cultures.

I was tickled that the phrase I heard most commonly upon sharing the news that I had been appointed a dean was "So sorry to hear that you've gone over to the dark side." Nonfolklorists and folklorists greeted me with this idiom of folk speech traceable to the tenaciously popular *Star Wars* franchise, itself a treasure trove of content for any well-schooled folklorist. Translated from its use in the movies, this phrase my colleagues used seemed to suggest I had been seduced away from the arena of the light—from the noble and altruistic pursuits of teaching and conducting scholarship—to the politically sinister and inherently evil but more personally lucrative world of university administration. The association of university leadership and the dark side of the Force extends beyond my professional network; in the literature of higher education, virtually every article, dissertation, or book that addresses the transition from faculty member to administrator evokes the *Star Wars* universe.

The classic light/dark dichotomy is perhaps even more interesting to me than it might be to other deans, since my scholarship includes the realm of racial stereotyping. As an African American folklorist/dean, I hear an all-too-familiar set of characterizations: light/white represents innocence, virtue, and benevolence, while dark/black connotes a preoccupation with power, vice, and evil. I devoted the better part of my book *Ceramic Uncles and Celluloid Mammies: Black Images and Their Influence on Culture* to the consequences of this cultural color-coding. But, of course, as a Black dean in major research universities, I was very much the ethnic exception. Nonetheless, I'm not sure the many faculty members who nonchalantly liken their deans to Darth Vader (voiced by James Earl Jones) think through the subtext of their commentary.

My training as a folklorist enabled me to do much more than analyze the stereotypes embedded in the offhand remarks of faculty members who no doubt consider themselves free from bias. What follows is a review of the tools I transferred from my folklorist tool kit to the one I put together to be a good dean.

Fieldwork: There's no doubt that I conducted a number of meetings in my office and the deans' suite conference rooms I had at my disposal. But more so than other colleagues in the deanship, I made time to go into the "field." I knew that when I went to the homes or churches of the quilters I was documenting, I was signaling to them a respect for their subject-matter expertise and a desire to learn from them. Similarly, I recall suggesting to the president of the student body that we alternate meeting locations. After he trekked over to the administration building to meet with me, for our next session I would make my way to the student services building and sit in his guest chair while he sat behind his big desk. The 2020 academic upheaval generated by the coronavirus pandemic threatened to fracture relations between the administration and the student body, but he and I have remained on good terms. Following his virtual commencement (an event he initially fought against), he texted me saying I was "the best administrator ever, no contest."

Centering the Folk: Scholars who are attracted to folklore studies are often those who take frequently marginalized individuals and communities seriously. In my focus on African American folklore, I have been invested in trying to place folk art renderings such as quilts and baskets in the same sphere as fine art painting and sculpture. And my years as a dean overlap with an era during which legal restrictions hampered efforts to situate students and faculty from underserved groups in the academy. When I moved into my first dean's office within three years of the passage of Proposition 209, a powerful impediment to programs that sought to provide access to people of color, I never allowed my colleagues in the administration to forget that diversity and excellence are paired attributes. When I was told I couldn't offer a mentoring program and undergraduate research conference just for students of color, I raised money to offer one to the entire student body but advertised it most heavily in the circles populated by students of color. I found ways to reward the faculty who took on the mentoring of these students. Today some of the alumni of that program are themselves in the academy—in the center, not the margins—creating the next set of opportunities for underserved students.

Deep Listening: Perhaps the most significant transferrable skill from my folklorist-to-dean tool kit is the ability to really listen and ensure that whomever I am listening to knows they have been heard. Often students, faculty, or alumni who find themselves pleading their case to a dean have made many other stops along the way: they have sought support or understanding from a department chair or the financial aid office or the president of the alumni association, and the dean is their last resort. And any dean will tell you we can't always solve the problems with which we are confronted. But in my experience, demonstrating to the afflicted party that I have a command of the issues and have really tried to see things from their perspective is always a productive step forward. At times, resolution can be achieved after circling back to the department chair, financial aid office, or president of the alumni association with a fuller picture.

Resource Wrangling: In the *Star Wars* films, Darth Vader and his partners in the Empire are conspicuously better financed than Luke Skywalker and the Rebels. It's probably true that deans have access to more resources than faculty, but I know few of my colleagues, particularly at public universities, who feel flush. Underwriting the academic aspirations of our community can be one of the most challenging aspects of these positions. Again, I found my life as a folklorist useful as I navigated the terrain of resource development. In order to mount a festival or conduct fieldwork, most folklorists become very adept at grant writing, and it is often the case that the grants we secure were originally intended for another purpose. Thus, we have to learn to sell our projects as viable; as a dean I had to do the same thing. When you look at a final spreadsheet for a festival or a conference, the resources have often been patched together from disparate sources, and most of the projects I initiated as dean required me to ferret out funds from a wide array of stakeholders.

Performance Studies: Over the years I've witnessed and documented the performance dexterity of gospel singers, preachers, quilters, hair braiders, and many other folk who know how to sway an audience. At the Smithsonian Folklife Festival and elsewhere, I have presented such performers, introducing them and their art form to a live audience. And in hotel conference rooms, on the stages used for university rituals of convocation and commencement, and in the private homes of donors, I have been charged with making remarks intended to inspire an audience.

Many of my fellow administrators found the public-speaking aspect of our roles the most intimidating. I liked nothing better than walking up to the podium at graduation and overseeing a ninety-minute ceremony aimed at about eight thousand students and an arena filled with their friends and family.

Like many folklorists, I bemoan the size of our field, wishing there were more scholars who understood how personally and professionally satisfying it is to study the cultural manifestations of everyday life. I am now an ex-dean and once again a full-time folklorist. And I think it will be the case that I will be able to use my administrative experience in service to the field of folklore, for I have become very strong in the ways of the Force.

CHAIRING A DEPARTMENT: DEBRA LATTANZI SHUTIKA

Debra Lattanzi Shutika earned her PhD in folklore and folklife at the University of Pennsylvania and is Professor in, and Chair of, the Department of English at George Mason University.

Folklore is my second career. I spent my twenties working as a registered nurse until I discovered folklore. My passions—ethnographic research and teaching—became my life goals. I was fortunate to find a tenure-track position in folklore in the English Department at George Mason University (or Mason, as we call it) as I finished my PhD. I spent the next six years working toward tenure and never considered a leadership position. Like many new associate professors, achieving tenure was not the nirvana I imagined. I ticked off a series of goals: matriculating at the right grad school, writing a dissertation, finding a job, writing a book, and achieving tenure, but when it was all done, I felt aimless.

That same year the English Department appointed a new department chair, who asked me to be the coordinator of the department's undergraduate curriculum. The job offered a new challenge that allowed me to think strategically about effective teaching. As a member of the department's leadership team, I was tasked with revising our department's undergraduate curriculum. The position allowed me to develop ties with colleagues across our large, diverse department. Within this framework, my leadership style emerged based largely on my ethnographic practice: observing, listening, and building consensus for all major decisions. It was a liberating process, as I learned that leadership isn't about having the answers so much as it is developing a problem-solving matrix and allowing colleagues to share their opinions and ideas. This produced a larger pool of possible solutions to any given issue and increased buy-in to whatever action we eventually took. By the end of my term as undergraduate curriculum coordinator, the department had successfully renumbered our courses; created a logical progression through the major, updated course topics; and deleted courses that were no longer effective. I felt a sense of accomplishment about that work.

When the department chair position opened, I was encouraged by many of my colleagues to run. My first concern was the folklore program. My senior colleague Margaret (Peggy) Yocom had recently retired, and while we were granted a search to replace her, this move would leave the program short-staffed for a year. As chair, however, I could reshape the department and the position of folklore in it. I decided to run for the position.

Among my first priorities was communicating my vision for the department. For most of the history of Mason's English Department, "the department" meant tenure-track faculty who taught literature. With the growth of full-time non-tenure-track positions, the department had transformed. I decided that all full-time faculty should be engaged in department decision-making and that, to the degree possible, graduate student teachers and adjuncts should participate in issues that affected them directly. It was still challenging to lead the largest academic unit on campus (including 220 teaching faculty), composed of seven academic disciplines (creative writing, cultural studies, film and media studies, folklore, linguistics, literature, and writing and rhetoric). In order to expand engagement, I invited representatives from each of the disciplines to join the Chair's Advisory Committee, whose members assist the chair with major decisions. These seemingly small changes made a significant difference in the intellectual life of the department. They forced tenure-track colleagues to see other full-time faculty as a permanent part of the department and equalized representation for disciplines with smaller faculty cohorts.

As I reflect on my seven years as department chair, I find that my approach to leadership is an extension of my work as an ethnographer and folklorist. All academics, at one time or another, rail against university administrators. Their decision-making processes are opaque, poorly communicated, and rarely understood. We assume, sometimes correctly, that university administrators' values are in opposition to our own. But rarely do professors take the time to learn the culture of administration and how decision-making processes work. I decided to try to understand how my dean and upper administrators made decisions: to try, in other words, to become a participant-observer of the culture of higher education administration.

That first year was tough. I found negotiating with my dean nearly impossible. She was a lovely person, but no matter how I framed my requests, her answer was a resolute no. After a few failed attempts, I asked a more experienced chair how I might be more successful. He had observed that our dean favored data-driven requests. When I prepared my request for new full-time positions for composition instructors, I provided a spreadsheet with our enrollments and highlighted the hundreds of students who had been wait-listed for our writing classes the previous semester. That additional student-centered data made the pitch successful. From that experience I started to observe my superiors not merely as gatekeepers but as stakeholders with their own priorities and biases. As a social scientist, the dean was not convinced by a compelling narrative; the data made the difference.

Understanding the goals and priorities of university administrators is immensely important. It is my job as chair to support the aspirational goals of faculty. When colleagues come to me requesting to launch an initiative—designing a new academic program, sponsoring a colloquium series, or creating a new study abroad—I work with them to frame the request so it aligns with the goals of our college and university and is more likely to succeed.

In my first year as chair, it was clear I would have to make unpopular decisions, but I didn't anticipate how difficult it would be to square off with the dean or provost. Much as I had developed relationships during my fieldwork, I cultivated alliances with university leaders and valued those professional relationships. I had to make a decision: would I be an advocate for faculty and students and possibly risk the goodwill of my superiors? I concluded that at its core the chair's role is to advocate for faculty and students. If the department chair doesn't do this, it's likely no one will.

As I enter my final year as department chair, it's clear that my time in this role has been well spent. I attribute my effectiveness as a department chair to my folklore training. Folklorists are astute observers, effective communicators, and skilled cultural negotiators. This is ideal preparation for leadership. Assuming a leadership position is also good for folklore as a field. Our numbers are small, but when folklorists lead academic departments, they demonstrate the value of our field to academic institutions in a way that is tangible and clear. We offer humane leadership in a time when it is much too rare.

DIRECTING AN ACADEMIC PROGRAM:
MICHAEL ANN WILLIAMS

Michael Ann Williams earned her PhD in folklore and folklife at the University of Pennsylvania and is University Distinguished Professor of Folk Studies and Anthropology Emeritus at Western Kentucky University and a past president of the American Folklore Society.

I never aspired to be a program director. When I was a child, I rather doubt that any of my teachers thought, *There's a girl with real leadership potential!* (although my siblings would probably attest to a certain requisite bossiness on my part). Still, I spent well over half my career in academia as a program director or department head.

Personally, I hold a rather healthy skepticism that leadership skills can be taught. I also do not believe any particular innate personality characteristics are required to be a leader. Rather, leadership is something you step up to. Or, as some folklorists once defined performance, it's an act of taking responsibility. Although there are certainly exceptions, in academia leadership is often thrust upon unwitting victims (in my own case, generational shifts put me in the director's position at a fairly early point in my career). You don't know how well you are going to do until you do it. The first, and perhaps the only, requisite is that you must care passionately about the fate of your program.

Certain folklorists, for good reasons, resist genealogical approaches to the history of our discipline. However, as folklorists we need to never lose sight of the roles real individuals play in shaping history. If we look at the vast majority of academic folklore programs, we can easily identify the individual or individuals who—out of sheer stubbornness, ability to wield certain administrative powers, or force of personality—built those programs. When I came to Western Kentucky University, the graduate program in folk studies had existed for less than a decade and a half. However, the teaching of folklore there had a history that stretched for over sixty years. Gordon Wilson, an early student of Stith Thompson's at Indiana, used his power as head of the English Department for over thirty years to make folklore a respected part of the teaching curriculum. Then, for over a decade, during the 1950s and into the 1960s, D. K. Wilgus fought the good fight alongside Wilson before marching off to UCLA. Even in retirement, Gordon Wilson worked behind the scenes to ensure the hiring of folklorists who became the core faculty of a new graduate program that emerged during the early 1970s.

Of course, only so much can be done to protect any program from external forces. Having gained departmental status in the mid-1970s, folk studies at Western Kentucky University lost this status in the early 1980s, when a new state governor (a businessman) decreed it was inefficient to have university departments with fewer than ten faculty members. When I joined the faculty in 1986, folk studies existed within the Department of Modern Languages and Intercultural Studies. With no direct contact with the university's higher-level administration, the program director became especially important in ensuring the program was visible and received an equitable piece of the departmental budget. Only once during this odd marriage of language teaching and folklore was the department head a folklorist (Larry Danielson). Among my own proudest moments as director was the negotiation of the creation of the new Department of Folk Studies and Anthropology in

2004. Of course, periodic budget cuts and calls for "efficiency" have and will continue to threaten this autonomy.

Although the histories of academic programs and the experiences of program directors are always unique, can generalizations be made that may be of use to others? Perhaps not, but I will give it a try. Academics, and especially folklorists, tend toward idealism. Typically, academic bureaucracies provide almost constant fuel for moral outrage. I believe that to best serve our programs, directors and department heads need to avoid becoming mired in either sanctimony or cynicism. Balancing pragmatism and idealism makes for a difficult tightrope walk, but we need to constantly ask ourselves what will best serve our programs at the time. I know that my choices as a department head diverged from positions I might have taken as a faculty member.

When I became a department head, the variety of ways the number crunchers in the academic bureaucracy came up with to harass programs came as a rude awakening. The process was unpredictable: would this semester's issue be student credit-hour production, faculty teaching load, or graduation rates? As a predominantly graduate-level program at a university that largely emphasized undergraduate education, our program was in a precarious position. Even with the most sympathetic higher-level administrators, numbers often ruled. While it's easy to dismiss the "butts in seats" mentality, we couldn't afford not to care about undergraduate enrollments, even when we did not have an undergraduate major. During the revision of the general education system, we had to claim a piece of that turf to ensure full undergraduate classrooms since only through this process could we ensure the variety of small seminars our graduate students deserved. Furthermore, general education courses invariably brought us the majority of the undergraduate minors who flocked to our other non-gen-ed courses. Similarly, online classes (typically fulfilling gen-ed requirements) brought us cash incentives, ultimately funding faculty and graduate student travel and other niceties not fully provided for in our operating budget. While I am personally not a fan of teaching large classes (luckily our department had no big lecture halls) or online classes run amok, in this case the gains outweighed the disadvantages.

As I have argued elsewhere, folklorists have an unfortunate tendency toward bemoaning the fact that no one understands us. The folklorist's blues serves neither the profession nor (especially) its program directors well. We have to be avid spokespeople for our discipline and stay positive in our message. If I have one piece of advice for new program directors or department heads, it would be to brag, brag, and brag some more. While we must focus on recruitment of students and visibility within the profession, we also need to actively engage in the critical activity of explaining our discipline to the administration and converting individual administrators into fans of our programs. Perhaps I was unusually lucky. During my tenure as a director and department head, I fortunately encountered a number of administrators who actively supported our program either because they actually really liked the discipline (one told me that if she had to do it all over again, she would become a folklorist) or because our visibility served their own purposes. Two different provosts fought hard for us to gain better funding and visibility within the statewide system. Ultimately they did not prevail (due largely to politics outside our university and unrelated to our discipline), but they brought us a heightened profile and goodwill. As one provost constantly told me, "Folk studies will always be a program of distinction to me."

So perhaps there do exist innate qualities that make for a good academic program leader: a deep well of (perhaps naive) optimism and a healthy dose of resilience. When those run out, it's time to pass on the reins and/or retire. I, in fact, had no idea what lay ahead when I decided to retire: a new governor hostile to higher education (who luckily was not reelected), budget cuts, new administrators at the highest level, more budget cuts, and COVID-19. I worry that others think I foresaw the future and fled, but after almost two decades of leadership, I was just weary of the sillier aspects of bureaucracy. At some point I had to face the fact that no program, no matter how good, is invulnerable to the whims of academia (and, for public schools, those of state government). Still, although I realize there was no way I could build a program that could withstand all the unseen forces of external change, I remain ultimately optimistic. D. K. Wilgus left Kentucky in the early 1960s bemoaning the fact that he didn't see the support for folklore in the universities of the Commonwealth that had existed in the previous decade. Gordon Wilson died not knowing that a standalone folklore program for which he spent half a century laying the foundation would come into existence within a couple of years. As a holder of a PhD from the University of Pennsylvania's Department of Folklore and Folklife, I know well that not all programs survive. Still, we have to keep believing.

Managing an Academic Program:
Cassie Rosita Patterson

Cassie Rosita Patterson earned her PhD in English and folklore at The Ohio State University and is Assistant Director of Ohio State's Center for Folklore Studies and Director of the center's folklore archives.

Snapshot of a "typical" afternoon: submit eRequests for Educator Committee honoraria. Denied: not really an "honorarium." Rebuttal: explain

the purpose of the payment and describe how it aligns with the supplied definition of "honorarium." Allowable, but add comments to eRequest explaining the rationale. Approved. Resubmit eRequest as purchase order for Time
Out for Me, a nonprofit organization, since honoraria can only be paid to
individuals. (Consultant texted me saying she prefers the money go to her
organization since they recently lost funding.) End goal: five educators in
Scioto County receive $1,000 each (and two continuing education units,
a different snapshot altogether) for participating in a workshop to develop
K–12 and after-school program curricula based on the *Placemaking in Scioto
County, Ohio* traveling exhibition (the project webpage is http://go.osu.edu
/sciotoplacemaking). The Educator Committee will create place-based curricula tailored to the COVID-19 pandemic as it plays out in a mostly rural
county where a number of students do not have stable access to the internet. Next up: adjust time line to reflect designing, printing, and distributing
physical curricula that can be mailed or picked up at school.

As an academic program assistant director who codirects a university-
and community-engaged project, my roles range from navigating university
bureaucracy (as illustrated previously) to conducting year-round fieldwork,
conceptualizing projects, writing grants, maintaining donor relationships,
nurturing collaborations, teaching ethnographic methods, and maintaining
the project archives. I regularly navigate university bureaucracy to enable
fieldwork and develop public programming using methods that balance collaborative decision-making processes with participants' busy schedules. As
a collaborator, I work with people to develop meeting and program agendas that facilitate inclusive dialogue, keep participants engaged, and work
toward meaningful outcomes. As a program manager, I discuss programming options with my director, considering faculty and student research
interests as well as strategies for recruitment to our program and visibility for
the field of folklore.

When I started graduate school in 2007, I had never heard of "alt-ac," or
alternative academic careers. While my dream had always been to become a
university professor, I continually found myself gravitating toward projects
in which my organizational skills supported the back-end work of bringing intellectual ideals to fruition. In 2012, I was hired as the assistant director of the Center for Folklore Studies, where my duties include program
management, outreach and engagement, research, teaching, administrative
oversight, and serving as director of our folklore archives. Woven throughout these duties are my roles as collaborator, coordinator, engaged scholar,
scholar-activist, and value-driven administrator. This essay focuses on my
role as codirector of the Ohio Field School (OFS), which draws upon all my

capacities in ways that both fulfill me and illustrate the importance of academic administrators within the field of folklore.

The OFS (its webpage is http://go.osu.edu/ofs), based on practicing and teaching collaborative ethnography, is a course focused on integrated archival collection development and university-community engagement, primarily for Scioto County in southern Ohio's Appalachian region. My codirector, Dr. Katherine Borland, and I developed the OFS in order to reframe experiential learning, which she found had the capacity to recreate the inequalities it sought to disrupt. Defining aspects of the OFS include year-round team-based fieldwork, advisory committees made up of community partners and former field school participants (students, postdocs, contracted public folklorists), university-community co-ownership of the OFS archival collection, the inclusion of community partners in presentations at academic conferences, and support of community- and student-led grant proposals and spin-off projects.

My approach to collaboratively building the infrastructure of the OFS is directly informed by my folklore training, which leads me to investigate and document the value of everyday cultural practices people use to navigate complex social and political dynamics, demonstrate the inherent worth and contextual nature of differential knowledges and meaning-making practices, prioritize community-led projects and center community partners in decision-making processes, and listen to, understand, and articulate these knowledges and practices in critical and impactful ways.

A foundational and enduring structure of the OFS is the Community Partner Advisory Committee (CPAC), which is made up of a wide range of local stakeholders and is regularly consulted to guide and ground our work. Throughout the year and leading up to events and project deadlines, I craft emails that are as informative as they are brief (truly, this is an art!) to seek input from collaborators who are eager to participate but also busy with their own lives and leading their organizations.

For instance, when we consulted the CPAC to develop themes for the traveling exhibit, we generated preliminary ideas based on fieldwork and interviews, drawing topic bubbles on large Post-it notes and leaving several topic bubbles empty for the CPAC to contribute its own topics. Rather than asking our community partners to generate all the content, we presented what we thought we heard while making space for their ideas and feedback. During these meetings, the CPAC said our most useful work was providing opportunities to connect diverse groups across the county who often have little time to connect, so, for a few months, I focused on logistical planning that resulted in a World Café at which over sixty community members and ten folklore students workshopped possible exhibit themes and designs. I hired independent folklorist Sue Eleuterio to work with us on the exhibition and arranged for her to meet with our students so they would gain exposure to public folklore work. I reserved the ballroom, ordered food, made travel and lodging arrangements, coordinated with the designer to produce mock posters, wrote agendas, recruited student table hosts, and asked highly net-worked locals to help recruit participants. I coordinated with the CPAC and local churches in the North End of Portsmouth, the seat of Scioto County, to ensure that the Black community was represented in a predominately White county. Community partner attendees discussed important topics, contributed feedback that directly influenced the final exhibit design, and engaged in problem-solving that extended into the following year's program-ming. Students directly participated in processes of gathering and synthesiz-ing community feedback as well as discussing strategies for developing an engaging exhibit.

The goal of our work has been to create deep, ongoing relationships with community partners built on an understanding of our capacities as folklor-ists so that community partners know the role folklorists can play in their project. We want to interrupt the model of extractive university-imposed initiatives and reorient institutions of higher education to be responsive collaborators. Conducting regular fieldwork—showing up—is critical for building the relationships from which community-led projects can emerge, so OFS participants and I made trips to Scioto County at least once a month, sometimes staying for a weekend or more at a time, between 2016 and 2019. Each trip required getting university approval for all travelers through OSU's eTravel system, coordinating emails to arrange visits and meetings for myself and fellow fieldworkers, creating an agenda, making lodging arrangements, and, upon returning to the office, processing reimbursements, writing field notes, and carrying out follow-up communication and tasks.

Although administratively cumbersome, these frequent visits enabled relationships to be built and sustained, laying the groundwork for responsive projects: documenting a neighborhood reunion, purchasing a greenhouse for a newly initiated urban homesteading program, arranging for participants to visit the OSU Student Farm, installing vinyl narratives on the windows of a community center, and digitizing early twentieth-century love letters. Indeed, the projects most aligned with the intentions of the OFS are those that have emerged out of our planned work but were unforeseen at the start. They draw directly on the skills of those involved and respond to needs and interests expressed in informal conversations. While universities are often slower at addressing emergent needs than community organizations, my job is to keep the project flexible and open to the unforeseen, make the necessary connections as the project takes on its own life, and then turn good ideas from all sources into reality.

BUILDING AN ONLINE SCHOOL:
SARA CLETO AND BRITTANY WARMAN

Sara Cleto and Brittany Warman earned their PhDs in English and folklore at The Ohio State University and co-own and operate the Carterhaugh School of Folklore and the Fantastic (https://carterhaughschool.com/).

"What if we had our own school?" We have no idea who said it first, but we do remember laughing wildly at the idea. Our *own* school? It was absurd. Had it not been for a potent cocktail of jet lag and anxiety, it might have remained unsaid. Earlier that day, we'd arrived in England for a conference, and our internal clocks were so confused that sleep was impossible. So, instead, we sat in the dark on our twin-sized hotel beds and talked about all the things grad students talk about, including the inevitable specter of the Academic Job Market.

If you're reading this book, you likely already know about the Academic Job Market (and understand why we're capitalizing it), so we won't dwell on it here. But we were finishing our dissertations and approaching the end of our graduate school funding, so it was a near constant in our minds. We'd watched our astoundingly brilliant friends and colleagues compete for a vanishingly small number of tenure-track jobs and even tentatively dipped our own toes in as well. It's not a revelation to say that it was all very demoralizing and soul crushing. So when one of us said, "What if we had our own school?" we had a good laugh . . . but it was quickly followed by, "Well, what do we really have to lose?"

Throughout our master's degrees at George Mason University and our PhDs at The Ohio State University, our professors impressed on us intellectual rigor and clarity of writing; even more important, they taught us the necessity of curiosity and instilled in us a willingness to think outside the box. They taught us *scrappiness*, and we had great examples of what that scrappiness could look like all around us. Our George Mason mentor, Dr. Margaret Yocom, founded a folklore department at her university when one didn't exist. Through her actions and words, she taught us to be advocates for our discipline and encouraged creativity every step of the way, showing us again and again that there's no one right path, no one right way to be a folklorist. (Which is, of course, what this book is all about!)

With all these factors in mind, we decided to see if we could make a new path. Later that year, we tentatively founded a (mostly) online school, called it the Carterhaugh School of Folklore and the Fantastic after a place mentioned in "Tam Lin," our favorite ballad from Francis James Child's late 19th-century collection *The English and Scottish Popular Ballads*, and crossed our fingers that our core belief—that people really do want to learn about folklore—was true.

And it was. Our first class had fifteen people in it, mostly friends or friends of friends, but now we teach hundreds of students from all over the world: the United States, France, India, Canada, Brazil, Italy, Singapore, Spain, Australia, England, Mexico, New Zealand, and more. We also write for magazines and blogs, present live lectures at venues as diverse as the Maryland Renaissance Festival and the Providence Athenæum, and recently won the Dorothy Howard Prize from the Folklore and Education Section of the American Folklore Society.

Our students tell us how excited they are to have a chance to study folklore seriously from teachers with academic chops and terrifying enthusiasm. These are people who never got to study folklore formally: some are ex-CEOs whose parents made them go to business school, and some are older women who never got to go to college at all. We've taught grocery cashiers, doctors, home-makers, high school students, teachers, and retirees: people from all walks of life who are drawn to folklore. All of them tell us how much they love learning about fairy tales, ballads, legends, personal narratives—all the things we love, too. We bring that to them in a way we never would have anticipated when we started studying folklore, and that's one of the best feelings in the world.

We couldn't have done it without our academic background in folklore. First and most obviously, there's the content of our courses. We draw from the lessons we learned as graduate students and our experience teaching courses at Ohio State. We know how to do research, evaluate sources, and impart knowledge in a way that will stick because of our fabulous folklore professors, friends, and colleagues.

But folklore also informs our work in much less obvious ways. Although folklore studies is, of course, its own discipline, it is also interdisciplinary by nature. And because of this, folklorists are pros at learning and adapting to communicate their work to a wider audience. To be understood, we as a discipline rely on clarity and connection. We're used to bridging fields, com-munities, and audiences, and that has been invaluable training for running a business.

Full disclosure: if you had told us five years ago that we'd be "web entre-preneurs," we would have laughed until we cried and then said, "You *must* have the wrong girls." We were (and are) dedicated teachers and enthusiastic researchers. We didn't know anything at all about running a business at first. But we also loved collaborating, something not often encouraged in academia—at least not so much in the humanities, and especially not for early-career academics. We coauthored articles as graduate students only to be told they wouldn't be taken seriously by hiring committees because they weren't single authored. A beloved professor told us we'd never get academic jobs because our CVs were too similar and we worked together too frequently.

Carterhaugh has been an exercise in taking this perceived flaw and making it a superpower. Once we decided to take the plunge and work on Carterhaugh full time, we did what academics do best: we dove into learning everything we could. We found teachers, took courses, watched lectures, read articles, and spent countless hours researching how to run a profitable business. We did things we never thought we would ever have to do, like registering an LLC with an attorney, engaging the services of an accountant, and learning how to translate our academic writing to marketing copy, which is far more difficult than you might imagine!

Mercifully, we've found that our skill sets and interests continue to overlap and complement each other. Sara (in a complete nondeparture from academia) writes thousands of emails, and she covers the student engagement and customer service aspects of the job. Brittany, who has always loved technology and design, researches and runs all the software and programs that allow the business to exist. Building courses and teaching remain, as ever, joint projects. We continue to learn more on the job every day. It's a future we never imagined for ourselves, one that was first proposed as a joke. But we couldn't feel luckier or happier that we stumbled sideways into it or that our background in folklore did so much to equip us for this wild ride.

Performing Diplomacy: Valdimar Hafstein

Valdimar Hafstein earned his PhD in Scandinavian at the University of California, Berkeley, and is Professor of Folkloristics and Ethnology at the University of Iceland.

In March 2019, I returned to the United Nations for the first time in years, this time to screen my film *The Flight of the Condor* as a lunchtime event for delegates at the World Intellectual Property Organization (WIPO). The film recounts a story of WIPO's genesis and showcases storytelling among diplomats in two organizations of the United Nations: WIPO and the United

Nations Educational, Scientific, and Cultural Organization (UNESCO). "This film is about you, brought to you, and screened for you," I announced in the desk microphone from the back rows of the meeting hall, my head larger than life on the vast screen up front. From their glass booths above my head, translators interpreted my sales pitch simultaneously into French, Spanish, Chinese, Russian, and Arabic. Wearing headsets, delegates grinned (after the translation time lag) at the hard sell, so out of character for the meeting proceedings. But it worked. Such events usually bring in twenty to thirty of the roughly one hundred delegates in attendance, but this one sold out: more than fifty delegates fought for seats. After the screening, we had another time for discussion. Had I only brought a couple of cameras and a directional microphone, I could have shot all the footage and audio necessary for a sequel. The film prominently features the conflicting claims of Peru and Bolivia on a melody from the Andes that hit the charts in the 1970s when Simon and Garfunkel released it as "El Condor Pasa (If I Could)" on their best-selling album *Bridge over Troubled Water.* The Q&A session after the screening found the delegates from Bolivia and Peru, both well-spoken and knowledgeable diplomats, arguing back and forth over the authorship and origins of the melody with eloquence and surprising intensity, leaving little room for other considerations. As they debated for a raptured audience of fifty diplomats unable to get a word in edgewise, I thought: "Wow! This is precisely what attracted me to the topic and summoned me into the field in the first place."

My field: My folk roam the hallways of Place Fontenoy, UNESCO's headquarters in Paris, and they ride elevators in WIPO's sapphire-blue highrise in Geneva. They have their own forms of folk speech (distinguishable by the use of the third-person national: "Iceland finds that . . . ," "Greece supports . . . ," "the United States believe . . . ," etc.), their folk rituals and customs ("As this is the first time that Iceland takes the floor during this meeting, I'd like to congratulate you, Mr. Chairman, on your reelection," etc.), their foodways (coffee/tea and biscuits, anyone?), and their traditional gestures and postures (shaking of hands, waving of the country badge, applause, congratulations, etc.), all very much on display during diplomatic gatherings. Few communications are as deliberate, thought out, and pregnant with meaning as diplomatic exchanges. As the saying goes, a diplomat thinks twice before saying nothing. That is because, in their meetings, words and actions are one; the debates and negotiations of diplomats in these settings are clothed with the power to fix rules and shape practice outside the walls of the conference room. Their traditional folk costume is the dark suit and tie and the skirt suit: uniforms that connote power at work, authority, and respect while deemphasizing differences of gender, class, race, and ethnicity by adhering (with slight variations and a few exceptions) to an unmarked Euro-American norm of bourgeois masculinity. (There is also a more marked and colorful festive garb for times of celebration, worn especially by female delegates in connection, for example, with the listing of intangible heritage from their country.)

By the time I took part in UNESCO's General Conference in 2011, I had been attending UN meetings for a decade and was already steeped in diplomatic folkways. Representing Iceland, I wore a suit of my own. Call it power dressing, call it camouflage, but, being a folklorist, I only had the one suit. On the second day, my fly broke. As luck would have it, there was a tailor next to my hotel, and he was kind enough to fix the zipper right away. I must have put on weight since I had bought the suit, for two hours later, the fly broke again. So I danced around Place Fontenoy for two weeks, debating world heritage and the freedom of the press, greeting ambassadors and heads of states, conferring with colleagues, and casting votes—always with an open fly. I wore my shirt untucked over my trousers, the best I could do under the circumstances.

It was an awkward moment of clarity. It spoke to questions of dress and material culture, to questions of etiquette, propriety, and the body; it opened to scrutiny the cultural norms of everyday life in this particular setting. Not culture in its solemn, monumental, highbrow denotation, as in the concept of world heritage, but the more prosaic and commonplace culture of daily life. But it is within the latter that the former is made. Debates about intangible heritage and traditional knowledge are framed by the cultural practices of the body that this (slightly embarrassing) anecdote spotlights. Because, if you give it a second thought, most things big or small take place in everyday life and take shape through everyday practices and expressions. That is where folklorists come in.

I attended my first diplomatic meeting in 2002. At the time, I did not have much on which to model my work. In the years since, many superb ethnographic studies of UN meetings and organizations have seen the light of day. Their authors bring their own sets of questions, and their own research agendas and priorities, to the field site. As is usual with fieldwork, what they discover on site reforms their agendas, reshuffles their priorities, and reframes their questions. That goes for me, too. But it also changed my position in the field, as I moved from participant-observer to observing participant and from NGO observer to sidekick on a national delegation and eventually to the chair of the national commission before going back where I started. Having represented the scholarly societies the American Folklore Society (AFS) and the International Society for Ethnology and Folklore (SIEF) at the back of the room in WIPO since 2002, I observed as part of

Iceland's national delegation the negotiations for what became UNESCO's Intangible Heritage Convention in 2003; once the convention entered into force in 2006, I served as Iceland's national delegate to some meetings. On various occasions, I also acted as a consultant on the convention's implementation to both the Swedish and Icelandic governments. Then, in 2011–2012, I chaired Iceland's National Commission for UNESCO. The chairmanship of the National Commission was a thought-provoking experience with a steep learning curve. The most memorable moments were at UNESCO's General Conference in 2011, when I voted (along with an overwhelming majority) for the accession of Palestine as a member state. But such highlights do not overshadow the mundane work done in countless meetings and consultations. From these I learned much that informs my broader understanding of how multilateral diplomacy works: the conflicts and debates, the underhanded maneuvers and open-minded discussions, the divergence of views, and the convergence of positions. It was often tedious, technical, and time-consuming; I recall more than once sitting in meetings with no clear agenda and no end in sight, thinking that if I swallowed my keys, I might get out. But, in truth, I remain deeply impressed that delegations from 195 different member states are sometimes able to work out their differences and reach consensus. No wonder it takes time and patience.

I am convinced we should follow the topics we study wherever they go. It is incumbent on folklorists, in my view, to follow the concepts we have a hand in shaping—folklore, tradition, performance, traditional knowledge, expressive culture, cultural spaces, cultural heritage—not only into the street, the plaza, the farm, or the home but also into the studio and the pharmaceutical industry, into government offices and electoral politics, and, yes, into intergovernmental committees. I do sympathize with the concerns of colleagues who prefer to maintain critical distance. I agree that we must protect the space for academic inquiry; theory and critical analysis are crucial for reflective societies. But folklorists must also be willing to have their skin in the game. Now, as much as ever, we need an operational nexus between theory and policy, between analysis and practice: an open channel of communication among intellectual workers in higher education, government, administration, and civil society. The field of folklore is good at this, particularly in the United States, with its well-developed and self-reflective practice under the signpost of public folklore. When committees and cultural workers in government or in the UN engage with the expressions and creative capacities the field of folklore is all about, then folklorists should be there on every side of the game: in the councils and secretariat, on national commissions, on expert committees, and as external commentators and critics. With a critical touch and a sharp eye but also with a constructive spirit and an open mind. But not necessarily an open fly.

Leading a Federal Government Agency: Bill Ivey

Bill Ivey remains ABD in folklore and history at Indiana University, where he now serves as Visiting Research Scholar in the Department of Folklore and Ethnomusicology, and is a past president of the American Folklore Society.

In September 1997, while attending a Georgetown University conference on historic preservation, I received a message that the Office of White House Personnel was trying to track me down. Following up, I agreed to a three o'clock meeting with Bob Nash, director of personnel for the Clinton administration. After clearing security, I found my way to the Eisenhower Executive Office Building. Nash opened the door, walked in briskly, perched casually on the corner of his deputy's desk, and said: "You're on the president's short list as chairman of the National Endowment for the Arts. The NEA has big, big problems: relations between the agency and Congress are terrible, staff morale is abysmal, and arts organizations around the country have lost confidence. Do you have anything in your background that would embarrass President Clinton? If nominated, will you take the job?" I quickly revealed everything in my personal history that might be disqualifying and said yes, I'd take the job. Dazed and excited, I flew home to Nashville. Two days later, Nash phoned. President Clinton had selected me as the nominee for the NEA post.

Over the next few months, FBI agents conducted discreet interviews with friends and associates in Nashville. The national press hovered, eager to learn who might replace actress Jane Alexander as head of our national arts agency. Just before Christmas a White House staffer leaked my name; the *New York Times* announced that President Bill Clinton intended to nominate me as the seventh chairman of our federal cultural agency.

The National Endowment for the Arts was and remains a rare, perhaps unique feature of the US national government. Not really an endowment at all, the NEA receives an annual appropriation from the US Congress, disburses a portion of the money in block grants to state arts agencies, and then manages programs through which nonprofits from all over the country compete for direct grants targeting specific artistic disciplines. Created in 1965, the endowment launched a modest Folk Arts Program in the mid-1970s, but it retained its original tilt toward what could be called mainstream fine arts: classical music, dance, painting, literary writing, sculpture, and so on.

I lacked the fine arts background the arts community wanted. Trained in folklore studies at Indiana University, I had been director of Nashville's Country Music Foundation (CMF) for more than two decades. The CMF and its Country Music Hall of Fame stood tall within America's museum and library communities, but directing an institution focused on country— a popular music genre rooted in American folk tradition—scarcely seemed credentialing for the NEA chairmanship. The Clinton team knew I understood how the agency worked from my service on endowment grant-review panels. But Nash and the White House were taking a risk, hoping my training in folklore and ethnomusicology and my country music résumé, built far from the coastal cities, would disarm vocal critics while garnering at least grudging support from our national fine arts sector.

The endowment chairmanship is a PAS position: presidential appointment with Senate confirmation. Usually Senate approval is routine, but the NEA presented a challenge since the agency had for some become a symbol of irresponsible government. Stoked by right-wing activists and conservative Christians, opposition to the NEA had been festering in Congress for decades, and antagonists seized on the fact that most grant money went to East Coast cities, where funds sometimes supported offensive art. Critics gained traction when Republicans gained control of Congress in 1994. Funding for the endowment was cut by a third in phase one of a three-year planned elimination. This controversy meant Congress cared about who would now direct the NEA. To secure confirmation, I had to deflect congressional concerns, in either one-on-one member meetings or a public hearing. One way or another, my path to the chairmanship meant winning the approval of the Senate Committee on Health, Education, Labor, and Pensions.

One of my first preconfirmation meetings was with North Carolina senator Jesse Helms. The darling of Republican conservatives, Helms was a stern anti-communist, an advocate of school prayer, and an avowed racist who had led a days-long filibuster opposing the creation of Martin Luther King Jr. Day in 1983. The NEA had drawn Helms's ire in the early 1990s, and he had stayed on the case, opining that art funded by the agency (like the photographs of artist Robert Mapplethorpe) would turn "the stomach of any normal person." Helms's positions tracked to the right of the American mainstream, but through the 1990s, he mounted a well-crafted letter-writing and speech-making campaign criticizing the NEA and its grant making. To my surprise and dismay, Helms was one of the first to request a meeting. I did not know what to expect. Would Helms again attack the NEA? Would he demand that I disavow the work of my predecessors? Would he oppose my nomination?

We met on the Senate side of the Capitol building. After courteous small talk, we spoke about country music, and especially about the senator's constituent Randy Travis, back then a freshly minted Nashville star. We spoke about folklore studies and the folklore archives at the University of North Carolina and my commitment to engaging and supporting the widest range of American art making. My background in folklore enabled me to speak expansively and legitimately about the diverse and broadly dispersed American arts scene. This was a new way of talking about art and the NEA. Helms liked it.

I had learned a valuable lesson: as I met face-to-face with congressional legislators, folklore bridged difference and distance. It made sense. Most of the United States is not big city; most of it is not rich; most art making is small-time, amateur, and threadbare; and traditional artistry connects with community. I met one-on-one with every committee member, and in the end, they didn't demand testimony in a public hearing. Majority Leader (and Tennessean) Bill Frist put in good words, and Senator Helms told an NEA staffer that he'd "like to see me approved by a unanimous vote of the Senate"; the committee sent my appointment on to the floor. Toward the end of May, my name came up for a Friday-night vote. Fingers crossed, I watched the session live on C-SPAN. It was after eleven when Tennessee senator Fred Thompson called me at my Nashville apartment: six months after my name had leaked to the *Times*; I was confirmed as NEA chair.

From then on, I played my "folklore card" in every one-on-one. Empowered by folklore's potent connection to everyday artistic practice, I could encourage supporters and answer critics and skeptics in a new way. In the spring of 1999, about a year after my Helms meeting, I was before the Senate Committee on Health, Education, Labor, and Pensions. Here's how I opened my prepared testimony:

> I am a folklorist by training and conviction, and I believe creative expression commands a central role in all societies and civilizations, past and present. I believe our living cultural heritage is a priceless creative reflection of the American experience that deserves to be treasured, carefully preserved in all its variety and richness, and securely passed on to our children and grandchildren. Whether it is in the form of films and musical recordings, dance and folk arts, or songs and drawings, these creative expressions contribute to the vibrant color, texture, and design of that magnificent mosaic of cultures we call America.

The chairmanship of the Arts Endowment was my job; strengthening the NEA while repositioning it in the eyes of Congress, the arts community, and the American people became my mission. Folklore provided the edge that allowed my argument to resonate. Armed with the perspective I had gained from folklore studies, I was working to fulfill the administration's challenge to make things better. Gradually, my folklore argument wormed its way into the rhetoric of the endowment. Our NEA five-year plan now highlighted "Living Cultural Heritage," not "The Arts." The agency's new Challenge America Initiative brought small, quick-turnaround grants to small communities all over the country.

On a wintry February night in 2000, the endowment celebrated its thirty-fifth anniversary with a Harvard University colloquium. Five former chairmen formed a panel, the great Jessye Norman vocalized, and I seized the opportunity to frame the character of our nation's expressive life. Quoting folklorists Richard Dorson, Dell Hymes, and others, I advanced an idea of culture that was nonhierarchical and not beholden to black-tie European art making but organized around the lively bazaar of America's metaphorical borderland. It was what I thought I'd been hired to do—talk differently about what the NEA did—and while I never felt the earth shudder over the months, things did quietly change. Attacks from the Hill quieted; Congress stopped calling for the end of the Arts Endowment. Although Senator Helms remained a negative vote, he never again wrote about the NEA and never criticized the endowment or me on the Senate floor. Elimination was set aside, and in the fall of 2000, our nation's tiny cultural agency received its first budget increase in more than a decade. Folklore had turned things around.

DIRECTING A FEDERAL GOVERNMENT OFFICE: ELIZABETH PETERSON

Elizabeth Peterson earned her PhD in folklore from Indiana University and is Director of the American Folklife Center at the Library of Congress.

I've spent most of my professional life roaming the nonprofit universe. Before becoming the director of the American Folklife Center (AFC) at the Library of Congress, I worked in a range of situations: cofounding the nonprofit Texas Folklife Resources with my colleagues Pat Jasper and Kay Turner, working at the New England Foundation for the Arts, serving as director of the Fund for Folk Culture, and consulting for many years through writing and editing, conducting fieldwork, working on media and programming projects, and conducting assessments and developing planning documents for small organizations, government agencies, and large national foundations. A little bit of this, a little bit of that. Along the way, I know my training and values as a folklorist have been fundamental to how I approach my work: deep listening, rock-solid commitment to the importance of expression in cultural context and motion, and a continued striving to understand multiple perspectives. Of course, it also helps to have cultivated an appetite for ambiguity.

How does this pertain to managing a large federal agency? The values and skills of a folklorist work equally well in small organizations or in large federal agencies, in places where you are a lone folklorist or in cultural institutions that hold a special place in the history and development of the folklore field. At the library, I interact with colleagues with varied expertise who represent multiple fields, diverse interests, and different constituents. Of course, part of my job involves advocating for the needs and interests of the center and competing for limited resources, but, more important, I am also translating the work of the center into terms that connect to other people's interests and concerns. I am connecting and collaborating with diverse organizations and individuals on a daily basis.

The stated mission of the American Folklife Center is "to preserve and present" American folklife. The summary sentence from my official job description lists the director's duties as "full managerial and professional responsibility for the development and growth of research programs, public & scholarly service programs, collection development, preservation and custodial management, interpretive and other special programs of education and presentation (including publications, exhibits and events) of the AFC." That covers a lot of territory and leaves much unsaid, but if you dig deeper, you understand quickly that the AFC mission "to preserve and present" is accomplished through managing and working with people. You bring ideas of folk heritage and cultural equity to life by working with, directing, and hiring talented staff with the right expertise. You map out new directions for an ethnographic archives and a national folklife program by testing, refining, and adapting ways of working collaboratively with diverse cultural communities over decades—for example, as the AFC has done through its ongoing work with Native American tribal communities. You try to strengthen ties and expand resources and opportunities for the AFC and the field by establishing research fellowships and paid internships, and you build collaborations with other programs and institutions by developing field-wide resources such as the *AFS Ethnographic Thesaurus* project we undertook with the American Folklore Society and Indiana University.

When the AFC was established in 1976 through an act of Congress, founding director Alan Jabbour was shaping a federal institution that didn't exist and creating, with a generation of folklorists and countless allies, a field of public-sector folklore that continues to evolve. In doing so, Alan and his staff helped establish standards for public folklore field research and helped found some state folk arts programs. With his guidance, AFC refined methods and ideas related to cultural conservation and collaboration with cultural communities through projects like the Federal Cylinder Project. Then, under Peggy Bulger's leadership, the AFC staff expanded and the growth of the folklore collections exploded through important additions to the Alan Lomax collections, ongoing partnerships with organizations such as StoryCorps, and the establishment of the Veterans History Project. Bulger involved the center as a federal representative in international discussions focused on intangible cultural heritage, intellectual property rights, and copyright law and highlighted issues of digital preservation and access for cultural heritage collections.

In my time at the helm, I have worked to move the AFC toward a more concerted emphasis on access by broadening our reach and connecting individuals and communities to our rich collections and our folkloric and archival expertise in the twenty-first century. For AFC, this means racing the clock to digitize important archival collections before they deteriorate and exploring digital tools and systems for preservation and presentation (such as crowd-sourcing, voice recognition transcription, and digital platforms enabling real collaboration with interpretive authority from cultural communities). It also means building a staff with diverse expertise and experimenting with ways to combine online and face-to-face presentation in complementary and ethical ways. Under my direction, we are increasing our collaborations with other programs at the Library of Congress and growing and strengthening AFC's archives by expanding narrative and oral history collections, with a focus on community memory. The AIDS Memorial Quilt Archive collection is one such example.

While our circumstances and styles are different, Alan, Peggy, and I have each tried to walk in step with the universe we live in. We are mindful of the past, but the problems and concerns we engage are in the here and now. On a daily basis, I find there is much in my job I cannot control: an international pandemic; a federal budget cut; a staff member who takes a new job; financial windfalls; presidential elections; members of Congress proposing, without your knowledge, legislation that affects your agency. All these have a tremendous impact on my work. What I can do, however, is set the tone, shape the organizational culture of the center, and determine and craft a vision in concert with the staff who will carry AFC forward.

In the prior paragraph, I alluded to politics. Politics—writ large or small—are part of any job. Understanding the multiple power centers within institutions and knowing how to overcome obstacles to make things happen are essential to being effective in any job. But in a government context, the notion of politics takes on specific meanings and permeates most decision-making. It can make you go the extra mile, and it can make you more risk averse, but it always makes you realize you are fulfilling a mission that is greater than yourself. At the library, our primary constituency is Congress. We take their concerns and requests seriously, as we serve their communities and constituents and a broader public. And, as corny as it may sound, the idea of serving the public is the defining characteristic of managing a government agency or working in a government job. It motivates everyone at the AFC and the library as an aspiration and a trust we strive to earn and keep every day.

At the beginning of every AFC board meeting, we start with a ritual public reading of Public Law 94–201, the legislation that created the American Folklife Center in 1976. Under Section 2 (a) of the American Folklife Preservation Act, describing the findings and purpose of the act, there's a passage that says:

> SEC. 2. (a) The Congress hereby finds and declares --
>
> (1) that the diversity inherent in American folklife has contributed greatly to the cultural richness of the Nation and has fostered a sense of individuality and identity among the American people;
>
> (2) that the history of the United States effectively demonstrates that building a strong nation does not require the sacrifice of cultural differences;
>
> (3) that American folklife has a fundamental influence on the desires, beliefs, values, and character of the American people;
>
> (4) that it is appropriate and necessary for the Federal Government to support research and scholarship in American folklife in order to contribute to an understanding of the complex problems of the basic desires, beliefs, and values of the American people in both rural and urban areas;
>
> (5) that the encouragement and support of American folklife, while primarily a matter for private and local initiative, is also an appropriate matter of concern to the Federal Government; and
>
> (6) that it is in the interest of the general welfare of the Nation to preserve, support, revitalize, and disseminate American folklife traditions and arts.

Powerful stuff, indeed. How do you do that in a federal agency? By building a great staff, talking and listening to people, finding the necessary resources (financial and otherwise) and being creative with what resources you have, building bridges and alliances, pushing back when necessary, and making sure your aspirations, interests, and resources connect to the people and the world around you. In other words, through management, budgets, personnel, planning, cajoling, negotiating, connecting, and keeping your eyes on the future.

LEADING IN A CONSULTING FIRM: MALACHI O'CONNOR

Malachi O'Connor earned his PhD in folklore and folklife at the University of Pennsylvania and is an owner and vice president of CFAR, Inc., a consulting firm based in Philadelphia.

"He sold out to management."
I had just shared the exciting news with a noted professor in the folklore department that I had landed a job at a consulting firm. He said, "I have to tell [another senior folklorist]," and called him up. How nice that he wanted to share the good news. Wrong. The words he spoke on the phone— as we sat side by side—were a gut punch. They became a recurring undertone for several years as I discovered that many other folklorists believed I had sold out, too.

I completed my dissertation about the intersection of work and play at Penn's Department of Folklore and Folklife in 1988 and began exploring teaching and public-sector opportunities. Most required a move that was impossible at the time, so I explored other things to do. Julie Vick, a folklorist working in Penn's On-Campus Recruiting Service, helped me frame the job search as a fieldwork project. I would interview people with PhDs in one field who had found work outside that field's usual boundaries. My eyes were opened to a new world of opportunities. I met people doing fascinating things and had a chance to see what felt like a fit and what didn't.

I returned repeatedly to one firm, the Center for Applied Research (CFAR). Among those I interviewed there were an economist intrigued by the psychodynamics of organizations, an architect attracted to systems thinking and organizational design, and a clinical psychologist who had pursued an MBA at Penn's Wharton School of Business. They were three of five founders of this small consulting firm spun out of the Wharton School, applying knowledge and capabilities from their graduate disciplines to organizational dilemmas. They invited me to work on a few small projects while completing my dissertation. But this was the business world, not the think tank I had first presumed. I spent hours talking with the firm's president about how consulting works and the connections between ethnography and consulting. After a few months, I had to ask: would they consider hiring a folklorist? Other firms had said no. If they said yes, I would be their first non-founder hire.

When the job offer arrived, I was surprised and thrilled. I went straight to the folklore department to share the news with one of my professors. That's when the tables turned. Suddenly my identity as a member of a community I had belonged to for eight years was being challenged. Having spent most of the previous few years doing dissertation fieldwork in the Amish and Mennonite communities in Lancaster County, Pennsylvania, I felt like I was being shunned.

What to do? Perhaps I'd work at CFAR for a couple of years while my wife completed her dissertation, and then I'd write an ethnography of consulting and find an academic job. Thirty years later at CFAR, consulting is still captivating. There is always more to learn about leadership and authority, self and other, person and role, and artistry in the interaction of individuals and groups.

I attribute much of my ability to do this work to my Penn mentors, Henry Glassie and Ray Birdwhistell, brilliant scholars with opposing worldviews. The former taught me to hear the voice of the artifact and understand the value of the individual to community; the latter, the workings of social communication codes and the roles people play in social systems. Like folklore studies, consulting holds these two ways of seeing—person and role, individual and system—in dynamic tension all the time.

At first consulting felt like culture shock: unfamiliar language, norms, and customs about what counted as "interesting" or "valuable." The rules for operating in client organizations and the communication forms consultants use (memo, report, financial statement) were unknowns. Learning to communicate in the language of organizational development and business strategy was more than challenging, but folklore skills helped me navigate.

My CFAR colleagues wondered what an ethnographic lens could contribute. We proposed to a retail business that they could better understand their customers through an ethnographic study of one of their major products, a waterproof boot. For a large insurance company, we shadowed agents and their support staff for over a year to help the company move from individual to team support of their seventeen thousand independent agents. They called this "riding shotgun," since we spent so much "windshield time" together.

There was so much to learn those first few years, but still I wondered whom I had "sold out" *to* and what I had sold out *from*. Was what I sold out *from* some sense of studying folklore as a pure, sacred activity with clear moral and political boundaries between right and wrong? Had I sold out *to* management because that's who usually holds the power and pays the bill? The continuous, steady drone remained: other folklorists believed I had broken some sacred rule or crossed a boundary, and that meant there were moral and ethical considerations at play.

And there are. In the late 1980s, we started working with a US government–hired client planning the implementation of President Reagan's so-called Star Wars initiative. At CFAR, anyone who had ethical concerns with a project could turn it down or withdraw. I was among several who did; ultimately, we decided to discontinue our involvement.

I learned that consulting work is never value free, and if you don't believe in the mission of an organization you might work for, saying no is an important option. I believe this is true for all of us, including academic and public folklorists, when being paid by someone else for the work we do. It's not easy, and I have made some mistakes along the way. The white hat I started out with is grayer now.

I learned that people don't work together and form organizations simply to accomplish a task or get paid; there is a lot more going on. In the messy world of organizational life, as in all of life, people work and struggle with each other in groups for much of their waking lives. Throughout organizations, people try their best to learn how to take up their personal as well as positional leadership and authority. It gets risky and uncomfortable sometimes, whether that discomfort is about race, equity, the use and abuse of power, or simply respect.

Sometimes the discomfort is about identity. The American Psychological Association was a CFAR client at a time when the association and some of its members had been accused of participating in torture at Abu Ghraib and other "dark sites." This spotlighted an important identity question: is the APA an organization whose task is to support its members' study and the creation of new knowledge, or is it a social justice organization? This is an ongoing dilemma that membership associations need to work through. It's easy to get stuck, for years, imagining that the answer lies at one or the other end of the polarity.

The American Folklore Society has also grappled with questions of purpose, as have a burgeoning number of folklore nonprofits and regional folklore organizations. I have been fortunate to work with many of them. Folklore organizations grapple with the same problems all organizations face: survival and growth, leadership and succession, stakeholder engagement and strategy, funding, governance, and board development, among others.

Organizations like Texas Folklife, CityLore, and the Philadelphia Folklore Project (all founded in the mid-1980s) create new knowledge for the field by collaborating with artists and their cultural communities *and* advocating for social justice at the same time. Working with South Arts recently, I loved hearing folklorists from around the country emphasize the importance of partnerships with arts and other organizations in connecting folk and traditional arts to critical issues people face in their communities. This, to me, is "applied folklore."

Organizational consulting is applied folklore when methods and materials of folklore are applied to address practical problems. Most of the work we do at CFAR depends on understanding how culture works in organizations so we can help people learn how to take up their roles each day to fulfill or unravel strategic commitments made by the organization. As folklorists we bring specific, ethnographic skills needed for consulting, including the ability to:

- Understand how people see their (work) world from wherever they sit in the system
- Accurately articulate that understanding to others
- Show how culture is enacted in the everyday performance of decision making, information sharing, creating budgets, etc.
- Explain the ways in which context influences events of all kinds
- Identify and articulate tacit assumptions that are reinforced over time and that— once articulated—can be discussed, reinvigorated, or changed
- Reflexively get out of our own way
- Read artifacts in useful ways; e.g., a balance sheet as a story told with numbers
- Elicit and understand the stories people in an organization tell themselves about the organization and how it works

Folklorists are exquisitely trained for this work.

Directing Communications Strategy: Katy Clune

Katy Clune earned her MA in folklore at the University of North Carolina and is Communications Director for Duke Arts, Duke University's arts initiative.

"You help folks get to know other folks." It's a shame I can't remember who said this to me, but this passing comment has stuck with me and grown in my mind to be a succinct and accurate description of my career.

In my last year of college, I found folklore, a field—with degrees, institutions, and jobs—that drew together my interests and worldview. I graduated during the 2008 financial crisis with trepidations about how limited professional folklore opportunities seemed to be. I am only now embracing "folklorist" alongside "communications director," after spending five years in a full-time museum job, the following two years earning my MA in folklore, and the next five years consistently reminding colleagues of my folklore training. Over the years, however, I've learned that I bring the skills, values, and curiosity of a folklorist to all the work I do. I lift up individual human stories (the people behind creative work), I advocate for programs and opportunities to be designed to meet community needs with equity and transparency,

I seek to demonstrate that all forms of creative expression are worth honoring, and I create opportunities for makers to enjoy a spotlight and platform—all from behind the scenes, without inserting my personal voice.

I am the daughter of a career US Foreign Service diplomat. I grew up in Jakarta, Indonesia; Nassau, Bahamas; and Paris, France, with a few years in the Washington, DC, area in between. At my elementary school in Jakarta, we had a language and culture class that taught me the *Ramayana*, the folk Hindu epic that is the basis for much of Indonesia's puppet theater. When my parents took me along on weekend day trips, we'd stop in search of *wayang golek* (the wooden, three-dimensional puppets; *wayang kulit* are the better-known shadow puppets) to add to my little collection. (The gilded bird crown and velvet sequined skirt of Sita, the forlorn princess, beat out my Barbies.) In Paris, my parents took me to museums and historic sites, ignoring my bored thirteen-year-old protests. Each time we moved, my mom would unpack our rugs, books, and decorations and conjure home in a new country. My love of cultural objects landed me in an art history course my freshman year at UC Berkeley. The discipline gave me a secret vocabulary to understand the architecture and design around me. However, I kept wanting to write about art outside the canon and not often found on museum walls: Indonesian batik, Navajo weaving, contemporary Aboriginal painting. I focused my major on twentieth-century art and politics, realizing later it was because I was more interested in the particular stories and contexts of artists than in the artwork alone.

Graduating from college a year early enabled me to work as an unpaid intern for the Smithsonian Institution, splitting my time between the Hirschhorn Museum and Sculpture Garden and the Center for Folklife and Cultural Heritage. I was at home at "the Center," whose Smithsonian Folklife Festival honors the artistry of everyday practices—there, the very people doing the making share their own stories. I supported curator Betty Belanus in researching, editing, and acquiring photographs for educational text panels and drew on these skills in my application for a communications assistant position at The Textile Museum, where I worked for four years, leaving the communications manager post for graduate school.

As communications manager for this mid-sized museum with a mostly international (sometimes anthropological) collection, I found a role that suited me. I played public ambassador for the collection: while the curators provided expert interpretation and storytelling, I had to distill exhibitions into press releases, brochures, and advertisements. I worked with the fundraising team as we articulated why studying textiles—and all the cultural, historical, and technical history textile arts embody—mattered. I pitched new ways to invite visitors into exhibitions. For our 2012 show *Woven Treasures of Japan's Tawaraya Workshop*, we hosted "Bento Box Office," a picnic dinner and Japanese film screening in the museum's garden that expanded our young professional audience. I helped land an exhibition review, "Far Eastern Dream Weavers," in the *Wall Street Journal*, extending the reach of the imperial silks on view to readers around the world. I also found satisfying ways to engage with the real content of the exhibitions: editing features written by our curators or interviewing longtime staff for our *Members' Magazine*. (It is one of the thrills of my life that my desk was next to the office of our Southeast Asian researcher, Mattiebelle Gittinger: I had checked out her book *Splendid Symbols: Textiles and Tradition in Indonesia* from the UC Berkeley library.) I began to see the power of being the institutional public messenger.

My pathway into loving and practicing folklore evolved from admiring objects to helping share the stories of the people behind the objects to believing that individual-focused culture work can meaningfully connect peoples. It is here that I find some parallels in my career to that of my diplomat dad. Sometimes this can feel naively idealistic. But I have little mantras I repeat to remind myself of my public folklorist values and guideposts: Steve Zeitlin's characterization of folklore as "the activist pursuit of beauty in the ordinary"; the potter Mark Hewitt telling me he makes work with the kitchen windowsill in mind, as important a space as any museum; and "Different kinds of work, performed with different sets of tools, can disclose the different faces of the world," a line by Michael Pollan that I love. Words like these orient me to the roots of folklore and remind me that it is worth striving for ideals.

Graduate school gave me the freedom to practice these ideas outside an institutional framework. I partnered with the Phappayboun family of Morganton, North Carolina, for my thesis, and I documented how these Lao immigrants expressed and nurtured their cultural identity through food traditions at home, in their restaurant, and at a Theravada Buddhist temple they helped found in a double-wide trailer and carport in the foothills of the Blue Ridge Mountains. I saw how my writing, conference presentations, and photos tangibly increased awareness of western North Carolina's Lao community. In February 2017, the Venerable Say Mathmanivong, a Buddhist monk, attended the opening of an exhibition of my fieldwork photography in Morganton City Hall, catered by the Phappayboun family restaurant, Asian Fusion Kitchen. The mayor invited him to open that evening's city council meeting with a Buddhist prayer—the first in the city's history.

Now I work as communications director for Duke University's arts initiative. Communications—how an organization connects with its audience—is central to the success of any business or mission-driven non-profit, and it has put me in a leadership role where I can pursue some of my ideals in a professional context. Strategic communication essentially asks, What do you want to say, how do you want to say it, and to whom do you want to say it? I enjoy being the ambassador in translating organizational priorities into the many ways, big and small, our work touches the public. Our office is tasked with increasing awareness of the arts at Duke, and I choose to give primacy to artists. I train undergraduates in interview techniques and pair them with faculty and visiting artists, sending their phone recordings off to be transcribed and coaching them through the editing process, always encouraging them to represent their interviewee in his or her own words, in the best and most gracious light possible, as a folklorist would. I recognize the power of the prestigious platforms I manage and work to represent as many forms of art making as I can in the features I publish, the speaker series we present, and the other public art experiences I support.

I have also had the opportunity to forge institutional partnerships. In 2018–2019, I codirected a collaboration between Duke University and the North Carolina Arts Council that resulted in an exhibition of documentary portraits of regional emerging traditional artists taken by student photographers (many from the Duke experimental and documentary arts MFA program). The artists gained professionally valuable photos while the students enjoyed a unique educational experience and service opportunity. The project also fulfilled one of Duke's key priorities—to forge purposeful partnerships in the region—which meant the university shone its bright spotlight on these artists. I learned lately that one of the MFA photographers has kept in touch with the artist she documented and has included him in her thesis project. This program was successful because it grew directly from listening to artists: the Arts Council conducted hundreds of interviews with the rising generation of traditional artists to understand how to design opportunities to fit their needs.

There is a graceful advocacy involved in understanding your audiences and finding ways to serve them through your mission and then building consensus among staff and administrators to make it happen. Organizations that do this well have a bounty of good stories to share, which makes a communications director's job easy. I truly believe in the transformative power of individual connection and that experiencing a culture different from your own brings empathy into focus. As much as possible, I design communications and programs that introduce people to others, that "help folks get to know other folks."

Directing a Learned Society: Jessica A. Turner

Jessica A. Turner earned her PhD in folklore at Indiana University and is Executive Director of the American Folklore Society.

At its simplest, a learned society is a collective of people working to advance knowledge in an academic discipline. In 1888, the American Folklore Society (AFS) was founded by three groups of people—academics in the humanities, museum anthropologists, and private citizens interested in the subject—all of whom wanted to advance the study of folklore and elevate its place within the academy and society. The reality of a learned society is somewhat more complex: tangled up in the disciplinary history of an academic field and those within it, those who led the field, and those who left; its position adjacent to sister disciplines; and the perception and reality of its job prospects and public value. AFS has a broad portfolio of activities but primarily serves as a nonprofit organization, a learned society, and a professional association to advance the field of folklore studies through scholarly publications, convenings, advocacy, and special programs. It networks our field.

In 2016, when AFS's previous executive director, Tim Lloyd, wrote to the AFS membership to announce his retirement and the search for the next executive director, I wrote him a note of congratulations and said, "I hope AFS finds someone as good as you in your replacement." Tim replied with a thanks and added, "Your name has come up in our discussions. You should consider applying." While those of us who know Tim recognize that in his thoughtful approach to members and his highly organized workstyle he undoubtedly wrote such a note of recruitment to many of us in the field, nonetheless his kind note drove me to open the link to the job description.

In that moment I realized I had gathered the skills necessary for this position following several years of teaching, program development, and administrative work in the field. The previous eight years of my work had been a whirlwind of developing skills in academic program design, teaching, fundraising, civic engagement, advocacy, and institution building. The tenure-track position I held as coordinator of an undergraduate program in cultural heritage studies at a small liberal arts college (Virginia Intermont College) melted in the economic reckoning after the 2008–2009 recession, which ended in the school's closure. Because I had also become involved in a community nonprofit in which I was truly invested as a scholar of Appalachian culture and traditional music, I stayed in the community to work with this organization on a museum startup. I found myself in meetings focused on the "creative economy" and "cultural asset development" where I regularly advocated for our field's methods of ethnographic inquiry and community-driven work as solid investments into successful community development projects. Over those years after completing my PhD, I had worked in academic program development and teaching, museum development and administration, exhibition curation, program and funding development, and nonprofit management.

I realized that through my own work in the field—some academic, some public, all the while advocating for our field as a critical intersection point with the projects in which I was involved—I had built professional skills, a knowledge of program development, a keen eye for advocacy and partnerships, and a desire to serve. The skills needed to lead AFS are not unlike the skills needed to run any other nonprofit: raise enough funds to cover expenses, work closely with the board on governance and vision, advocate for the field and its people and institutions, manage the organization's legal requirements and steward its finances, work with staff to carry out programs and services, and maintain existing relationships (with board, donors, staff, and stakeholders) while also building new ones.

AFS is one of seventy-five learned-society members of the American Council of Learned Societies (ACLS), and, like any other peer group, the directors of those societies share information, data, and wisdom about learned-society activities and leadership. The director of another ACLS member society described, for example, the two primary duties of the job: be a cheerleader for the field and serve as its human complaint box. Cheerleaders amplify and rally, literally from a position in and alongside the field. Complaint boxes absorb, aggregate, and act upon suggestions and ideas. Both are useful analogies of the core functions of this work and further reminders to avoid arrogance.

My approach to leadership is in the vein of the servant leadership model, and I believe that serving well recognizes the many stakeholder voices that make up AFS: the president and board; past, present, and future leaders; members; and conference participants. My idea of a strong organization is one in which the staff and the board work as partners to advance the organizational mission. Such a relationship takes trust, communication, and effort; regular work toward understanding the various management and governance duties of board and staff is important to creating an organizational culture in which everyone feels they have a voice and a role in the effort. Beyond the board, numerous stakeholders exist, and a strong board and staff will consider these stakeholders regularly. Because AFS is a membership organization, members are the clearest example of stakeholders in our organization, but they are not the only ones. Advocacy, financial stewardship, and program development are other key areas of my work, and they requires constant nurturing to maintain my knowledge and skills. If I added up the continuing education hours I have put into learning to be a nonprofit leader, they would certainly amount to an MBA.

Fortunately, the values necessary to get all this right are already built into the values and practices of our field. Acknowledging elders and other bearers of knowledge as experts is an important part of disciplinary and organizational stewardship. Collaborative research, ethnographic methods including deep listening, and the centering of voices besides our own are important ways to sustain relevance as a learned society as we look toward the future of inclusive scholarship. Communicating impact helps us advocate for our field within the arts and higher education structures within which we work. Finally, practicing ethnography helps us avoid complacency; it is useful in acknowledging histories while also recognizing acute situations that require that we not rest on our successes (or in our failures, for that matter).

A skill I have to practice regularly is my ability to sit with discomfort, not retreating from conversations or ideas that make me feel uncomfortable or inadequate. A key component to developing resilience (which is itself an important part of organizational strategy), sitting with discomfort asks us to make brave spaces for the conversations that matter to the field right now. As economic and social fissures continue to challenge our world and the ways folklorists have worked previously in the world, sitting with discomfort gives us the opportunity to reflect, improve, advocate, and serve more broadly. Inequities born from systemic racism and structural inequalities, funding gaps in the field of folk and traditional arts, and the future of the humanities in higher education each are broad areas of concern that require thoughtful, collective effort. Part of the job of the AFS director is to steward such important conversations, reaching out to our mentors as we reach forward into the future. Recognizing that this period is not the first to require deep listening and structural change in our field, such stewarding will make a better network to keep folklorists connected and speaking effectively from our values to the world.

DIRECTING A MUSEUM: JASON BAIRD JACKSON

Jason Baird Jackson earned his PhD in folklore at Indiana University, where he is Ruth N. Halls Professor of Folklore Studies and Anthropology.

A folklorist who serves as a museum director will likely still be involved in doing some frontline folklore work of the sort a museum curator, state folklorist, or undergraduate teacher does, but there is a strong likelihood that much of the director's time will be spent in activities aimed at supporting the work of others within the museum. These include not only the museum's staff but also its larger circle of supporters and partners. Museums around the world vary greatly in size and scope, but museums with strong folklore studies programs tend to be smaller and more grassroots in style. This characteristic is what usually enables the director of such a museum to keep a hand in the work of teaching, curating temporary exhibitions, or undertaking research projects. The ability to stay involved in such activities helps keep a director energized and in touch with the purposes of the work. They are also a kind of reward for the other kinds of work a museum director is called upon to do, from making sure the museum's lights are kept on to making sure robust policies are in place to protect children participating in museum programs. The range of activities with which a museum director must engage is vast, and this too can be one of the pleasures of the job. Even in small institutions, the museum director in a folklore-oriented museum is a manager of staff, budgets, and facilities and of projects, research, and relationships.

Between the beginning of 2013 and the end of 2019, I served as director of Indiana University's museum of ethnography, ethnology, and cultural history. Known then as the Mathers Museum of World Cultures, this museum had a long history of involvement in the work of folklore studies. This fact is reflected in its original name—the Indiana University Museum of History, Anthropology, and Folklore—and in the ways the museum had historically articulated with the work of students and faculty in the university's Department of Folklore and Ethnomusicology. My directorship of the Mathers Museum of World Cultures was informed by my earlier work as a museum curator. While museum directors can come initially to that role from a wide range of previous experiences, curatorship remains a particularly common stepping- stone to directorship. Being a curator is good preparation for leading a museum as director, but directors typically become involved in a much wider range of activities. To illustrate, I rely here on my calendar for April 2019, which was a typical month in my directorship.

A museum director in a folklore-oriented museum is a kind of diplomat, representing the museum to various external groups and individuals with an aim to strengthen relationships. Thus, that April, I welcomed the Executive Board of the American Folklore Society when they held part of their biannual board meetings at the museum. Hosting this meeting was an important opportunity to share the work of the museum with this group of leaders in the field. Two days before hosting the AFS board, I welcomed an ambassador to the museum. A representative of his home country to the United States, he visited our museum to see an exhibition we were presenting related to his homeland and to attend a talk by the exhibition's curator. Meeting interesting people is definitely one of the perks of this job!

A museum director in a folklore-oriented museum is also a strategic planner and project manager. But if the museum's staff (inclusive of volunteers, students, and others working to advance its goals) gets bigger than a handful of individuals, the museum director will also be guiding and overseeing the work of other staff who themselves will be project managers and project doers. Much of my calendar for April 2019 was filled with events (lectures, exhibition openings, concerts, and community receptions—the list goes on and on) that responded to strategic goals and served the museum mission but were organized by other staff members. Museum directors are thus participants in events they are not technically leading but for which they are ultimately responsible as workaday managers and higher-level agenda setters. For example, in April 2019, our museum's curator of folklife and cultural heritage, Jon Kay, was producing a set of documentary videos he would debut at the Traditional Arts Indiana Heritage Fellows Celebration held at the museum at the end of that month. As director I was an enabler of this work, but Jon was at the center of leading his team and making it and the associated event happen. At the strategic level, April saw me reporting to the museum's faculty advisory board on our progress toward our strategic plan goals and our participation in a university fundraising campaign.

A museum director in a folklore-oriented museum is also a fundraiser. While some museums are large enough to have their own development staff, such professionals will be few in number or nonexistent in most museums with folklore programs. Even in museums with advancement staff, it falls to the director to lead such efforts, as they will be shaped by the museum's strategic goals, community needs, and ongoing relationships. In this particular April, on the same day I hosted the ambassador, I spent the morning doing what fundraisers call "prospect review." While fundraising provokes awkward feelings in many of us, folklorist-museum directors have to train themselves to get over such feelings. It helps to remember that the funds we seek will support good work and that those who are willing want to help advance the museum's mission. Prospect review involves thinking through all the people who are committed to, or might be drawn into commitment to, the museum and thinking about how they might be particularly open to contributing in particular ways to meet specific needs. Might the collector of beautiful textiles be willing to sponsor an artist residency with a weaver? Might the longtime participant in museum programs be open to funding internships in which students are trained to organize the kinds of programs the potential donor loves? Might the object donor be willing to purchase new cabinets to store such collections safely for generations to come?

A museum director in a folklore-oriented museum is also a media and marketing manager. A museum needs funders to achieve its mission and serve its community, but it also really needs to get the word out. Paid advertising is one effective way to do this. But few museums with folklore programs can afford to do much of it. With or without advertising, other modes of communication need to be pursued. Social media is now a big part of this work. Older forms of messaging (newsletters, for instance) remain valuable. But a key activity for a museum director, and those who are assisting the director, is to generate news stories in whatever media venues the museum can connect with. The increasing absence of local newspapers is a growing challenge in this regard. One tries to tell the museum's stories as systematically and as widely as possible. That April, for instance, I did an interview with our local National Public Radio affiliate about the work of our museum. Eighteen days later it appeared as a wonderful long essay overviewing all our work. It is in the nature of such media that it can be repackaged and reused; this online NPR story could be shared by the museum on social media, passed on to a university administrator, or given to a faculty member seeking information on the museum as a teaching resource.

One of the greatest pleasures of doing folklore studies work of any kind in a museum is that a large percentage of the activities captured in the table of contents to this volume are a part of the work. As director that April, I was active as a publisher, an author, a research coordinator, a blogger, a university-community partner, a local advocate, a digital humanist, and an internationalist. I also had the pleasure of working closely with folklore colleagues across the full span of the roles evoked in this collection. This is the joy of museum work in general and of directorships in particular. There is a clothing practice that speaks to this diversity. The museum director may wear business clothes to work each day, but a pair of jeans and a work shirt should hang behind the office door to be changed into when the morning of donor meetings is followed by all-hands-on-deck physical labor. Similarly, the curator may come to work wearing jeans in anticipation of working with a team of volunteers to unpack a dusty collection, but business wear needs to hang behind the door, too, ready to be jumped into when the governor shows up unexpectedly and wants a gallery tour. Folklorists are uniquely prepared for such diverse duties.

Directing a Nonprofit Organization: Ellen McHale

Ellen McHale earned her PhD in folklore and folklife at the University of Pennsylvania and is Executive Director of New York Folklore.

The New York Folklore Society (now New York Folklore) was formed in 1944 as a scholarly society. At its inception, the society welcomed as members anyone who had an interest in folklore: those who taught folklore in the academy; collectors of folklore material; librarians and archivists; schoolteachers; musicians, writers, actors, and artists who used folk material in their own work; and community members who recognized the importance of their own or others' heritage and traditions. As an association, the New York Folklore Society was inspired by early civil rights activity in the metropolitan New York City area, educational reform movements, progressive politics, and the expanding globalization that was a result of World War II. In its current form, New York Folklore has remained true to the founders' original mission to draw attention to the diverse cultural heritage found in New York State and to strive for cultural equity in the state's expression of heritage.

In my history with the organization, I have been a member, board member, officer, and paid membership director; since 1999 I've been executive director. While this long engagement with an organization is unusual, I feel it has provided me an institutional memory for the period of time (1990 to the present) during which New York Folklore (NYF) transitioned from a board-run academic "society" to a nonprofit public folklore organization. While New York Folklore's programs of journal publishing and conferences remain from its earlier mission, as a nonprofit service organization, New York Folklore has expanded its reach to provide services to artists, community leaders, and researchers.

An effective executive director of any cultural organization should be versed in a wide variety of skills. When I left my staff folklorist job at the Rensselaer County Arts Council in 1990 to take a new job as a historical museum director, I was told that to be "successful" as an executive director, I must always know about "the money." I have taken this to heart, as I believe financial stability is the key to any strong organization. Fiscal management is not something I learned in my studies in college or graduate school. Recognizing my own deficits when I became NYF executive director in 1999, I enrolled in graduate courses in nonprofit accounting and marketing. However, even with prior academic training in business subjects, the nonprofit director of a cultural organization still learns on the job.

As executive director I benefitted from the strong groundwork laid by my predecessor, John Suter, who had previously moved NYF from an all-volunteer organization with folklore at the heart of its mission to a statewide service organization with a paid staff. After having worked in the history museum field for several years before taking the job at New York Folklore, I found it refreshing to be once again involved intimately with folklore, now as the leader of an organization dedicated to folk culture. I found that the skills I learned as a folklorist—including deep listening and the examination of "community" as dynamic and innovative—are important skills for any executive director.

As an undergraduate major in world music and American studies at Wesleyan University, I was encouraged by my advisor, Mark Slobin, to consider folklore as a career. As an undergraduate, I had conducted a successful senior thesis fieldwork project to document French American performers in northern Vermont—my first entrée into ethnography. While I had always considered my major interests to be musical, I was genuinely interested in how music and dance operated within community settings and in the role of music and dance in the intersection of heritage and place. Folklore and folklife studies at the University of Pennsylvania seemed like a great fit, and I completed the program to receive my PhD. As a graduate student, I had always intended to return to rural New York State. I was also more interested in working in the "public sector" than in becoming an academically based folklorist. While still a graduate student, I had been encouraged by the knowledge that the New York State Council on the Arts (NYSCA) was creating regional and county public folklore positions across the state.

My first jobs in the field were as researcher and programmer; I worked within school settings and museums and as the regional and county folklorist. Prior to my job at New York Folklore, I had initiated regional folklife positions at the Rensselaer County Arts Council and at the Dutchess County Council on the Arts, and I had been the staff folklorist at the Tri-County Arts Council in Cobleskill, New York. These positions focused on ethnographic field research and public programming. While folk arts programming is not a paramount part of my current role as executive director, research and programming are still part of my job description. New York Folklore participates in cultural activities at the local level, where we collaborate with existing opportunities to infuse folk arts and artists into public exhibitions, festivals, and city initiatives. To expand our footprint in Schenectady, for example, we opened a changing exhibition gallery in 2019 that has greatly expanded our programming opportunities. As the New York Folklore gallery exhibits the work of folk artists from New York State, we can augment each exhibit with workshops and public programming that provide a context and amplification for the art forms being exhibited.

New York Folklore is a service organization; therefore, much of our programming revolves around providing technical assistance and professional development for the folk arts field in New York State, and we partner with the New York State Council on the Arts to implement several of the ongoing folk arts programs they support. For over thirty-five years, one of our signature programs has been the annual New York State Folk Arts Roundtable, which brings together more than forty-five folklorists and cultural specialists for professional development on topics and issues pertinent to the field. Another is the Mentoring and Professional Development Program, which supports one-on-one mentoring exchanges, travel to visit model programs to learn from colleagues, and targeted small-group workshops.

The technical assistance programs of New York Folklore address issues in the field of folklore and provide opportunities for the dissemination of best practices. Through managing these two professional development programs, I can personally play a strong role in affecting positive change throughout our state. In partnership with NYSCA, I am responsive to the changing needs of the field and the issues facing my folklore colleagues, and I directly assist folk and traditional artists in our state. A few of the initiatives of which I am particularly proud are the Latino Dance Summit, which brought together dance leaders in the Latino communities of New York to discuss pedagogy and develop recruitment and retention strategies; an ethnographic marketing project for Mohawk basket makers and Tuscarora beadworkers; and a microenterprise project for immigrant and refugee artists. These projects originated from needs expressed by members of the communities for which they were designed. Because they were community initiated, these technical assistance or professional development opportunities were wide reaching, impactful, and replicable. In general, because of the technical assistance provided by New York Folklore in partnership with the New York State Council on the Arts, New York State has a strong and committed folk arts network.

As a young person growing up in rural northern New York State, I often felt that my community did not recognize its worth. The desire to help communities and their members realize the value of their traditional culture and their own unique histories has inspired me throughout my career. As the leader of New York's statewide folk cultural organization, I continue to work with artists and leaders in New York's communities to recognize and amplify their folk cultural assets. I can conduct fieldwork, design programming, strategize an issue, or advocate for traditional heritage and culture, all in the same day. I am never bored, and there is never a moment when I feel I have nothing to do. In doing this work, I continue to be pleased that each day I can engage with my chosen field and actively work to further the field of folk and traditional culture.

DIRECTING A RECORDING LABEL: DANIEL SHEEHY

Daniel Sheehy earned his PhD in ethnomusicology at UCLA and is Director and Curator Emeritus of Smithsonian Folkways Recordings.

I have jumped into several career abysses-of-the-unknown in my lifetime, but taking on the directorship of Smithsonian Folkways Recordings may have been the deepest. On the face of it, it sounds easy. I had been a working trumpet player since the late 1960s. I played Broadway musicals in theaters, rhythm and blues in nightclubs, mariachi music and Veracruz *son jarocho* in restaurants, pop rock and Balkan music in recording studios, park concerts with the musician's union band, and more. I played bass drum in the UCLA marching band. I *loved* playing "The Star-Spangled Banner," especially the "rockets' red glare" part when the bass drum and cymbals had solo booms and crashes for all to admire. While I was a music education student at UCLA, I took performance courses in Ashanti drumming, Persian *setar*, Japanese *shakuhachi*, and Russian balalaika. I took a half-time job in the Institute for Ethnomusicology's audio laboratory and learned about recording technology. Later, I produced records of traditional music from Chile and Veracruz.

Then things started to change. I realized there was no place in my planned career as a high school band director for the musics I had come to admire: those of James Brown, Mariachi Vargas de Tecalitlán, Veracruz *son jarocho* by Conjunto Medellín de Lino Chávez, royal court drumming by Ashanti prince drummer Kwasi Badu, and so many others. They weren't in the public-school classroom, and they weren't valued by mainstream America. I came to feel that biased social hierarchies and institutional inertia shaped the content of music education more than inherent aesthetic worth. In a word, anger fairly described how I felt about this cultural exclusion. It was social injustice, pure and simple, and I had to do something about it. I could not stay in the band director box. In graduate school, I switched to ethnomusicology.

Then, as I was studying ethnomusicology, I was kidnapped by folklorists. (Willingly, of course.) In 1974, Bess Lomax Hawes and her folklore protégée, Barbara Rahm, recruited me to do fieldwork among Southern

California Mexican musicians for the Smithsonian Institution's 1975 Festival of American Folklife. The fieldwork fed into the 1976 Bicentennial Festival of American Folklife, twelve weeks of multiple concurrent festival programs featuring more than five thousand participants from all US states and thirty-eight countries around the world. The implied social justice agenda of the festival and the high-flying rhetoric by Ralph Rinzler, Margaret Mead, Alan Lomax, and others appealed to me. I was amazed to be able to play a part in giving some of those excluded musicians a forum on the National Mall in Washington, DC! And a major epiphany was that I got paid to do it! The idea that there might be a career in there somewhere started to take shape.

In 1978, Bess hired me to be the staff ethnomusicologist in the budding Folk Arts program she directed at the National Endowment for the Arts. I finished my PhD fieldwork in Veracruz, packed up all my worldly belongings, drove to DC, and learned how to do the job. There was a lot of learning to do. The best part was hanging around with Bess and learning by osmosis. We had long talks similar to those we had in putting together the 1976 Bicentennial Festival of American Folklife, discussing programmatic strategies to honor and fortify traditions and their practitioners throughout the United States. We talked about "in-reach" and "outreach" programs to connect communities to their own traditions and to project traditional arts to broad audiences. We talked about Alan Lomax's media efforts at cultural equity, which worked to counter the deleterious effects of a centralized, domineering media industry that ignored "smaller" cultures that didn't play into the mass media's revenue plans. Through grants, we helped launch dozens of state-based folk arts programs and state apprenticeship programs, the National Heritage Fellowships, in-reach concerts connecting communities to their traditions, outreach efforts such as television documentaries and documentary recordings aimed at a national audience, and more. When Bess retired in 1992, the director reins passed to me until I moved to the Smithsonian in 2000.

What does all this have to do with my work as the director and curator of Smithsonian Folkways Recordings? Everything. All the cultural strategizing with Bess over the previous twenty-five years served me well in my new job; in fact, strategy became my central axis when selecting recordings to publish. The main tool of my trade switched from grant money to recordings. Bess occasionally would say that "money is a blunt instrument," which I took to mean that the application of money to an issue only got you so far. The broader cultural agenda, strategy, goals, and people doing on-the-ground work really made things happen. So how to translate this notion to recordings? How could recordings play into cultural-social agendas?

Over time, several lines of thinking shaped my actions. I translated the Folk Arts Program in-reach and outreach notions into mission statement rhetoric: "supporting cultural diversity and increased understanding among peoples through the documentation, preservation, and dissemination of sound" and "strengthen[ing] people's engagement with their own cultural heritage and enhance[ing] their awareness and appreciation of the cultural heritage of others." I prioritized the publication of recordings that played into a particular cultural agenda, and I used slogans such as "music that is more than music" and "great music and a great story," pointing to a social-cultural "storyline" issue surrounding the music recording. One example was the album *¡Soy Salvadoreño!: Chanchona Music from Eastern El Salvador*, the first recording with educational liner notes of music from the Oriente region of El Salvador, which was hit hardest by the civil war of the early 1990s and was the place of origin of many Salvadoran refugees in the United States. Another was *Singing for Life: Songs of Hope, Healing, and HIV/AIDS in Uganda*, spotlighting the application of traditional music to the battle with the AIDS pandemic. Most of the more than two hundred recordings published during my Folkways tenure had such a storyline.

This was the fun part. Other things made it even more fun—and impactful. The Harris Poll regularly ranked the Smithsonian as one of the most trusted brand names in the United States, alongside the Mayo Clinic. Having the word *Smithsonian* in Smithsonian Folkways Recordings gave a generous dose of visibility to our efforts. And we had a marketing department to give our recordings even more dynamic presence in the world. For me—a "make the world a better place through public impact" type of person—this was a dream come true.

But there were not-so-fun parts, too. Folkways staff and production expenses were paid almost exclusively from revenues. Overnight, I found myself running a $4 million business. This meant we had to bring in nearly that much each year to cover our costs. Believe me, every morning when I went to work, I felt the pressure of making enough revenues to pay my colleagues' salaries. I also learned quickly that the music industry, on which Folkways depended for those revenues, is highly complex and litigious. Release-date deadlines; distributors; profit margins; contracts for artists, producers, and notes writers; production music licensing; and threatening letters from all sorts of alleged intellectual property owners were daily topics. My predecessor, Anthony Seeger, told me of how a friend of the family and agent for a prominent folk singer congratulated him on his new job and followed by saying that he would soon be suing him! How did I deal with this onslaught of responsibility? The name-brand slogan "Just do it!" came to mind, but I mainly leaned hard on the expertise of our talented staff. I also lucked out. Filling big shoes such as those of Bess Lomax Hawes at the NEA and Tony Seeger at Smithsonian Folkways was intimidating, but I came to realize in both cases that they had put in place a basic plan for me to follow and tweak as necessary. I thought of them as the architects and myself as a carpenter.

I close big, answering the question "What is the meaning of life?" In my time with Folkways between 2000 and 2016, I often started talks with the trope, "Music has no meaning at all [dramatic pause] . . . except the meaning that people give it." In doing this, I took a cue from Folkways founder Moses Asch, who stuffed those heavy cardboard record sleeves with album notes that placed the sounds into a cultural-social-historical context. So, in a way, I found my answer in the Folkways legacy. What is the meaning of life? The meaning you give it! And what can be better than living a life filled with joy and purpose?

Coordinating Research Projects: Diana Baird N'Diaye

Diana Baird N'Diaye earned her PhD in anthropology and visual studies from The Union Institute and is a cultural specialist and senior curator at the Smithsonian Institution's Center for Folklife and Cultural Heritage.

As the goals and products of folklore research have expanded within the larger contexts of public, digital, and community engagement, the role of research coordinator has also expanded in scope. When I began graduate school in 1972, the paradigm for a cultural researcher was to be a lone individual "in the field," accompanied by a tape recorder, camera, and notepad to document the ways of "the folk." After writing up field notes, he or she would then analyze them, place the speakers' narratives in an interpretive framework informed by the work of folklorists, and present the bounty of wisdom and the rich experience of community "bearers of tradition" to other folklorists and, occasionally, to the public. Some of the best examples of the genre of individual research projects with autoethnographic themes are the work of Zora Neale Hurston, who translated her research into essays, novels, and even theatrical presentations; Kathryn Morgan's *Children of Strangers*; and Gladys-Marie Fry's *Night Riders in Black Folk History*.

The advent of the Smithsonian Institution's Folklife Festival in 1967 heralded the rise of public folklore; it was revolutionary at the time because it put the skills and practices of folklore research—particularly team research—at the service of public presentation. In 1990, my first year as a curator for the Smithsonian Folklife Festival, I shared the role of research coordinator with my husband, Gorgui N'Diaye; we worked in collaboration with a team of folklorists at the Centre Civilisations et Culture, located in Dakar, Senegal, a division of the Senegalese Cultural Ministry. Each folklorist was an expert in the traditions of an ethnic/language group in Senegal and was, more often than not, from the region or ethnic group whose traditions she or he was documenting. Our task as festival research coordinators was not to train these seasoned folklorists how to do the important work they had already done and had published for decades but rather to orient them toward the specific requirements of the Folklife Festival.

For this, Gorgui and I translated and adapted a set of guidelines we had received from the festival director that had been tweaked, updated, translated, and passed on from curator to curator throughout much of the festival's then twenty-three-year history. These guidelines outlined the general purposes of the festival—to "present the practitioners of living community-based cultural traditions within the context of a particular program"—and described the goal of our research efforts: facilitating "the identification and selection of traditions and their bearers, the identification and selection of Festival participants who represent those traditions, the development of presentational formats and interpretive materials for selected traditions and participants and the development of thematic concepts, aesthetic and functional designs, and staging logistics." The guidelines also outlined the role of the researcher: to provide documentation of local traditions and recommend local practitioners who might be appropriate for the festival.

Smithsonian Folklife Festival program curators are responsible for developing a thematic focus and integrating program components and may also often function as research coordinators. As was the case with the Senegal program, discussions about festival program development took place through field researchers, curators, and research coordinators working together. As the 1990 festival took place on the National Mall in front of the Smithsonian Castle, another role for the folklorist as research coordinator—that of research facilitator—was emerging. My folklorist colleague—curator and education specialist Dr. Betty Belanus—had received an internal Smithsonian grant to use the festival as a training ground for cultural activists from small heritage organizations who wanted to learn the foundations of folklore research and presentation to create similar programs in their own communities. For the Smithsonian Summer Institute for Community

Scholars, Betty enlisted the services of several folklorists to train these individuals in an intensive introduction to the fundamentals of research-based programs.

During the festival, Cameroonian journalist and economist Dominic Ntube, who began and ran the annual African Festival on Freedom Plaza in downtown Washington, DC, each year, asked for help in learning about producing a festival more along the lines of the Smithsonian's, and members of the local Senegalese support society had already expressed interest in continuing to produce programs on Senegalese culture after the 1990 festival was over. Gorgui was already active in the cultural and social life of New York City's Senegalese community. Given my long-term interest in what I called "community self-definition," I was inspired by Betty's community-scholar project and started to think about a research and presentation initiative to recruit and train African immigrant cultural activists and educators from various countries of origin who lived in the Washington, DC, area to coordinate research and produce their own public programs. Betty and I worked together to train the researchers/coordinators who would then, in turn, coordinate study groups. This facilitation, and the work of community scholars/research coordinators, eventually resulted in the 1997 African Immigrant Folklife Smithsonian program, in which our roles as cocurators were actually a form of research coordination. Dominic Ntube's African Festival continued in DC, eventually coming under the wing of the District of Columbia's African Affairs Division. It did not follow the pattern of the research-based Folklife Festival, but several of the artists, like Malian guitarist and kora musician Cheikh Hamala Diabate, who performed or demonstrated at the African Immigrant Folklife program for the first time, became regular performers at the African Festival.

The African Immigrant Folklife program was the precursor to the Smithsonian's 2010–2019 Will to Adorn project, which offered another set of challenges and new opportunities with the emergence of digital communities of research practice. The project's original goals were to document African American aesthetics of style across regional, ethnic, gender, faith, and class boundaries. We sought to answer the question: What are the common elements of African American dress? Early in the project, we determined that the project was really about the diversity of African American identity as seen through the lens of dress.

The Will to Adorn project, like the African Immigrant Folklife project, was grounded in participatory research and community cultural autobiography. With the support of study grants from the Smithsonian Scholarly Studies program, a craft research grant from the Center for Craft, and a series of Smithsonian Youth Access grants, we were able to involve researchers at all levels of experience and training—from established scholars to middle school students—in documenting African American style.

For example, Smithsonian Folklife Festival alumnus Camila Bryce-Laporte organized a group of adults and young people from her church to do the documentation work in Washington, DC, and Baltimore. Her Mustard Seed Ministry cohort interviewed African American milliners, shoemakers, tailors, dressmakers, braiders, cosmetologists, and many others. Not only was the work invaluable to the overall project, but the introduction to conducting research was excellent precollege training for young people, who thereby strengthened their connections to an older generation of makers. Other researchers/coordinators, such as Deirdre Holland and Jade Banks at the Bronx-based Mind Builders Creative Arts, Inc., led their organizations' internship programs through many seasons of excellent cultural documentation work with community icons like clothing designer/maker Brenda Brunson-Bey.

The growing capabilities of cell phones and the expansion of social media into proprietary platforms made it possible to organize and coordinate cultural documentation work at multiple sites. Researchers could record and share still and moving images and sound in real time. We could hold and record meetings across wide distances on a daily basis at minimum expense. When the Will to Adorn project began, this technology was still imperfect and awkward; as the principal investigator and research coordinator, I learned the upsides and downsides of technology, since there were many glitches. Sometimes great images were taken at too small a resolution. Sound recordings captured important voices and thoughts but were sometimes lost or recorded at too low a volume. The sheer volume of work could be overwhelming to coordinate. Years into the project, new institutional review board processes were put into place, and new web safety protocols made online platforms unusable. Nevertheless, the idea of training local research coordinators to create and sustain researcher groups enabled young people, as well as adults who previously had no experience in folklife research, to learn valuable research skills.

To be successful, research coordinators need to be effective teachers and mentors: setting and communicating research goals; recruiting, convening, monitoring, supervising, framing, and motivating researchers; knowing equipment; creating or adapting research guidelines to a project; and suggesting or pursuing outcomes and deliverables. At the end of a project, they are additionally responsible for evaluating and critiquing the work and making sure all participating voices are heard.

Managing Regional Arts Programs: Teresa Hollingsworth

Teresa Hollingsworth earned her MA in folk studies at Western Kentucky University and is Director, Film & Traditional Arts at South Arts.

Few students in graduate folklore programs probably consider becoming, or aspire to become, arts administrators. Some may envision themselves in academia (with a professorship and all that it entails) while others may anticipate a career in public-sector folklore (as a state folklorist, festival director, museum curator, fieldworker, filmmaker, podcaster, etc.). My young graduate-student self never contemplated a career trajectory that would lead me to arts administration—but here I am. As a folklorist whose work as an arts administrator is consistently challenging, sometimes frustrating, and always rewarding, I've been a staff member at South Arts in Atlanta since 1999. To the credit of the leadership at South Arts, one of six nonprofit regional arts organizations in the United States, the work of folklorists has been integral to our endeavors since the 1980s.

My first ten years as a public-sector folklorist were spent at the Kentucky Folklife Program, the Maine Folklife Center, and the Florida Folklife Program, where my work was heavily directed toward documentation. I had lots of different titles, including "folklife specialist" and "folklife coordinator." Fieldwork was our cornerstone: we used it to create or contribute to such public programs as exhibits, publications, festivals, educational resources, public workshops, and teacher trainings. Then I organized the documentary materials I created during fieldwork, and they eventually were moved from my office to the appropriate archival collection. It was pretty straightforward: Fieldwork. Public program. Archive.

In 1999 I accepted a position at South Arts (formerly the Southern Arts Federation) as the director of traditional arts. My transition from fieldworker and participatory programmer to arts administrator provided new opportunities and a different, broader perspective. I left a large state government agency for a regional arts nonprofit organization (working in nine Southern states) that provided flexibility, encouraged staff creativity, and actively sought partnerships. For my first ten years at South Arts, I guided traditional arts programming and was given autonomy to sunset some projects and create new ones. There was little to no fieldwork for me personally as I planned convenings, traveling exhibits, and artist trainings. Frequently, I outsourced components of this work to curators, fieldworkers, and educators so I could address the infrastructural and long-term aspects of projects.

As South Arts expanded its portfolio of work, my administrative responsibilities grew to include film. My new, and still current, title—program director for film and traditional arts—reflects the two proverbial programming caps I now wear. My time is split; others may say "shared." The two disciplines naturally mesh. I've been able to connect documentary filmmakers to traditional artists and cultural community gatekeepers, and during my term as film editor for the *Journal of American Folklore*, my media contacts provided access to a steady stream of ethnographic films that otherwise might have been overlooked by folklorist peers.

To continue to move the robust South Arts traditional arts program forward, but now, with less time, I have to undertake even more administrative planning. I work with our development team to secure funding for programs, projects, and initiatives. I devote time to establishing new contacts and partnerships while I continue to strengthen long-standing relationships. These responsibilities require time for planning, implementing, and reporting, including developing and balancing budgets; producing contracts and guidelines; monitoring time lines and progress; supervising administrative assistants, interns, and contractors; providing content for marketing and access (including website and social media information); and creating, executing, and compiling evaluation. These tasks are core components of arts administration.

Arts administrative work provides the infrastructure for traditional arts programming to exist. A recent example is our In These Mountains: Central Appalachian Folk Arts and Culture initiative, a multiyear endeavor with activities in the Appalachian Regional Commission counties of Kentucky, North Carolina, and Tennessee. The administrative elements of this project include securing funding, establishing partnerships, writing awards guidelines, developing time lines, contracting community scholars and interns, coordinating partner memos of agreement, confirming timely payments, participating in meetings and preparing reports, and designing evaluation. Attention to many administrative decisions and details is required to produce useful outcomes: elementary students who have access to after-school traditional arts programs, instructors who are being compensated, undergraduate students who are participating in paid internships, graduate students who are receiving fellowship stipends and tuition assistance, the expansion of existing state arts agency mentor/apprenticeship programs, and master traditional artists who are receiving cash awards to help them pursue lifelong learning opportunities.

Although I spend numerous hours at a computer, attend multiple daily meetings (in person and by video conference), and experience periods of substantial travel, I also have opportunities to advocate for the inclusion of folklife and the traditional arts in other programming and resource areas within my organization. The stealth work of a folklorist as arts administrator is not by accident. This realization happened soon after my arrival at South Arts. Two colleagues appeared in my office doorway and asked me to define bluegrass music because I was "a folklorist, and my academic degree sounded like I should know." They were working on a funding proposal for our former annual performing arts conference and needed to provide detail about the genre. I shared information about the roots and evolution of bluegrass and offered to loan them several CDs. It was more information than they wanted or needed, but my experience and knowledge as a folklorist superseded my role as an arts administrator in that moment. This was the first of countless informal but important office encounters that gave me opportunities to share insight about the traditional arts. Whether to provide context and definitions for grant application reviews, to distinguish between the work of a traditional string musician and a singer-songwriter, or to offer insight about classical Chinese dance, I continue to be called upon to contribute my knowledge as a folklorist to the larger work of our organization. Opportunities for me to strategically align the traditional arts with South Arts' other organizational programming and resources arise more commonly than most might think.

As of this writing, South Arts has twelve funding categories for individual artists and nonprofit organizations. Although only one is specifically directed at presenting traditional arts and artists, other opportunities provide potential for traditional arts participation. As an arts administrator, I constantly (sometimes to the chagrin of my colleagues) advocate for the inclusion of the traditional arts for consideration in other grant categories. For example, a potential grantee might apply to our Performing Arts Touring Grant category for support to present a traditional zydeco group or a blues singer. Performing arts includes more than presentations of classical music or ballet.

Over the years, I've also become the default archivist and oral historian for my organization. I've retained copies of reports, notes, and publications (or at least I know where they are in storage) that reflect the organizational history and breadth of South Arts programs and projects. I find holding a beautiful exhibit catalog in my hands is personally much more appealing than scrolling through the same catalog online (if it's even available). I like paper. Without fail, colleagues call upon me to recall a funding source or a project partner, or to request a copy of an old grant narrative. Institutional knowledge isn't always recognized as important—until it's necessary.

Technically I'm an arts administrator. Some days I'm an advocate, archivist, consultant, or educator. But every day I'm a folklorist.

Managing a State Government Program: Steven Hatcher

Steven Hatcher earned his MA in American studies at Utah State University and is Folk and Traditional Arts Director at the Idaho Commission on the Arts.

It is not an unusual life-curve for Westerners—to live in and be
shaped by the bigness, sparseness, space, clarity, and hopefulness of
the West, to go away for study and enlargement and the perspective
that distance and dissatisfaction can give, and then to return to what
pleases the sight and enlists the loyalty and demands the commitment.
(Wallace Stegner, *Finding the Place: A Migrant Childhood*)

I dreamed of Idaho while living in Switzerland. On an overnight hike in the
Uri Alps, on our way up to the Surenen Pass, we stayed the night at an *alp*,
a high-altitude working farm. As I was walking around the property, on the
side of a barn I spied a small, painted Swiss Confederation flag—chipped,
faded, and receding into the grain of the wood. After three years of living
outside Geneva, the idea of "Swissness" finally made sense to me. I took the
idea with me when I returned to Idaho a year later.

Swissness is a word created sometime in the early 1990s, although I would
wager the idea dates to the formation of the Swiss Confederacy centuries
before. The concept has been mangled and twisted and is now a tool for marketing, cultural tourism, and political nationalism, but its intent, I believe,
is a way to unify and define a small geographic region with a surprisingly
diverse population and a wealth of natural and cultural resources. In an area
roughly the same size as Elko County, Nevada, or New Hampshire and Vermont combined, Switzerland maintains four national languages as well as a
bevy of cultural trappings—food, music, architecture, customs, occupations,
and beliefs—that often bear little resemblance to one another. Smack in the
middle of Europe, Switzerland could have easily been consumed by cultural
traditions more dominant. But it hasn't, and it won't. There is no doubt that
when you cross the demarcated border, you have entered or exited a defined
sense of place that is unique among its neighbors. This is Swissness, and this
is what I brought back to Idaho.

Two years after crossing the Surenen Pass, I was hired as the state folklorist at the Idaho Commission on the Arts. At that point, I wasn't entirely
sure what an arts administrator was supposed to do. I didn't know a thing
about writing (or reviewing) grant applications. I never curated an exhibit,
budgeted for public programming, managed grant programs, or planned
for multiyear projects. I returned to Idaho, however, with a collection of

experiences from ten years in four countries on four continents and a newly acquired vision for a state of "Idahoness."

More relevant was that I returned to a place I knew and understood. In past lives, I fought forest fires in the northern Panhandle, and I worked as a ranch hand on a homesteaded family property at the threshold of the Pioneer Mountains and the lava-encrusted Snake River Plain. I waited tables in the capital city, witnessed my son's birth in Sun Valley, and traversed the state from top to bottom, desert to range, city to ghost town, and all points in between. I felt I could speak several of Idaho's cultural languages.

I knew I had big shoes to fill. Within the unique and often singular world of a state folklorist, successive folklorists leave their mark on the communities they engage in, or not, and the ways they choose to focus their interest and attention. Whether through fieldwork surveys, exhibits, demonstrations, or other projects, a state folklorist is given the opportunity to discover and present the state in a way that makes the most sense to him or her. Patterns emerged as I browsed shelves, filtered through filing cabinets, and dug into dusty boxes.

The first state folklorist, Barbara Rahm, like many inaugural state folklorists, focused on fieldwork surveys. In 1985 she instituted and managed the state's Traditional Arts Apprenticeship Program, which is still a keystone project. About a dozen years before I studied with him at Utah State University, Steve Siporin curated a statewide folk arts exhibit and book that eventually traveled overseas to the Middle East. Bob McCarl concentrated outreach for the Traditional Arts Apprenticeship Program in Idaho's five Native American tribes and devoted much of his work to occupational lore that would sustain his later career at Boise State University. Debbie Fant worked extensively with Boise's Basque community and explored avenues to introduce folklife into arts education curriculum. Maria Carmen Gambliel helped connect the stories of Boise's refugee population to the larger demographics of the state and looked beyond documentation to offer professional development opportunities to traditional arts practitioners.

With a small budget, limited time, and other work requirements (like reviewing grant applications), every state folklorist wants to support as many cultural communities as possible. It is a hefty task, and you soon realize you cannot do it all, but somehow, someway, I wanted—and still do—to level the playing field. Only through equity, or an honest attempt at fair representation, is the creation of a distinctive and unique collective identity possible. This is what I want from the place I call home, and this is what I have tried to achieve since returning. This is part and parcel of what I call Idahoness.

The vision is idealistic, maybe naive, and certainly setting high standards, but I believe there is a connective element between a logger in St. Maries, a refugee in Twin Falls, and a farmhand in Grace that defines the cultural dynamic of the state and is not replicated outside its somewhat arbitrary borders. Idahoness is an idea that requires cultivation, but, once sown, I believe it is a self-fulfilling prophecy and not something for which I can take credit. After ten years working inside and alongside US embassies and consulates, I adopted the values of civil service—working for the good of the whole, not the individual or party—and returned to the United States to work on behalf of the citizens of Idaho. I see myself as a facilitator and promoter rather than a director or author of projects and programs. I feel an obligation to stay anonymous.

Thus, I want those I work for to speak for themselves and tell me how to spend my annual programming budget. I want community scholars to reveal to me what and whom they find meaningful in their communities. I want the musicians, performers, and tradition bearers in places like Soda Springs, Elk City, and Bonners Ferry to have the same opportunities to perform, demonstrate, and perpetuate their traditions as those in Boise, Idaho Falls, and Coeur d'Alene.

I was fortunate enough to study at Utah State University with both Steve Siporin and Barre Toelken. As I reflect on my work and the vision that drives me, I often recall Barre's words from his book *The Dynamics of Folklore*. For folklorists, defining what we do and why we do it seems to occupy an inordinate amount of time, and, like a rite of passage, we must each go about the task on our own. Barre helped me define my role for myself when he separated the idea of the *dynamic* from that of *tradition*.

"*Tradition*," he writes, "is a compendium of those pre-existing culture-specific materials, assumptions, and options that bear upon the performer more heavily than do his or her own personal tastes and talents. . . . *Dynamic* recognizes, on the other hand, that in the processing of these ideas in performance, the artist's own unique talents of inventiveness *within* the tradition are highly valued and are expected to operate strongly."

My vision for Idahoness is borne in the tension between the tradition and the dynamic: although within the Gem State there are few cultural expressions not found elsewhere, the exact combination and exact performance of those expressions creates a place and people and legacy like no other. The same customs, rituals, behaviors, and occupations just on the other side of the Snake River, the Palouse, or Lolo Pass are somehow rendered differently than those from within.

It is a vague assertion at best, and probably impossible to prove, but it also inspires my day-to-day ideas, tasks, and projects. And to spend a career in pursuit of the minute but palpable differences is to participate in its own dynamic. The commitment and practice required to understand, appreciate, and support the identities of collected communities within a geographic border are not unlike the dedication and performance required to uphold the value systems and community-specific expressions found throughout the state. I returned from Switzerland prepared to accept the burden of Idaho's preexisting culture-specific conditions and have since dedicated myself to the challenge of inventiveness within the tradition of the state folklorist.

CHAPTER 3
Communicating and Curating

ARCHIVING FOR PRESERVATION, ACCESS, AND UNDERSTANDING:
TERRI M. JORDAN

*Terri M. Jordan earned her MA in folklore and her MLS at Indiana University
and is Fife Folklore Archives Curator at Utah State University.*

When I arrived at Indiana University as a folklore graduate student,
I didn't know what I wanted to do in the discipline. I only knew that
I wanted to work with the stories people tell about the world around them
and learn about the ways these stories connect with a broad spectrum of
audiences. Although I didn't realize it at first, working in folklore archives
is a natural way to accomplish this goal: at the core of folklore archiving,
stories in various iterations—narrative, song, dance, and many others—are
captured on archival media and preserved so they may be connected to individuals and communities of all stripes.

One and a half years into my folklore degree, I took my first steps down
the path to archives work when I concurrently enrolled in Indiana University's Library and Information Science graduate program. As a lifelong lover
of books and other texts and a witness to the role that oral histories, story
collections, and other primary resources play in the transmission of folklore,
I believed the discipline of library science would enable me to combine a
number of my personal and professional interests.

The same semester I began coursework in the library science program,
I began work at Indiana University's Mathers Museum of World Cultures
under the supervision of curator Dr. Ellen Sieber. Because of my library interests, one of the major collections I was given to work with was a subset of the

Wanamaker Collection of American Indian Photographs containing photographic materials related to Native American World War I veterans. While photographic prints were part of these materials, most of the items I handled were the papers of the photographer Joseph Dixon. Dixon had not only photographed veterans but also had many of them complete questionnaires on their tribal and military affiliations, and he compiled histories and conversations he collected from them less formally.

In cataloging this collection, I came to understand how the intersection of different types of archival materials can tell a more well-rounded story. The soldiers in the photographs were of the most visual interest, but it was the information contained in the documents that gave researchers a more complete picture of these veterans' experiences and made the materials easier to locate. It was this increased findability that led to the discovery of the collection by members of the Otoe-Missouria chapter of the American War Mothers, which in turn led to my own MA thesis project that connected the museum's images and stories of veterans with the War Mothers' own recollections.

One of the most delightful aspects of being a folklore archivist is that one can find lore—the documentation of traditions and of innovation within those traditions, as practiced and passed on by those outside the mainstream—in many different kinds of collections. Thus, once my graduate studies concluded, like many other twenty-first-century archivists, I pursued a professional path that has led to opportunities at a wide range of cultural and archival organizations.

The Department of Native American Languages at the Sam Noble Museum was one such institution. Situated within the University of Oklahoma's natural history museum, the department maintains collections primarily composed of textual and audiovisual recordings of Native American languages. Language is, of course, a critical source of cultural information: regardless of the stories, music, or other information passed along when language is spoken, the words themselves document the structure of the speaker's world and connect that individual with a community of other speakers. For some endangered languages that have few or no speakers—as was the case for many of those represented in the Native American Languages collection—archival recordings may preserve some of the last examples of this spoken lore.

The Department of Native American Languages was and continues to be a research resource for academic scholars, but it is also a resource for Native language speakers (some of whom are also scholars of those languages). Although the language collections themselves are its major attraction, the archive also offers many other events and services, including an audiovisual studio for recording speakers and musicians and the Oklahoma Native American Youth Language Fair, an annual competition that showcases language performances, art, videos, and other media from young language learners.

These and other activities I was involved in during my tenure at the museum—and that are ongoing—served to build goodwill with language speakers and communities and encouraged the creation of important new language recordings. This, in turn, frequently generated contributions to the Department of Native American Languages. For instance, although it was not required, speakers who used the audiovisual studio frequently chose to provide copies of their recordings to the archive. In addition, each Youth Language Fair was recorded on video for the archive by museum staff, with the knowledge and permission of the participants.

I learned many things at the Department of Native American Languages as a budding folklore archivist. I developed audiovisual preservation and digitization skills. I gained experience in the ways cultural archives can work directly with communities to create and collect new materials. Most importantly, however, I learned about the significance of building mutually beneficial connections between an archive and the individuals and communities its collections document.

The ability to create rapport with collaborators stood me in good stead throughout my time as an archival consultant in the Oklahoma City metropolitan area. I worked primarily with individual artists and art collectors, as well as with local art galleries and small nonprofits, to organize art and associated archival material (correspondence, exhibit catalogs, sales records, public relations documents, and so forth) and conduct collections research.

One of the major professional relationships I developed through this work was with Nicole Poole, the daughter of Oklahoma artist O. Gail Poole, a longtime fixture in the Oklahoma City arts community. When Nicole and I met, her father had passed away unexpectedly and left her hundreds of his paintings, dozens of sketchbooks, and boxes full of personal effects. I was originally connected to the O. Gail Poole Collection to manage the collection database. However, as I began creating catalog records and reviewing the art itself, patterns in Poole's work began to emerge: art styles, motifs, particular landscapes, and specific people all appeared repeatedly in various incarnations.

Nicole Poole was interested in exploring her father's art to tell the story of his professional life and artistic development. As we discussed the themes that were portrayed in Poole's art, we began to document his personal history through Nicole's remembrances and Poole's own words, preserved in his archive of personal papers and the notes he'd written alongside the sketches in his sketchbooks. In partnership with Nicole, I began to collect additional stories from others who had worked with him: his longtime studio partner and other peers in the Oklahoma arts community, his personal friends, and even some of the models who appeared in his paintings.

Poole's innovations within various artistic traditions, his depictions of people and places that were important to him, and the major events in his life were all personal lore that deeply influenced his substantial body of work. Through my collaboration with his daughter and through our story-centered efforts to document this information, his art has been further contextualized; this contextualization has, in turn, been used to enhance gallery exhibitions, news articles, and other means of connecting his works to the larger arts community of the state and region.

As I've established such connections with a wide range of archival collections—historic, institutional, and personal—I've also maintained connections with the folklore community, primarily via active involvement with regional organizations and the American Folklore Society. The pinnacle of these efforts has been my role as convener of the American Folklore Society's Archives and Libraries Section, a position I have filled for several years: in this capacity, I work to link fellow folklore archivists to each other and to other professionals within the discipline. Throughout all of my archival endeavors, a folklore-informed approach has fulfilled my original goal: to use the stories documented in archival collections to connect to individuals and communities in an ever-changing world.

The most substantial change to my own life in recent years has been accepting the position of Fife Folklore Archives curator at Utah State University starting in fall 2020. The wealth of lore in the Fife Folklore Archives offers up a wide array of possibilities for community collaboration through work with archival materials. I look forward to learning the stories these new collections have to tell. And as I consider my professional journeys, I rest secure in the knowledge that regardless of wherever I may find myself, as a folklore archivist I will always find new stories to experience and new connections to make.

BUILDING AND PROVIDING ACCESS TO LIBRARY
COLLECTIONS: MOIRA MARSH

Moira Marsh earned her MLS and PhD in folklore at Indiana University and is the folklore subject librarian at the Indiana University Libraries.

I am an accidental librarian. I trained to be a folklorist and a scholar, not a librarian, but for most of my career, I have happily been all three. As the subject librarian for folklore at Indiana University Bloomington, I care for a library collection that also came about almost by accident. As a subject librarian, I am both a collection curator and a research whisperer.

Great library collections are not created overnight; they're curated and grown over many years. Put another way, the IU folklore collection is the living culmination of a decades-long tradition. It began, literally, as the books that IU folklore program founder Stith Thompson put on reserve for his students to use in comparative folktale studies courses. Initially confined to a small room, this reserve collection was moved intact to the current library building in 1969. At the same time, Polly Grimshaw was appointed as the first subject librarian for folklore. She was still there years later when I entered the IU graduate folklore program, and I worked as Polly's folklore student assistant for most of my graduate studies. I thought I knew a thing or two about library research when I started, but she soon put me straight.

The folklore collection at the Indiana University Libraries is unique. In most academic libraries in the United States, "folklore" is understood as composed of the Library of Congress classifications beginning GR (folk literature) and GT (costume, food, calendar customs, and life-cycle rituals from birth to death). At Indiana University, these ranges make up barely two-thirds of the folklore collection, while the rest runs from A (museums) through Z (bibliography). If it is of interest to folklorists, we include it in the collection. Few of the individual books there are either rare or particularly valuable; what makes the collection unique and priceless is that everything that pertains to folklore, broadly conceived, is shelved together. This collocation is the outstanding feature of the collection, which now numbers almost 56,000 titles (and counting).

Institutional libraries operate on a massive scale by rationalizing their operations as much as possible: cataloging materials according to the same schemes, shelving them in order, and so on. By this standard, fully one-third of our folklore collection is shelved "out of place." It runs crosswise of normal library operations, causing headaches for library patrons and staff, especially shelvers. If I were to approach the dean of libraries today and suggest creating a special collection on another subject from scratch by moving books from their proper locations so they could all be together, I am confident the proposal would go nowhere. The IU folklore collection began quietly and then just continued.

Curating this legacy involves managing finite space—and a generous but finite acquisitions budget. I decide which books need conservation treatment and which ones should be replaced because of loss or damage. As space for physical library collections is increasingly scarce, I work with catalogers to use metadata to create a "virtual" folklore collection encompassing everything that would interest folklorists, even though different parts of it may be shelved in remote storage or online rather than in traditional open-stacks library space.

Most important, though, is my daily work to identify and acquire new materials for the collection, including some gifts. The collection's scope is intended to include any academic book, journal, or database that pertains to the study of folklore, encompassing all genres, all parts of the field and related disciplines, all parts of the world, and all languages. I also acquire a selected number of popular publications as primary material for folkloristic study. Accordingly, I cannot rely solely on the usual collection development tools. Drawing on my direct knowledge of the scope of research in folklore and ethnomusicology, I scour monograph catalogs in several western European languages, from both academic or popular publishers and small or regional presses. Book reviews and social media posts are another source. I also rely on gifts and tips from folklorist colleagues from around the world.

The *Jokebooks* by Frog are one example. One day, IU alumnus Jens Lund, then the Washington State folklorist, sent me a parcel of homemade, paper-bound jokebooks he had bought from a peddler at an Oregon street fair. The peddler, known everywhere as Frog, made his living in part by compiling, copying, and selling cheap jokebooks on the street. For years, Jens has bought all of them on behalf of the Indiana University Libraries, and our collection now holds at least eighty of them. The University of Oregon Library is the only other library in the world that holds the complete set. One folklorist's eye at a street fair and another folklorist's eye in the library together recognized this one of-a-kind gem and ensured it would be preserved and made accessible for folkloristic research now and in the future.

Many people think librarians get to read books all day. Ironically, although I work in a building packed with three million volumes, I rarely have time to read. Most often, when I open a book, it is only for a few fleeting minutes—just long enough to glean the fact or quote I am looking for, usually on behalf of somebody else. When a library collection achieves the strong reputation that the Indiana University folklore collection has, it attracts researchers from all walks of life and all around the globe. I provide research consultations and answer reference questions for anyone interested in folklore, including students, folklorists, and members of the public. Sometimes I use these interactions as clues for further collection development directions or refer inquiries to colleagues in folklore archives and other special collections both at Indiana University and elsewhere. My knowledge of the collection, my awareness of current work in folklore, and my own practice as folkloristic researcher and writer all contribute to my role as a research whisperer. Handling reference questions requires the librarian to transform the patron's query into an answerable question. This transformation is accomplished in the reference interview, where my folklorist's training in how to listen, ask questions, and elucidate context comes into play. I do not just answer questions: I show people how to find the answers for themselves and recommend information management tools with which they can manage their research.

Although my official constituency is made up of Indiana University faculty and students, I see my work as building a research collection for the entire field of folklore. In addition, my mission as both folklorist and librarian is to serve the source communities whose traditions are presented, described, and analyzed in the works in the collection. The sheer size and comprehensiveness of the collection attracts queries from both lay and academic researchers worldwide. It also creates unique opportunities for collaborative projects, including the Indiana University Folklore Archives, the Modern Language Association Bibliography Project, and the Open Folklore Project.

I am not an archivist, but libraries and archives are closely related. I have had the privilege of referring numerous people to IU's Folklore Archives and the Archives of Traditional Music to find the stories and recordings some folklorist collected from his or her grandparents a generation ago. I mediated between the folklorists and archivists on our campus to find a permanent home for the folklore archives, which began life as a file cabinet in Richard Dorson's office. We have improved access to the holdings of the archives, started an active acquisitions program, and mentored student interns who have worked in the archives.

The *Modern Language Association International Bibliography* (MLAIB) is the go-to index for scholarly publications in folklore studies. I was a graduate student working in the folklore collection in the 1980s when the MLA approached Indiana University for assistance in getting access to publications in folklore. Simply put, our collection included many things the MLA could not access. I helped create a kind of bibliographer field office for contributing bibliographic records to the MLAIB, with support from both the MLA and the American Folklore Society and drawing on a small army of folklore graduate student bibliographers.

The greatest folklore access project the folklore collection has given rise to is the Open Folklore project (http://openfolklore.org). Although Google Books digitized the entire IU folklore collection in 2009, copyright laws killed their dream of an open digital library for all. Beginning in 2010, however, I have been part of a team of folklorists and librarians from the American Folklore Society and the Indiana University campus who have leveraged that corpus of digitized material with other online tools and content to create an open-access portal to folklore scholarship available online. Open Folklore's mission is to deliver open-access folklore content from a single portal and to encourage more open access in our field and for the world.

CURATING IN A CHANGING MUSEUM WORLD:
CARRIE HERTZ

Carrie Hertz earned her PhD in folklore at Indiana University and is Curator of Textiles and Dress at the Museum of International Folk Art.

As a scholar and curator of dress, I spend a lot of time in other people's closets. There is a good reason "the closet" is a common metaphor for stashing skeletons and secret selves. Like any collection, the contents of closets can include artifacts representing many times and places: treasured memories, lost connections, forgotten obligations, former life chapters, past mistakes, and hidden identities, all waiting to be rediscovered again. They comingle, anachronistically accessible all at once. Private wardrobes are not so different from museum storage vaults, but in museums the scandalous skeletons are not always metaphorical.

I've always loved museums. Big-city museums in Louisville, Cincinnati, Indianapolis, Chicago, and further afield felt like portals of discovery to me, a middle-class White girl from a fairly homogenous small town in southern Indiana. They presented the world as a vast and complex place and its cultural and artistic traditions as manifold. I found this presumption of diversity thrilling and comforting but uncomplicated. It was only later that I came to understand the limitations, hierarchical biases, and structures of oppression baked into the very founding of the Western museum as an institutional form. Despite notable strides made over the last decades, the museum field still has much work ahead to reckon with its role in a history of White supremacy rooted in colonial expansion, nation building, economic exploitation, and scientific racism. However, although museums are commonly recognized today as an invention of the West, culturally specific methods for caretaking material culture and knowledge have long existed in many societies. I sincerely believe that, like some other imperfect social institutions, the mainstream museum model is worth innovating and remaking through greater respect for and incorporation of indigenous heritage and care practices developed throughout the world.

I take inspiration from interdisciplinary colleagues who look beyond "fixing" museums to also reimagine and reinvent them. Anthropologist Christina Kreps, in her promotion of "appropriate museologies," reminds us that goals for honoring diversity should encompass issues of representation beyond content, audiences, staffing, and administration to also include diversity in terms of how we even make sense of the museum idea itself and how it can be enacted. Through my own participation in collaborative research on the iterative development of ecomuseums in southwest China, initiated jointly by the Chinese and American folklore societies, I have been fortunate to witness the kind of grassroots museologies that Kreps advocates: those emerging from local communities and compatible with local traditions, values, protocols, and heritage systems.

Similarly, in a recent webinar, "Striving Towards an Equitable Future," hosted on the museum technology and engagement platform Cuseum, Damon Reaves of the Philadelphia Museum of Art argued that most mainstream museums in the West, in light of their origins, can never be truly "decolonized," but like most movements on behalf of inclusion and social justice, the goal should not be to reach such an unlikely utopian state (some differences being simply irreconcilable) but rather to see our work as an open-ended active process and realize that these museums will always be decolonizing. Because the boundaries of inclusion and exclusion, the targets of oppression, and the contours of privilege constantly shift through time and space, the business of challenging, disrupting, and dismantling injustice has no end. And although scholarship and consultation can help transform museum paradigms, radical transformations cannot be achieved without individuals also working for collective change from within.

I've spent much of my career trying to reconcile my youthful appreciation for museums with a maturing professional awareness of both their failings and their potential. And while my professional life may be situated within museums, my identity as a folklorist has remained primary to my approach by advocating for ever more inclusive and accountable museum practices informed by folklore theories and methodologies, particularly ethnographic fieldwork and the prioritization of vernacular modes and epistemologies. In my role as curator, many of my disciplinary interests meet at the intersections of dress, identity, performance, and politics.

As one of the most intimate genres of folk art, dress is what anthropologist Terence S. Turner called the "social skin," and getting dressed is what my Indiana University mentor, Pravina Shukla, described as "the most common of artistic acts." If private wardrobes are not so different from museum storage vaults, then a body dressed for public view is not so different from an exhibition. From the perspective of contemporary folklorists, dress persists as a powerful medium for self-definition, for asserting agency over one's own experience with, interpretation of, and positionality in the world. The daily act of dressing helps mediate the tensions between traditional expectation and individual expression, purposeful repetition and creative reinvention, public performance and private reflection.

Yet the taxonomies of dress employed within many Western museums today still perpetuate modernist ideas about cultural change, echoing debunked theories of universal human evolution in which historical or disappearing cultures of "traditional" people wear costumes while "advanced" civilizations of modern individuals produce fashion. Such subjective, externally imposed, elitist, and hierarchical categorizations of people's clothes helped support even more disturbing and specious classifications of human groups based on skull measurements and collections of human remains. While contemporary museology has been moving away from its universalist Eurocentric foundations and—increasingly and rightfully—repatriating sacred artifacts and bodies, the manner in which dress is collected and represented in mainstream US institutions has largely not kept pace, replicating Western conceptual and aesthetic imperialism. It should come as no surprise that classifications of the "social skin" tend to fall along similar lines as that of human skin: examples of dress from non-Western, indigenous, and ethnic minority cultures are represented disproportionately in historic or ethnographic "costume collections" as opposed to "fashion collections" housed in museums of contemporary fine art. When I accepted my position as curator of textiles and costume at the Museum of International Folk Art, one of my first acts on the job was to successfully petition for a title change, replacing the term *costume* with *dress*. I have similarly sought to establish ever more inclusive and interdisciplinary collecting, care, and interpretive practices that understand dress as dynamic, artistic, performative, multisensory, and contextually meaningful; as simultaneously personal and cultural, rhetorical and functional, traditional and fashionable; and as potentially sacred, animate, or inappropriate for us to own. I still, and will always, have much more to learn.

My folkloristic training has helped me hone my ability to look for absences and listen for silences, to tease out the hidden assumptions underpinning discourses and social structures, and to question established histories, canons, taxonomies, and terminology. Nothing has transformed my perspectives more consequentially than engaging in the dialogic process of ethnographic fieldwork. Fieldwork strikes me as an ideal methodology for curatorship because, in essence, it is the practice of deep listening and holistic observation, of bearing witness to the lives of others. When it comes to the principles that guide my work, I have learned the most important lessons from my collaborators, particularly how distorted museum classifications and representations of dress can often seem to their makers and wearers. Private wardrobes are not so different from museum storage vaults, and the keepers of vernacular family collections and dress traditions are no less expert than professional curators. That people are willing to open up their closets honors me, humbles me, and instills in me a profound sense of shared responsibility. With every curatorial project, I take my lead from the caretakers of traditions: the makers and practitioners who give artistic traditions life by sharing them willingly with others.

Descriptions of the curatorial profession commonly focus on its relationship to collections and exhibitions, and these certainly remain important components, but I consider the personal and intellectual relationships I cultivate with artists and their communities far more central to what I do. Curators can fill many roles: researcher, biographer, educator, student, public scholar, mediator, facilitator, event producer, arts promoter and patron, collector, and cultural steward. However, I most often imagine the mission of my work as amplification and dialogue. Folklore studies taught me that all ways of knowing require a coming together of minds, but mutual understanding will remain elusive if those minds cannot come together as equals. No human being should ever be reduced to a passive object of study. As a curator, I endeavor to amplify voices, identities, perspectives, and creative expressions too often excluded within master narratives and mainstream institutions of power, access, and authority. I see museums not only as places that care for diverse tangible and intangible cultural knowledges but also as sites where we as a society can pursue more transparent conversations on subjects critical to who we are and the communities we wish to create, together within the expansive interconnected world we inhabit.

Producing Audio Ethnography: Rachel Hopkin

Rachel Hopkin earned her PhD in English and folklore at The Ohio State University and is a folklorist and radio/audio/podcast producer.

My website byline reads, "Folklorist and Radio Producer," although I sometimes wonder about changing the latter part of that title to "Audio Producer" to reflect the many means besides conventional radio broadcasts through which my work now appears (podcasts are the most obvious example). I have worked on a wide range of audio productions, but not all of them have been based on audio ethnography. I'm originally from the UK, and my career there began when I joined the British Broadcasting Corporation, where I worked for six years. For the bulk of that time, I produced classical music–related output, including themed recorded-music-sequencing shows—such as *Composer of the Week*—and broadcasts of live events, such as the Cardiff

Singer of the World competition. While those projects certainly involved research, they did not require ethnographic fieldwork.

After leaving the BBC, I wound up in Argentina, where I set myself up as a freelance radio producer. I did some news reporting during that time but much preferred making non-news-based radio documentaries about music and culture whenever I had the opportunity to do so. The first project with which I had real success in this regard was called *Musical Migrants*. I now also consider it to be among the earliest of my "audio ethnography" productions, even though I doubt I knew what the word *ethnography* meant when I started work on the series. It also gave me one of my first professional opportunities to largely focus on vernacular cultural forms.

In all, I made fifteen *Musical Migrants* programs for the BBC between 2008 and 2012 via the UK-based company Falling Tree Productions. These were audio portraits of people who had relocated their lives for love of a particular musical genre. Each person had moved because the music they loved somehow conjured a sense of a life they felt unable to access in their native environment. Those featured included Ann Savoy, who was born and raised to be a Southern lady in Richmond, Virginia, but was drawn to Louisiana by the "wild freedom" of Cajun music; Yoke Noge, who experienced a raw emotion in Chicago's blues music that otherwise went largely unexpressed in her native Japan; and the Swedish violinist Daniel Sandén-Warg, who so adored the *hardanger* fiddle that he relocated to a rural valley in southern Norway.

The *Musical Migrants* were montage productions: presenter-less features, in the language of the audio world. Each episode was highly edited and constructed from my interviews with the migrants in question (minus my part of the conversations), relevant audio from the soundscapes of their daily lives, and excerpts of the music that so inspired them. To gather the raw material, I traveled to the migrants' locations and then spent a few days interviewing them and recording as many aspects of their daily lives as I could. At the end of each trip, I generally had around five to seven hours of audio files from which I was able to create a relatively short program. I have long likened the process to making a stock: you get all these ingredients, including huge quantities of water, and then you boil, boil, boil, until you're left with this (hopefully) wonderfully potent essence. It thrilled me when I later learned that that groundbreaking folklorist Zora Neale Hurston described folklore as being the "boiled-down juice of human living."

I don't generally consider myself a journalist, but I did cut my media production teeth in one of the world's most highly respected news organizations and have done some reporting for it, so this is part of my professional formation. A central tenet of ethical journalism is objectivity. Some believe that ethnographers should strive for the same. Now, whether objectivity is ever really possible is a debate outside the purview of this essay, but I will say that whenever I have worked in a "folklorist as audio ethnographer" capacity, I'm fairly unashamedly unobjective. In fact, I like to fall a little in love with every interviewee, and I usually choose to work on projects or approach subjects in such a way that allows me to feel that "everything in the garden is lovely."

As far as I can remember, the narrative arc of every *Musical Migrant* episode ended on an ultimately positive note. The same was not true of *Country Down Under*, another audio ethnography–based work. Again a Falling Tree production for the BBC, this documentary was about the popularity of American-style country music among Australia's Aboriginal peoples. During a two-week trip, I spent a few days with three of the key contributors, Auriel Andrew, Roger Knox, and Glenn Skuthorpe, and also recorded interviews with two more musicians, Kev Carmody and Sue Ray. These collaborators shared very personal accounts while also collectively relating the story of how this musical genre from half a world away became popular Down Under during the first half of the twentieth century. So pervasive was the style that it reached the bush, where many Aboriginal people were forced to live on missions and government-controlled reserves. At a time when their own cultural heritage was being systematically erased, country music became a medium through which they could maintain their oral tradition of sharing stories. The fact that many country music melodies tend toward the melancholic enhanced its appeal. As one person put it, "Country music was all about loss, and we'd lost everything."

And yet, despite the fact that the overall story the contributors collectively tell is a deeply tragic one, there is a lot of laughter in the piece. My collaborators were all witty conversationalists, and I've found that listeners find it easier to stay engaged when hearing of wretched circumstances—and therefore to feel empathy for those whose narratives they are hearing—if there is some element of lightheartedness. However, it would have inappropriate for me to ignore the ongoing and often institutionalized discrimination Aboriginal peoples endure, so that is discussed in various ways throughout the program.

Along with the aspiration to be objective, another central tenet of good journalism, as well as a good many other forms of media production, is that the journalist/producer does not give participants a say in how their contributions are used because of the need to retain editorial control. So when the manager of one of the musicians featured in *Country Down Under* asked for the right to approve the final product before it aired, I was surprised. I'd never received a similar request during my more than fifteen-year career.

As far as the BBC *Guidelines* are concerned, the material gathered during any openly conducted interview (i.e., whenever interviewees know they are being recorded) is available for use, as consent is understood to have been implicitly given. I believe most reputable media organizations take a similar approach. However, during my training as a folklorist—first at Western Kentucky University and then at The Ohio State University—I've become much more aware of the ways I am indebted to my collaborators, whether I'm working on a radio project, an academic paper, or something else. It has also made me far more conscious of how unequal power dynamics can play out during such collaborations. While, on one level, I wanted the freedom to make the program as I wished, at the same time, I did not want to put myself into a position in which I was exerting the privilege afforded me as an associate of an internationally respected institution over that of an individual from a population that has met with all manner of oppression since colonizing British forces first arrived on their land.

I therefore engaged in a negotiation process with the manager and the musician. I sent them both a draft of the program. They responded by asking that certain elements be cut and gave me their reasons for their request. I pushed back against some of those requests with my own counterexplanations. In the end, they approved the final version we broadcast and, in so doing, gave me permission to use a few lines they would otherwise have preferred be excised because they appreciated how they contributed to the overall picture. It was an uncomfortable process, but I'm glad we managed it while staying on good terms, and I remain grateful to them for their flexibility. In my career to date, my priorities have changed, not least because of all I've learned as a student of folklore. In the past, my main objective was to please my colleagues and, by extension, the general audience who received my work. I certainly continue to be thrilled whenever I receive positive feedback from such quarters, but what matters most to me now is that my collaborators are satisfied with the end result.

Translating Language, Place, and Performance: Levi S. Gibbs

Levi S. Gibbs earned his PhD in East Asian languages and literatures at The Ohio State University and is Associate Professor of Chinese Literature and Culture in the Asian Societies, Cultures, and Languages Program at Dartmouth College.

The first time I saw the "Folk Song King of Western China," Wang Xiangrong (born in 1952), was at a concert in Taipei on a warm summer evening in 1999. After a Chinese music orchestra had played the first half of the concert, Wang walked out to the middle of the stage dressed in the traditional clothes of Northern Shaanxi province—a sheepskin jacket and a white towel wrapped around his head—causing the audience to giggle and smile. He smiled back and started to sing. His voice was full of emotion, unlike anything I had heard before. He sang a love song in a regional dialect of Chinese about a woman across a valley standing on another mountain and the singer's desire to be with her or, at least, have her wave at him. Although the song was not in standard Mandarin, there were supertitles or perhaps a brief description in the program.

This experience led to a decades-long intellectual pursuit to learn more about Wang's life and songs and, more generally, the roles of singers in society. The day after the concert, I went to a bookstore in Taipei to buy a CD with Wang's songs. Listening at home to their dialect words and pronunciations, I tried to write down the lyrics syllable by syllable, learning to sing the song about the woman on the mountain before I understood what the words meant. In spite of the linguistic barriers, I felt a raw emotional expression in the songs that only increased my desire to learn more about their lyrics and the backstory of the man who sang them.

Ultimately, I was able to interview Wang about the stories of his songs, their connections to his life, and the meanings of those tricky (to the uninitiated) dialect words. Many of the love songs he learned as a child were intimately connected to the topography of his home village, located in northern China near the intersection of the Great Wall and the Yellow River, as well as to various stories of failed and successful romantic relationships and the struggles of his mother's generation for marriage reform. In Wang's village, there was also a tradition of esoteric songs sung by ritual specialists known as "spirit men," who serve as intermediaries making it possible for villagers to communicate with local gods and ancestors-turned-gods about illnesses and other afflictions and how to cure them with remedies using locally foraged herbs. Villagers regarded spirit men as respected arbiters of local knowledge and history, and my conversations with Wang about translating their songs tapped into the village's rich cultural history.

Although Wang grew up with sixty or seventy fellow villagers in the 1950s, only three elderly residents remained when I visited that mountain village in 2012. As with many Chinese villages today, young and middle-aged people have moved to cities to study and work. Yet as I walked up the main path of that empty village, it came alive with meaning accumulated from knowledge of Wang's songs. I saw local flowers and trees mentioned in love songs. I passed by the spirit man's cave home where he had conducted rituals.

I looked at the valley below the village that separated Wang's mountain from the neighboring mountain range, just like in the song about the woman. Seeing how the songs were so closely tied to local topography, flora, and fauna, I was reminded of my Ohio State doctoral advisor Mark Bender's stories about translating the ancient epics of ethnic minorities in southwest China—also rich in references to local knowledge, plants, and animals—which led him on extensive treks into a variety of landscapes and waterways to photograph flowers, trees, and wildlife mentioned in the epics and later to consult with local tradition bearers, botanists, and other specialists to identify species, all for the purpose of translation. He followed a similar pattern to learn more about local customs, material culture, and ritual behavior mentioned in the epics he studied. Because such expressive forms are intimately tied to local knowledge, this type of translation requires on-the-ground fieldwork and extended conversations with people familiar with the connotations of each word and turn of phrase. At the same time, my advisor's juxtaposition of hikes with local collaborators and subsequent visits to Beijing zoos to identify rare species highlights the way this sort of translation represents a conversation between different fields of knowledge.

I had initially envisioned myself as a translator who would allow the voices of Wang Xiangrong and other singers to shine through in appropriately styled English, albeit couched in research on the history of this regional song tradition as it evolved along with China's shifting cultural politics. What started as a desire to translate Wang's words into English, however, ended up requiring conversations between places, time periods, and worldviews, linking together conversations on different scales so new conversations could emerge. The work of translation was not just among different languages but also among academic fields as diverse as personal narrative studies, performance theory, and celebrity studies. Through the writing of my book *Song King: Connecting People, Places, and Past in Contemporary China*, I came to look at how Wang's life and songs could be viewed in relation to the localities in which he had lived but also as a case study for singers who emerge from local traditions to become national and international symbols—singers such as "The Voice of Latin America," Mercedes Sosa from Argentina; "The Voice of Egypt," Umm Kulthūm; and "The People's Singer," Hibari Misora from Japan.

In my experience, folklorists are constantly engaging in acts of translation on and across different scales, large and small. I saw this firsthand during the 2014 Smithsonian Folklife Festival in Washington, DC, where scholars of Chinese music, including folklorists and ethnomusicologists, were invited to serve as "presenters" for the festival's China program. Tasked with facilitating cultural exchange, we were in essence translators with knowledge of the cultural traditions being presented. At times, we would stand on the massive stage on the National Mall facing the Capitol Building and introduce audiences to folk singers, musicians, and dancers from across China. At other times, we were asked to stand in smaller venues next to individual artists who made traditional porcelain, kites, food, and paper cuttings and translate questions from passing festival visitors and the artists' answers. A visitor might pause for a moment, watching an elderly tradition bearer from Northern Shaanxi working on elaborate paper cuttings, then ask where she learned to do that, what the different designs meant, and what she thought about while she worked. This sort of person-to-person translation allowed two people from vastly different cultural backgrounds to speak to one another about a cultural expression being witnessed by both. It allowed them to make a human connection that could not otherwise be made.

On the one hand, folklorists facilitate conversations about creative expression on "big" stages when we introduce and translate performances for audiences at the Folklife Festival, give invited talks at American and Chinese universities, write books about how artists from "small" places become representatives of "big" ideas, and teach courses on traditional performance traditions past and present. Equally important, however, are the ways we translate on "small" stages. It may be facilitating conversations between festivalgoers and Chinese artists in Washington, DC. It may be translating explanations for visiting Chinese folklorists about the contrasting attitudes of Amish and Mennonites toward technology in rural Ohio or Catholic iconography in an old church outside Santa Fe. Or it may be helping a student compare Chinese crosstalk comedy (*xiangsheng*) to American stand-up during office hours in Hanover, New Hampshire. For me, translation among languages, cultures, and experiences forms an essential part of the folkloristic enterprise—it expands our view of the diverse ways we express ourselves to one another and brings us together through the shared experience of interpreting those expressive acts.

Critiquing Internet Culture: Andrea Kitta

Andrea Kitta earned her PhD in folklore at the Memorial University of Newfoundland and is Professor in the English Department at East Carolina University.

I consider it an honor and privilege to be a part of a microgeneration many on the internet have labeled as Xennials—people born in the late 1970s and early 1980s who have had an analog childhood and a digital adulthood. I love to tell people that I wrote my first undergraduate paper using the library's card catalog and my last paper using digital sources I found entirely online. I think those of us raised in two worlds—whatever those worlds are—need to move back and forth seamlessly between identities, and so we end up as natural folklorists because we're innately aware that we are actively participating in culture while also studying it. This double consciousness is also a key element in understanding how we can be critical of the cultures we study. While I do believe we need to accept cultures at their face value and practice cultural relativism, we also need to realize that there are times and places to make a stand and call out the elements of culture that are potentially unhealthy, dangerous, and deadly. This is certainly very true with the internet and how folklore and the related topics we study are portrayed there.

Unfortunately, we are not in charge of the narrative about folklore on the internet. Search online for *folklore* and some of the first hits lead you straight to White nationalist groups and authors. The work of folklorists can be used by such groups even when that is not the intention of the authors. At best, the online face of folklore is rarely in the hands of folklorists, is often misguided, uses out-of-date scholarship, and portrays folklore as an interesting series of anecdotes rather than a serious discipline of study. Changing that narrative requires a concerted effort, which is something professional organizations like the American Folklore Society are attending to by creating committees to review our online presence and undertake active work to make our work more accessible to the public.

We also need to be reflexive about our own discipline's historical role in providing scholarship that has been misused to strengthen this marginalization. This history shows that some of our work has been and continues to be used by oppressive movements and governments that pursue strategies of racism, misogyny, ableism, and homophobia. In addition, we have too often ignored or undervalued the contributions of underrepresented folklorists past and present. As a field we are now taking steps to highlight those colleagues and their work, but we should do more. At the very least, we must acknowledge that this is a part of our history as a discipline, and we must actively work to be inclusive both in our research and in who we promote and bring into the discipline.

As I write this essay, the world is learning to cope with the COVID-19 pandemic, and we are in the middle of protests surrounding the deaths of many members of the Black community. In this situation, it is easy to point out that conspiracy theories, legends, and rumors—on the internet and elsewhere—are detrimental to people's health and well-being. Right now, the role of the folklorist has shifted from complex analysis to collection and debunking. While these are not and should never be our only roles, in a time of crisis, our most important roles can shift. Many folklorists are also engaging in political activities and protests, and advocacy is and should be a part of what we do. However, this can be a complex situation for belief scholars who want to honor the deeply rooted beliefs of those they study. It is my opinion that we should honor those beliefs so long as they do not cause immediate harm to others. This is a slippery slope, of course, as it could be argued, for example, that centuries of the patriarchy of most religious institutions have caused harm. I wish I had an easy answer for this, but I do not, and it truly is up to each individual to decide where and when to make a stand. It is my hope that as a discipline and as individuals, we chose to take a strong stand on behalf of people who are marginalized.

I recognize that there are some folklorists who feel our role is not to advocate or judge, but merely to report and analyze. However, our privilege as academics, leaders in our field, museum and archival curators, and community leaders means that even by deciding which traditions to study, we are privileging some voices over others and undertaking a political act. We are both a part of culture as well as those who analyze and study culture, which means we participate and shape culture. Our analysis will always be tinged with our own biases, and we cannot pretend to be unbiased.

But how does this all link to the internet? None of us can separate ourselves from online culture; even if we don't perceive ourselves as active participants in it, we are still influenced by and influence what happens there. The old distinction between IRL (in real life) and what happens on the internet is no longer firm. We live our lives in both spaces, even more so now in the time of a pandemic when we cannot gather in person. These lines are only going to become blurrier, and we need to acknowledge that our online presence defines us as individuals and folklorists.

Folklorists need to be part of discussions about the content and impact of online culture, and one of the easiest ways to do this is to be active on social media. One need not be on every form of social media, and I do acknowledge that social media can be deeply problematic at times. However, this is why we need more folklorists using these tools. We need to let people know what folklore is and how we define it. We need to comment on news and cultural events. For too long we've let others define what folklore (the processes we study and the field itself) is and is not. We need to be a part of the narrative by taking on the double consciousness of individual and folklorist and informing others about what we do. Our discipline is rich and complex, and it connects in a completely different way to the public than so many other disciplines since there is a traditional dimension to all human activity. If anything, we should have an easy time communicating this: we're trained in ethnography, and we understand networks and how people communicate, so why are we doing so poorly online?

In some ways, this is a generational issue (although I see folklorists of all ages with fascinating online engagements). In other ways, it's a triviality issue, as many people feel social media are ephemeral and not important. Folklorists should certainly understand how untrue that is! Additionally, it's also an issue of work inequality. Many folklorists with a strong online presence are underemployed, while other folklorists do not have the time to engage online because their workplace does not see the value in an online presence. These are systematic issues that need our attention. As the lone folklorist in my department, I often turn to the internet for my engagement with the field. Social media is a wonderful place for those who have retired, for those without nearby colleagues, and for those just learning the discipline to connect, and the internet can be a wonderful place for mentoring, engagement, and connection. Due to my online presence, I've received multiple invitations to be a part of conferences, podcasts, community art projects, and publications. Do not fall prey to the idea that the internet is bad or useless. The internet is where folklore happens, where folklorists connect, and where folklorists connect with the public. It is a rich fieldwork site and a remarkably fertile place to observe and analyze culture and current events.

COMMUNICATING AND EDUCATING ONLINE:
JEANA JORGENSEN

Jeana Jorgensen earned her PhD in folklore at Indiana University and has since taught at universities all over Indiana, as well as the University of California at Berkeley; when not teaching, she writes and dances.

How did this folklorist create an online following for her writing, magically bringing her discipline's insights to the notice of totally new audiences on the internet? Click this link to learn more! In the ephemeral yet structured world of the internet, folklorists have found a foothold in many areas: studying forms of digital folklore such as memes and conspiracy theories, conducting fieldwork and moving academic journals online, and participating in online forums and discussions such as the immensely popular #FolkloreThursday hashtag on Twitter. And we blog.

A weblog or blog is a site meant for showcasing one's writing online and is hosted on a personal, commercial, or institutional web domain. Blogs can be more or less curated, which is important for my purposes; back in the day, it was free to have your own LiveJournal, and anyone can set up a Word-Press site these days, perhaps spending a few dollars a year to snag a domain name you like. In contrast, many university presses have blogs, and writing for them focuses on the press's publishing program—for instance, highlighting a work of yours they're publishing in order to translate its insights into lay terms to generate more interest. So, as in many areas of culture, there are more and less institutional ways to go about blogging, and even a work with a more formal frame can be of interest to folklorists.

I started blogging almost by accident. I've always been a writer: I began by penning novels, short stories, and poems in elementary school and continue to maintain a lifelong, almost-daily journal. Learning to write academic papers came naturally; while studying as an undergraduate at Berkeley with Alan Dundes, I learned this is a standard activity of folklore scholars. I presented my first paper at the American Folklore Society's annual conference while finishing my senior year at Berkeley, and I planned to go straight to grad school for a folklore PhD. Indiana University accepted me, and my first publication that wasn't a book review came out in 2006. I take joy in writing for my peers, but I also had many words I wanted to communicate that I didn't want to see tied up in the lengthy peer-review and publication process. I'd taken a PhD minor in gender studies, and I had tons to say on that front, as well, and while I've devoted a lot of time and energy to trying to get as much feminist and queer and gender and sexuality stuff into my folklore research (and vice versa), I still had more ideas to express that weren't quite fleshed out enough to become their own research projects.

In 2010 I started writing for a fellow Indiana University scholar's blog, MySexProfessor.com, run by Dr. Debby Herbenick—a sexual health rock star—of the School of Public Health. I wrote multiple posts per month (inserting folklore whenever I could, such as writing about breasts in the Grimms' fairy tales). However, I had still other thoughts to share with the world, so I created my own website and blog in 2011. While Dr. Herbenick's blog has wound down and my own blogging is now hosted at Patheos.com (on their nonreligious channel), I used those early experiences to learn how to create content quickly and how to find a balance between what's interesting to me and what might be interesting to others.

The irony, of course, is that my earliest folklore studies occurred under Alan Dundes, who did not think much of public/applied folklore and hence primed me for a career in the academy. Were he still alive, I am not sure what he would think of me translating my academic folklore knowledge into blog posts that thousands of people read, but I hope he would feel pride at my efforts to boost the discipline in the eyes of many.

While my folklore training (with a specialty in folk narrative—both my MA thesis and PhD dissertation focused on European fairy tales) prepared me to write about tons of interesting topics for my blog readers, I also find myself drawn to general activism. I write about misogyny, homophobia, and transphobia; racism and White supremacy in the United States; and how the lack of accessible health care is killing people. My training to look for patterns and identify the interplay of tradition and variation has given me a keen eye for connecting topics such as emotional labor and women's folklore. Knowing a bit about autoethnography has given me tools to write about my experiences in academia and translate for outsiders the bizarre politics of the ivory tower. My graduate training in fieldwork has helped me become a better listener when I engage with sex workers on Twitter so I can more accurately write about the topic for my readers when, for example, I'm critiquing laws criminalizing sex work that actually harm the people engaged in it. Learning to look at the overlooked—as we sometimes define what we do as folklorists—has opened my eyes to many marginalized perspectives that inform how I write about a variety of topics.

And, of course, sometimes I write from plain old rage. The co-opting of folklore studies by White supremacists is infuriating, and when I can write against it, I do. This does not come without its perils. When Carolyn Emerick, the self-styled "Völkish Folklorist," decided to quote my work in a blog post of hers on folklore, the Romantic era, and nationalism, I was angry at her appropriation of my work (and not just mine: she quoted Dundes and Marina Warner as well). I wrote a blog post refuting her work and buckled in for some conflict; her blog post was shared by White nationalist sites, and I'm aware that posts like mine can lead to doxing and other all-too-real threats. Nothing ever manifested, thankfully, but it was a disturbing reminder that for every use of folklore, there is also a potential to abuse it. When we're in the realm of blogging, we're sending missives into a world where even the informed public might not know when someone is using the trappings of our discipline to put a nice frock on a poisonous message of hatred.

So, blogging as a folklorist is not without its risks. In addition to having to face bigots appropriating my work, I share the same problems as every blogger: trolls who leave nasty comments, the specter of being horribly misunderstood, and the negotiation of boundaries when you write about people who can, as it turns out, read what you've written about them (although this is something folklorists face whenever we do ethnography).

I believe folklorists are especially well suited for blogging, and while I can think of colleagues who are already doing it, there's always room for more. The internet is vast, and the siren call of broadcasting one's thoughts and experiences is alluring, although not without peril. Besides, I cannot possibly refute every terrible invocation of Joseph Campbell's hero's journey on my own, so I shall end with the traditional blogging formula of the call to action: grab your Vladimir Propp and Max Lüthi books, your favorite *Journal of American Folklore* issues and theorists, and your best archival materials and join me on the web.

CREATING EDUCATIONAL CONTENT: JON KAY

Jon Kay earned his PhD in folklore at Indiana University, where he serves as Associate Professor in the Department of Folklore and Ethnomusicology and directs Traditional Arts Indiana.

From making field recordings to producing films, folklorists translate the fleeting moments of performance into more durable and shareable content. In this way they are meta makers, working with storytellers, artists, musicians, craftspeople, dancers, and other knowledge bearers to produce books, media, exhibitions, events, and more. While academic programs may train folklorists in research methods and theories, they also provide students with opportunities to develop or hone their skills in content creation. As the director of Traditional Arts Indiana (TAI: the state folklore program for Indiana, a partnership between the Indiana Arts Commission and Indiana University), I have collaborated with dozens of students to produce resources in many media for communities and tradition bearers.

Folklorists usually make content with a specific community, group, or individual in mind. Their projects may find a wider audience, but specificity makes production and design questions easier to answer. For example, when TAI began work on the exhibition *Indiana Folk Arts: 200 Years of Tradition and Innovation*, we initially struggled to decide on a format and design for the exhibition, but once we clearly identified the project's primary audience and purpose, these decisions became obvious. The exhibition aimed to introduce a general audience to the work of traditional artists in Indiana. Therefore, we decided against a traditional gallery or museum project but rather created a traveling exhibition that provided a context for presenting demonstrating artists at parks, festivals, and events. Knowing the artists would be working alongside interpretive panels meant our design had to create an interactive space where artists could share stories about the history, diversity, and vitality of their traditional art with the public. If we had not recognized the audience and the overt function of these interpretive panels, our exhibition design and production would have been difficult—and potentially ineffective.

A recent documentary project emerged from that bicentennial exhibition tour. Keith Ruble, a bowl hewer from Vigo County, Indiana, asked me to write a booklet about this distinctive regional tradition for potential bowl makers. I suggested that we collaborate on a video, which would be free and able to provide more visual detail than a booklet. Recognizing who we aimed to serve also informed the editing process: we included what the audience needed to know to make a bowl. During the project, Keith decided we should include how to make an adze bowl-hewing tool. To serve this specific group, we produced two videos, one on adze making and one on bowl hewing. Folklorists' understanding of folk groups, communities of practice, and social networks informs their work as content creators.

Nevertheless, folklorists must attend to the expectations of the community or individual with whom they collaborate, the funders of the project, and their colleagues, as well as the public they aim to reach. In 2019, TAI released *Music from the Home of Stephen and Nancy Dickey*, a free CD. The artists and their community were thrilled with the recording, and we distributed 750 CDs in the first three months. We chose to make this piece for the local community, rather than folklore colleagues, who may have wanted the recording to focus on different tunes or include more detailed ethnographic liner notes. The point is that if we make our content to please everyone, we usually please no one.

While folklorists sometimes make videos or exhibitions for a defined group or specific purpose, their work can find a wider audience. In 2015, I curated the exhibition *Willow Work* at Indiana University's Mathers Museum of World Cultures. The exhibit explored the art of Viki Graber, a willow-basket maker from Goshen, Indiana. We originally divided the video into segments that looped on six monitors mounted in the exhibition hall, each showing various stages of making a basket. The idea was to convey the construction process quickly. As an afterthought, I combined the clips into a single video and uploaded it to YouTube. To my surprise, the video has been viewed tens of thousands of times. This taught me to release content into the world. There are many reasons to decide not to share content, especially in the sensitive cultural work folklorists do, but all too often, it is only fear or perfectionism that inhibits us from releasing a work. I have made things I would make differently now or not produce at all, but I have also written pieces, shot video, and recorded podcasts I never released, and now their time has passed (as have, in some cases, my collaborators).

A maker at my core, I enjoy planning and producing events, making recordings, and shooting and editing video. While each of these requires specific skills, they follow a similar sequence of actions: research, create, review, revise, release, repeat. Here are a few observations about this six-step approach to creating content.

Folklorists create most of their content through the relationships they forge and the data they collect or produce in partnership with their interlocutors. While the folklorist may begin with an end product in mind, often this product is emergent, shaped in part by what she captures with her recorder, camera, or field notes and in part by what her collaborators want to share or foreground in their work together. Upon returning from the field, I usually process the materials in preparation for the project, which may include transcribing audio, logging photographs, and compiling videos into a working file. Then I work and rework it until the piece looks, sounds, or reads the way I want. For example, video projects start long, and my process is reductive. A recent documentary about the making of a rice basket in Guangxi province in southwest China started with more than eight hours of raw footage, which I edited to an hour, then to thirty minutes, and finally to its final length of fifteen minutes. Each draft cuts the excess video and smooths the transitions. Often when a project is around 90 percent complete, I share it with a trusted colleague who gives me feedback. After considering his or her comments, I make the needed edits and produce my first draft. Then I share the video, essay, or recording with the tradition bearers or community members featured in the piece and ask for their feedback, ideas, and concerns. With their comments in hand, I work to finish the piece.

Of course, this description is just one approach. I have done projects where artists or tradition bearers are involved in all aspects of the design and production of the work, such as the bowl-hewing project. For a recent exhibition with Miami Native American bead artist Katrina Mitten, *Reworked for Re-use: Tradition and Innovation in Great Lakes Style Beadwork*, I worked closely with Katrina to produce the exhibition she envisioned. I interviewed her about her personal history and about each of the pieces in the show, and then I transcribed the interview; finally, the two of us selected quotes and edited them for length and clarity.

Whether I'm making a video about basketmaking or an exhibition on beadwork, the time eventually comes to publish, install, or upload a piece. My current undertaking is a resource guide for older adults focused on traditional arts and creative aging. However, this print piece got stuck in a seemingly endless loop of reviews and edits. My team kept working, but the finish line remained beyond reach. When this happens, there are only two answers: quit or ship. If a project is not going to work, remove it from the to-do list and move on to something else. The other option, and the one we adopted for the creative-aging guide, is to pick a completion date, work to finish the project, and commit to publish it on that date. The ship date is still a month away, but now our team is working diligently because we have a defined time line. Once a project is finished, the content creator should start a new initiative. One project often points to the next, each leading to new insights and directions.

This is the work of the folklorist as content creator: we make things for the people we serve and through that process build a body of work and a career. My book *Folk Art and Aging: Life-Story Objects and Their Makers* emerged from several earlier projects: a video, two exhibitions, and a presentation. Each earlier project offered insights into the topic. The book then led to an edited volume, another exhibition, a series of workshops, and finally the resource guide I mentioned earlier. For me, content creation is not just about making things for people (which it does). Each project deepens my own knowledge and understanding, which I hope makes me a better public servant, scholar, and person.

Designing Visual Communications: Meredith A. E. McGriff

Meredith A. E. McGriff earned her PhD in folklore at Indiana University and is Membership Director of the American Folklore Society.

I came to folklore studies by way of art; I was an artist and graphic designer long before I was a folklorist. At this point, however, it's difficult to separate the skills of those professions: communicating visually and studying visual communication go hand in hand. As a folklorist I spend my time with contemporary potters and other professional artists, studying the ways they build a sense of community within their professions. Most of my work as a graphic designer has been freelance; my clients have varied, but I have mostly worked for small arts and cultural organizations. As a result, I've spent a great deal of time contemplating art as vocation. Most art, if made for consumption, is about communication between individuals, not about ego or individual pleasure. Professional artists don't simply create whatever they want, and it's a common misconception that being an artist means having complete creative freedom. People frequently do create for themselves alone, particularly as a therapeutic or leisure activity, but that doesn't mean the result will be successful in communicating to others. Doing good work in both folklore studies and design often means setting aside what you personally want to see and working toward a result—an article, a book, an exhibit, a website, or an advertisement—that places your collaborators in their own best light.

In all my work, observational and analytical skills are crucial. In addition to listening, I have to be in tune with visual and tactile experiences of the world. To work effectively as a graphic designer, I need to be able to connect words with actions and physical surroundings. When I start to develop a relationship with a new client, I begin by focusing on how they say they wish to represent themselves or their project, paying close attention to how this compares (or often contrasts) to existing assets, current print and digital materials, or even the décor of their physical spaces. This involves deep listening skills—most important, listening without judging—as well as being an effective visual observer. More often than not, being an effective designer means navigating among many differing personal preferences and goals within an organization that may not be stated outright. In doing this kind of observational work, researching and writing about artists is not so very different than designing materials for an organization or event. As a folklorist, I was taught to try to see through others' eyes, to seek understanding of how they perceive themselves and wish to be represented. I think of this as the academic practice of conscious empathy toward the goal of building an understanding that is true to life; not avoiding the truth or being uncritical, but knowing deeply and understanding flaws and shortcomings as part of a whole. My goal is to be respectful, considerate, and compassionate; to recognize that all humans are flawed; and to accept those flaws with grace.

That all might sound a bit lofty, but it comes to mind often in my design work. Educated and employed in small museums, arts organizations, nonprofits, and small businesses, folklorists like me are often quite attentive to the challenge of accomplishing much with a minimal budget, the need for employees to fill multiple roles, and the frustrations of having our time divided between disparate tasks. Familiarity with the inner workings of such institutions helps me effectively usher them through design projects. Sometimes it's as simple as noticing that the founder's favorite color is red and therefore many designs will be pushed toward warm tones, whether everyone else likes it or not! Sometimes it's being respectful of the project budget and not suggesting elaborate undertakings that are beyond the reach of a small organization. It can also be helpful in managing a project efficiently to remind clients to copyedit text before providing it for layout or make them aware of deadlines ahead of time; for example, a performance group I work with often needs a nudge to start early on the acknowledgments page of the program for their event since showing appreciation for donors and funders is so crucial and getting it right is a time-consuming project.

Often, my work entails communication with people who aren't familiar with the terminology for the visual aspects of the design work they need, but they do know what they like when they see it. On the face of it, this is a challenge: how to create a design without a description. My preferred method is usually to first create drafts or sketches of many possible ideas and/or variations on ideas so we can work together to narrow down the possibilities. I'll ask for specific likes or dislikes, often helping to clarify whether "I don't like it" means images, colors, fonts, sizes, proportions, and so on. Then follows another round of drafts, and another, as we refine every element of the design. I don't think I was aware, initially, how much my experiences of ethnographic fieldwork influenced this process, but the parallels are obvious now: when I begin doing fieldwork with artists, I usually have some loosely formed ideas, and my research involves a sort of intellectual circling around, theorizing, asking questions, and slowly working toward a more refined understanding.

From folkloristics, Elaine Lawless's concept of reciprocal ethnography—in which scholar and participant openly exchange ideas and learn from the other without privileging one's own perspective—has undoubtedly influenced my dialogic approach. From ceramics, Marvin Bartel's approach to critiquing student artwork is also helpful: by comparing two works and looking for what is better about each one, he can speak about the students' efforts in a positive manner. This strategy comes in handy, for example, when clients are looking for images to use in publications; if they provide multiple options, I can focus on the benefits of one choice without sounding unkind about the options that don't work. These kinds of things take time, though, and a tight deadline is my enemy in either line of work. Good ethnographic fieldwork cannot be done in a day; similarly, in situations where I've been expected to design something to go to print right away, with little or no time for revisions, inevitably my client and I are both dissatisfied with the results.

One of the benefits of being positioned between professions is the opportunity to facilitate collaboration on creative projects. In fact, a tremendous part of the work of a folklorist and a graphic designer can be thought of in terms of facilitation and translation. Both professions require maintaining multiple areas of expertise, and communicating with those who have differing expertise is crucial. For example, to write about the occupational folklife of contemporary potters, I need the skills of a folklorist and ethnographer along with substantial knowledge of ceramics. As a graphic designer, I often translate between my clients and other professionals: printers, web developers, and more. For example, a client may or may not know what a bleed is or why a printer requires it. If I show them a proof of their design that includes bleeds, I have to be sure to explain so they understand the final product will be cut to size. On the other hand, in communicating with printers about deadlines, I might be able to ease the process by explaining why an organization needs materials within a certain time frame, since someone in the printing world may not be familiar with logistics or staffing challenges that mean materials need to be ready in advance of an event.

Quite often, familiarity with the terminology of multiple fields enables me to communicate more clearly and efficiently about the work others are doing, thereby easing the work of management. As my career develops and I shift to less hands-on work and more time as an administrator and supervisor, I'd like to think that what I've learned from engagement with many different professionals helps me be a better and more empathetic leader. As a folklorist and ethnographer, I've learned to study people with care and look for the exceptional skills they bring to their work. I have developed an understanding of many different jobs in the visual, creative, and nonprofit worlds; I have seen the value of each of those roles and have benefitted greatly from collaboration with those who have expertise in different areas than I do.

Presenting Ethnography Graphically: Andy Kolovos

Andy Kolovos earned his MLS and PhD in folklore at Indiana University and is Associate Director and Archivist of the Vermont Folklife Center.

I'm not a cartoonist, just a lifelong comics fan. An early memory? Circa 1975, I found a *Superman* comic book among the jumble of men's magazines at Angelo's Barbershop in Glen Cove, New York. I was little—four or five years old, maybe—and fascinated. I remember holding on to that comic the whole time my hair was being cut, all the while perched on a board laid across the arms of a barber chair as a booster seat, hoping Angelo might just let me keep it. It wasn't to be, and with regret I returned it to the pile of *Sports Illustrated*s and *Playboy*s as my father paid and we headed home.

As I grew up in the 1970s and 1980s, comics were everywhere: supermarkets, 7-Elevens, and drug and stationery stores. I grew up reading them, failed miserably at trying to create and publish them throughout my extended adolescence, and I continue to collect them to this very day. Words and pictures together created a kind of magic—one that I am still in the thrall of all these years later.

Because the word *comics*, like the word *folklore*, carries so much baggage, I usually begin with a definition of the term. There are plenty out there, but I favor cartoonist Scott McCloud's from his *Understanding Comics*: "Juxtaposed pictorial and other images in deliberate sequence, intended to convey information and/or to produce an aesthetic response in the viewer." You'll notice this definition contains no mention of words, just pictures. That's okay! It is a minimal definition that focuses on the essence of the form, and I tend to augment it as follows: "Juxtaposed pictorial and other images in deliberate sequence"—*often with accompanying text.* A key thing excluded by McCloud's definition is the single-panel cartoon: think the *New Yorker* or Keith Basso's *Portraits of the Whiteman.* Following McCloud, "comics" are composed of multiple intentionally sequential images—and it's comics in this sense that I think most about.

How do folklore studies and comics connect? For a start, there is a long and rich history of the adaptation of folkloric texts into comics and of comics drawn from, inspired by, and incorporating traditional narrative themes and motifs. Comic adaptations of fairy tales merit an article and bibliography of their own, but I'll point you to *Walt Kelly's Fairy Tales,* a particularly stunning earlier example; Françoise Mouly and Art Spiegelman's *Little Lit* volumes; and the Jan Brunvand–edited *Big Book of Urban Legends: 200 True Stories, Too Good to Be True!* (1994), among others, as well as to the contemporary work of cartoonists such as Emily Carroll, Julia Gfrörer, Mike Mignola, and many more.

On top of this are a raft of other folkloric angles on comics provided by my folklore colleagues now establishing the Comics and Culture Section of the American Folklore Society: the occupational folklife of cartoonists, the cultures of comics fandom, the traditionalization of iconic characters, the study of the form across cultures, and even the idea that cartooning can be viewed as a kind of traditional art in itself. While I'm certainly interested in all this stuff, most compelling to me is the idea that comics can serve as a medium for ethnographic representation alongside our other established forms: written texts, exhibits, and audiovisual documentaries. Comics can be used to explore, present, and interpret culture.

My interest in seeing comics used to create ethnographic texts—what I like to call ethnographic cartooning—is undeniably rooted in my love of the form but also deeply informed by the directions taken by cartoonists over the last fifty-plus years, a period during which nonfiction cartooning in the areas of memoir, history, and journalism emerged in earnest and exploded in growth. When I look at this large body of literature—including powerful and evocative work like Alison Bechdel's *Fun Home,* Art Spiegelman's *Maus,* and Joe Sacco's *Palestine*—I have to ask myself why so few folklorists, anthropologists, and other ethnographers seem interested in exploring the potential of comics as a medium for sharing powerful and engaging ethnographic narratives.

For decades now comics have been viewed as a respectable focus of academic study, but only quite recently have comics come to be seen (even tentatively) as a respectable medium for presenting scholarly discourse itself. Anthropologist Sally Campbell Galman of the University of Massachusetts Amherst has been producing scholarly work in comics since at least 2007; see her *Shane, The Lone Ethnographer: A Beginner's Guide to Ethnography* for an example. The earliest self-consciously ethnographic comics I've found date to 1990 and were created by Cambridge University anthropology graduate student Gillian Cowther as "Fieldwork Cartoons" for the journal *Cambridge Anthropology*. Many others—including Michael Atkins, Dimitrios Theodossopoulos, Chitra Vankataramani, and Dana Walrath—have taken up this effort, particularly in this century; for a relatively recent example, see Sherine Hamdy, Coleman Nye, Sarula Bao, and Caroline Brewer's 2017 ethnographically based *Lissa: A Story about Medical Promise, Friendship, and Revolution*.

In 2014 I had my first real opportunity to participate in the creation of ethnographic comics when I was invited to be part of *El Viaje Mas Caro/ Most Costly Journey*, a project begun by nurses Julia Doucet of the Open Door Clinic in Middlebury, Vermont, and Naomi Wolcott-MacCausland of the University of Vermont, Middlebury Extension's Bridges to Health program. There are over a thousand migrant workers from Mexico and Guatemala working on dairy farms in Vermont, and they make up a large percentage of the patients seen by free clinics like Open Door. Doucet and Wolcott-MacCausland began to recognize that in addition to physical ailments and injuries, many of the migrant farm workers they saw were struggling with mental health issues such as depression and anxiety as well due to trauma, isolation, and fear. In search of a culturally appropriate way to provide them support, Doucet hit upon the idea of creating Spanish-language comics that depicted the personal experience narratives of individual farm workers who faced similar struggles and distributing them to farms. Through the comics, she hoped to let those suffering know they were not alone and point them toward help.

Working with University of Vermont anthropologist Teresa Mares and New Hampshire cartoonist Marek Bennett, I became part of the team that developed the project's collaborative ethnographic framework. By its conclusion we oversaw the creation of over twenty different comics that explored traumatic border crossings, interpersonal violence, communication issues, sexual and gender identity, loneliness, isolation, and substance abuse. The health-care team identified thematic content in the interviews. Depending upon cartoonists' language skills, we paired them with materials in either English or Spanish. Guided by input from the original storytellers, the cartoonists worked with these texts to craft the final stories, with the goal of representing as accurately as possible the perspectives of the original narrators on their personal lived experiences. It was an amazing effort that combined public folklore, applied anthropology, applied cartooning, and graphic medicine.

Since then, the Vermont Folklife Center has undertaken even more comics-related projects. Support from the National Endowment for the Arts has allowed us to create ethnographic comics about our Vermont Traditional Arts Apprenticeship Program and a collection of comics adaptations of stories from the life of Vermont African American storyteller Daisy Turner. We've held comics-focused events to bring together historians, journalists, ethnographers, and cartoonists to discuss nonfiction cartooning topics. I've been privileged to present annually at the Center for Cartoon Studies in White River Junction, Vermont, to introduce their students to an ethnographic perspective on nonfiction comics storytelling. Most important, I've met more folklorists, anthropologists, and others interested in comics and the exploration of ethnographic cartooning.

I am continually moved by the potential of comics for sharing ethnographic narrative and am inspired by ethnographically oriented cartoonists like Marek Bennett, Sally Campbell Galman, and Dana Walwrath, as well as by folklorist and anthropologist colleagues—like Erin Kathleen Bahl, Ian Brodie, Erika Hoffman-Dilloway, Nic Hartmann, and Lucy Wright—who have taken up the cause of using comics to share their research and perspectives. By connecting the work I love with the medium I love, I get to be that enthralled kid in the barbershop, the aspirational adolescent small-press publisher, and the grown-up public-sector folklorist all at the same time.

Portraying and Preserving Culture through Documentation: Tom Rankin

Tom Rankin earned his MFA in photography at Georgia State University and is Professor of the Practice of Art and Documentary Studies at Duke University, where he directs the MFA in experimental and documentary arts.

Throughout my childhood, my family—along with my aunts, uncles, and cousins—would gather every December 23 at my paternal grandmother's house in Louisville, Kentucky, for a combination Christmas dinner and birthday party. It was my grandmother's birthday and also her chance to have her three children—my father, my Aunt Caroline, and my Uncle Edwin—and all her grandchildren over for dinner at Christmastime. "The Twenty-Third," as the gathering was called, was such a fixed tradition that it continued for years after my grandmother's death in 1970, with subsequent generations trading off the hosting, attempting to keep extended-family fires burning even though some of us lived far from Louisville.

The most memorable December 23 gathering for me has always been 1967, when our great-aunt Annie Wardlow Rankin came from her home in Henderson, Kentucky. Auntie Ann, as everyone called her, was then in her nineties—an eccentric character we heard stories about but rarely saw. At the age of eight or nine, I had been given a small open-reel tape recorder that held three-inch reels. I recorded this and that but mostly just played with it. The older folks in the family decided I should try to record some of Auntie Ann's stories that evening after dinner. They particularly wanted me to record her telling a story she had told to them as children and to my generation as well: the story of a young boy and his two dogs living out in the country "on the big road." In the story, two ladies appear at his house asking for a drink of water and directions to the crossroads. After giving them some water from the cistern, his mother grants him permission to lead them to the crossroads. As they walk along together, the ladies transform into two panthers. It is a frightening, mysterious, and at times funny story—a tale with themes similar to some Jack tales and other stories but also a narrative I've yet to match with any other version. The boy's two dogs—one named Minnie Minnie Morris and the other Follow Linksgo—prevail in the end and save him from the panthers. My dad and his siblings were more excited than the children to hear her tell it—after all, they had listened to her tell it for years—and they insisted that if she knew she was being recorded, she would tell the story unnaturally or maybe even not at all. I accepted this premise and at the innocent age of nine found a way to hide my microphone inside the poinsettia plant on the coffee table in front of the couch where we planned to have her sit. I sat on the floor on the other side of the coffee table with my recorder at the ready. It all went off perfectly: a grand telling, with an audience of eighteen to twenty listening intently and responding all along the way. Auntie Ann never had any idea she was being recorded.

For better or worse, that is the only version I know or have of her story, the only telling. The story "lives" on in my telling it to my children, but the version I tell is nearly verbatim the version I recorded. I don't know another version, as any other rendering is completely obscured by the one fixed in my recording. I made my first documentary recording not only without the permission of the teller of the tale but in collusion with my elders, who were all so adamant to capture a piece of Auntie Ann's story gift that I don't think consent was ever a concern. If it was, it was only that getting consent would mean not getting their story. I think of this conundrum all too often and return to it when I hear someone oversimplify the rules of the documentary process, and I ponder the complexity when I see students leaning toward making documentary work about family to avoid the tangle of working with strangers, the complexities of otherness, transparency, and other ethical minefields.

In one sense, my tape recording of Auntie Ann was a strict violation of consent; in another sense, it's the product of a particular family moment, the convergence of her coming from Henderson, Kentucky, on a particular December 23, of my father and his siblings feeling this might well be the last time, of my having a tape recorder, of her willingness to tell the story one more time to her patient and adoring listeners, and more. Documentation is so often now or never, and this was perhaps the only possible moment.

My own documentary work began in this familial space, in the impulse to want to know what the older generations were talking about, to listen to their stories, to try to understand where they came from and the work they did, what they laughed about, and what they remembered from earlier days. It quickly extended beyond family to others around me whose storytelling seemed only to ask for a listener. In those same early years, I also was given a plastic Kodak Hawkeye camera, and soon I was taking pictures of my grandparents and uncles, the things they made, and their yards. Looking back on those early photographs, I see that what I was drawn to was the most mundane of subject matter: the day-to-day things everybody knew but to which no one was necessarily paying close attention. When I looked through the camera lens, what I saw was as fresh to me, as exotic and magical, as a traveler's new vista or a shopper's new wardrobe on display. I was simply drawn to the stories and landscapes within my reach—things that mattered in the moment.

What matters shifts as we move through time and space, and soon I was drawn to use documentary expression to explore worlds also troubling and offensive to me. I have found it much simpler to make documentary work about those things I'm drawn to out of an emotional and intellectual appreciation, using the documentary arts in praise of cultural riches I hope others will come to share. I've done that much of my career: working on folklife survey projects, documenting fishing families and their occupational histories on rivers and coasts, interviewing and recording musicians whose songs and tunes move me, and photographing sacred spaces in the American South for over thirty years, to name just some of my documentary obsessions. But I've felt equally drawn to use my documentary inquiries to peer into our more troubling cultural landscapes.

Several years ago, in my town of Hillsborough, North Carolina, we were surprised by an impromptu Ku Klux Klan gathering on a Sunday afternoon in front of the county courthouse. Without any time for prior thought, I went to witness and photograph, to confront and counter. Twenty or so Klan members gathered, some in their regalia, others sporting Confederate and White supremacist symbols on hats and T-shirts. Why the impulse to document, to photograph? I've heard for years that if we wouldn't pay attention to such folks, they would go away. And yet they haven't. How can we ignore such a moment—a moment filled with hate on the steps of a county courthouse, an intervention into the quiet decency of a town? While I always ask for permission to photograph—and did this time as well—my request may have been disingenuous, as I'd probably have taken pictures anyway. My confidence to be there and to photograph came in part from the privilege of being White; it also stemmed from having local knowledge of the space I was in, appearing like most any other weathered photojournalist, and my experiences in so many situations with my camera through the years. I was fueled in part by an anger—a defiant sense that I wanted to bear witness and look straight at the ugliness of reality in hopes of understanding the darkness. And so, I photographed.

For all the ability of our recordings and photographs to fix and freeze time and sentiment, it is remarkable how the meaning of our documentary expression shifts through the years. Our own personal collections of documentary materials and memories are a rich and evolving endowment of both personal journey and cultural representation. Eudora Welty said it best in her first book of photographs, *One Time, One Place*: "If exposure is essential, still more so is the reflection." Pondering the tension between the moment of documentation and the time later, she continued, "Insight doesn't happen often on the click of the moment, like a lucky snapshot, but comes in its own time and more slowly." And so does the rich promise of the documentary enterprise: of doing something in the here and now, in the moment, often propelled more by intuition than plan, as much by heart as head, with a faith that through later reflection, even more will be known, understood, felt, and revealed.

Becoming a Journalist: Russell Frank

Russell Frank earned his PhD in folklore and folklife at the University of Pennsylvania and is Associate Professor in the Bellisario College of Communications at Pennsylvania State University.

I'm writing this essay during a sabbatical leave in Greece, where, I am delighted and humbled to learn, the word for newspaper is εφημερίδα (*efimerida*), as in *ephemera*. The ephemeral nature of news is exactly why I had no interest in it as a man-child with literary aspirations. I wanted to write, but the writing I respected—fiction and poetry—had staying power. That is why I—a professor of journalism—neither studied journalism in college nor worked on either my high school or college newspaper.

So how did I get here? In 1984, having finished my coursework for the PhD in folklore and folklife at the University of Pennsylvania (an academic career seemed like a good backup plan should gainful employment as a poet never materialize), I moved to Sonora, California, to do my dissertation research on present-day gold miners. For the first few months, I lived in a teardrop trailer umbilically attached via extension cord to the mobile home of one Albert Norman "Bub" Dambacher, a fourth-generation miner assigned the lead role in my dissertation. Fieldwork mostly consisted of hitting the red button on a cassette recorder on Bub's kitchen table, thus preserving his conversations with the steady stream of friends who dropped by to drink coffee and shoot the breeze in exchange for a portion of whatever they grew in the garden or shot in the forest. As my pile of tapes grew, the balance in my checking account shrank.

Knowing I needed a job, one of Bub's friends suggested that the *Union Democrat* in Sonora needed help, which I incorrectly took to mean it was hiring; he meant he thought it was a pathetic excuse for a newspaper. (Avid readers often say unkind things about their local paper.) I applied and, I am proud to say, aced the editing test, even spelling *ukulele* correctly. But I was not hired, presumably out of concern about my total lack of experience.

A few months later, managing editor Sally Scott called me back. Was I still interested? Clearly she was desperate. Down to my last one hundred dollars, so was I. Still, publisher Harvey McGee was skeptical. Was it really the heart's desire of a guy getting a PhD from an Ivy League school to be a reporter at a small-town newspaper? I assured him there was nothing I would rather do.

It wasn't true. But it became true. I started at the *Union Democrat* in March 1985. My main beat was Sonora city government, which mostly entailed going to city council meetings on Monday nights and writing up every little thing they did, including granting parade permits, issuing toothless proclamations at the behest of one interest group or another, and rezoning a residential property so a homeowner could use her living room as a hair salon.

I was also assigned to "God, Wrecks, and Babies," which meant making weekly calls to churches to obtain sermon titles for the religion page and daily calls to the highway patrol to find out if there had been any accidents and to the birth center to find out if any babies had been born. Beyond those primary responsibilities, I was encouraged to pursue any local story that might interest our readers. That was where the job of being a reporter dovetailed with my sensibilities and training as a folklorist.

A while back, I offered students in my feature-writing class a list of defining attributes of the genre. The feature, my slide told them,

- Focuses on matters of ongoing interest rather than breaking news
- Provides a close-up view of individuals rather than an overview
- Focuses on ordinary people as well as movers and shakers
- Seeks out the extraordinary in the ordinary and the ordinary in the extraordinary
- Describes how people live and what they value
- Engages our empathy for other people
- Increases our understanding of other cultures and our own
- Makes us aware of the possibilities of life

Thus conceived, feature writers are fieldworkers who interview and observe their sources and then compose accounts of the words, deeds, and lifeways of those sources. Put another way, feature writers weave stories out of the stories they obtain from the people to whom they talk. Little wonder I loved the work. The only problem with it was that it took up so much of my time and energy that my dissertation languished. I even considered abandoning it: I had found my vocation. What did I need a PhD for? It is good to have an older sibling for moments such as these. Meryl urged me to consider the possibility that I might be really glad I had that doctorate someday.

Accordingly, I took a part-time reporting job at the *Modesto Bee*, put the finishing touches on "Bub's: Exchange and Talk of Change Among Oldtimers in California's Mother Lode Region," paid the university the back dissertation fees I owed, and became Dr. Frank. My newsroom colleagues asked me if I planned to add my title to my byline. Only if they let me write a medical advice column, I said.

By this time, I was the father of two daughters. Soon, I would also be the father of a son, and I was still working part-time, without health insurance. It was time to make a move. The pickings were slim. I applied for reporting jobs at the *Budapest Sun* and the *Anchorage Daily News* and for a teaching job at Southwest Louisiana State University. If offers had come from any of those places, I would have accepted. But the only folks who showed any interest were the editor and publisher of the *Centre Daily Times* in State College, Pennsylvania. I rationalized taking a job at a smaller paper by telling myself I was now management—the job was features editor—and that, who knows, maybe at some point I could connect with the big university down the street.

That happened sooner than I expected. I started at the paper in 1995, took on one journalism class as an adjunct instructor the following year, and applied for a tenure-track job the year after that. At this writing, I am in my twenty-first year on the faculty at Penn State: one of the old-timers. I have been extraordinarily lucky. I made the transition from newsroom to classroom at the very moment that the number of newspapers and the number of jobs in journalism began withering away. Pursuing a graduate degree in folklore studies did not seem like the most practical career choice at the time, yet journalism friends who lack PhDs in folklore have had to take public relations jobs of one kind or another when the axe fell in their newsrooms. I'd rather be a college professor.

There is much I love about academic life. As a scholar I have tried to make a bridge between the folklore and journalism worlds by considering the ways folk ideas and beliefs find their way into the news as well as the ways news and the rhetorical conventions that govern the presentation of news have been used as fodder for satire and parody. I also keep connected to the journalism world by writing a regular local column and pitching an occasional feature or commentary to a national paper or magazine.

Even now, though, I miss the daily routine of trotting around with a reporter's notebook in my back pocket; returning to the newsroom with that notebook full of quotes, factoids, and descriptive detail; banging out a modest work of literature on deadline; and seeing it in print the next morning.

EDITING A SCHOLARLY JOURNAL: ANN K. FERRELL

Ann K. Ferrell earned her PhD in English and folklore at The Ohio State University and is Associate Professor in Western Kentucky University's Department of Folk Studies and Anthropology.

The primary job of a journal editor is to shepherd into publication the best work the field has to offer. This involves day-to-day tasks as well as ongoing efforts to represent a field that includes members with diverse research topics, modes of inquiry, perspectives, and employment contexts. Much of this labor is often invisible.

The five years during which I served as editor-in-chief of the *Journal of American Folklore*, or *JAF* (2016–2020), can be illustrated in part by the structure of the editorship. I was fortunate to work with a team of excellent associate editors at Western Kentucky University (Brent Björkman, Erika Brady, Timothy Evans, Kate Parker Horigan, and Michael Ann Williams) and to always work with a coeditor (Erika Brady, Kate Parker Horigan, and Michael Ann Williams all rotated in and out of this role). The two editorships that preceded us demonstrate the evolution of this model. First, Harris M. Berger and Giovanna P. Del Negro of Texas A&M University were coeditors, followed by Thomas A. Dubois and James P. Leary of the University of Wisconsin, who served as coeditors along with a team of associate editors. Following our WKU-based editorship, Lisa Gilman has taken on the editor-in-chief position, and her George Mason University colleagues Benjamin Gatling, Debra Lattanzi Shutika, and Lijun Zhang are serving as associate editors. Movement away from a single-editor model, whether it is here to stay or not, in part reflects changing university priorities. As many universities impose larger course loads coupled with decreasing financial support, serving as the lone editor of a quarterly scholarly journal is no longer possible for many. However, working as part of an editorial team not only aims to lessen the workload but also brings a wider range of expertise to the process, and that's a good thing.

As researchers we submit our painstaking work to a journal and then, because so much of editing is invisible, we may be mystified by the long wait for a response and the further wait to final publication once a manuscript is accepted. Once submitted, the manuscript must undergo internal review to determine if it is a potential fit. During our editorial tenure, we worked hard to uphold our policy that articles published in *JAF* must be grounded in the methods and theories of the field of folklore. This means we spent a lot of time internally reviewing the surprising number of submissions with no engagement whatsoever with—or seemingly any knowledge of—folklore as a professional field of study.

Once the editors determine that a submission is a potential fit, they must then identify external readers (sometimes known as peer reviewers) with expertise in the topic/region/methodology and sometimes cajole them into completing reviews in a timely manner. Manuscript reviewers are truly the unsung heroes of journal publication: they too take on invisible work, putting their time (sometimes an astounding amount of it) into reviewing manuscripts, all the while knowing they will not receive public acknowledgment due to the double-sided anonymity required of the process. Editors must then review the recommendations of readers, make sometimes difficult decisions about acceptance, and wrestle with scheduling accepted publications when there are often numerous manuscripts (including special issues) in the pipeline. For some editors this means pulling together articles related in some way to create a thematic issue. Our editorial team's intention was often to include a variety of topics in each issue so that there would always be something of interest to a spectrum of readers.

The editorial team then works with authors to revise accepted articles, guided by the reviewers' recommendations and our own, and then must copyedit the final version with rounds of queries to authors. Meanwhile, the editors work with review editors and authors to finalize reviews of books, sound recordings, films, and exhibits, and with appropriate authors to write obituaries. In the case of *JAF*, once our work is done, our publisher, the University of Illinois Press, needs about six months to complete its careful production process. At any given time, we were working on three issues in varying stages of the editorial and production processes, as well as reviewing new submissions as they came in. As this overview makes clear, each issue of a journal represents the work of a large team, including not only editors but editorial assistants, manuscript reviewers, review editors, the staff of the press, and, of course, authors.

As editors negotiate the day-to-day, we also keep in mind the big questions: What are the pressing issues of the time? How do members of the field define the elusive thing we study under the identifier *folklore,* and what are the boundaries of the field? What work is out there that is not making it into the journal? Although I am certain editors in other fields face such questions, I believe journal editors in a field as attentive to (and often centered on) issues of inclusion and representation as folklore studies face them in profound ways.

One of the joys of editing a folklore journal is being so close to the vast range of research undertaken by our colleagues around the world. Take volume 131 (2018) of *JAF* as an example. The topics covered in this volume year included: Chinese folk drama, retrospectives on careers in public folklore, the fate of recordings made of the music of the Hammons family of West Virginia, contemporary jam sessions that engage musicians both online and face-to-face, critical thinking about intangible cultural heritage, Iberian *calenda* in Black American performance culture, grave-marking traditions of Chinese immigrants in Newfoundland, the role of the supernatural in political discourses in Russia and Ukraine, and a special issue devoted to the emergence of "fake news" in the wake of the 2016 presidential election.

Working closely with such a wide range of experts in our field makes serving as a journal editor an awesome (and I use the term not as slang but truly to mean awe-inspiring) opportunity to feel connected with the field. However, part of being a journal editor is knowing that parts of the field are under- or unrepresented for a host of reasons. For one, some folklorists (including public folklorists, independent scholars, and scholars of color) have less access to the necessary resources—particularly time—for writing up their work, and often there is no reward structure in place for publication by public folklorists and unaffiliated scholars as there is in the academy. Additionally, historical exclusion sometimes serves as a self-fulfilling barrier to inclusion in the present: "I won't submit this to *JAF* because the editors so rarely publish work by public-sector folklorists/folklorists of color/on the topic of my research." Editors' attempts to solicit a varied range of submissions are also part of the world of invisible work necessary to produce a scholarly journal, especially if those attempts are unsuccessful. The bottom line is that the best way to ensure work isn't published is not to submit it for consideration.

Meanwhile, we don't know how the work we publish will live on. *JAF* readers (and authors) might be surprised to learn that according to statistics on *JAF* access via the online scholarly journal access provider JSTOR during a three-month period in 2018, of the top one hundred most downloaded articles, only thirty-six were published after 1920. The most accessed (1,606 times) was an article by Adrian Recinos published in 1918 entitled "Cuentos Populares de Guatemala." Online access through databases such as JSTOR is exciting in that folklore scholarship—past and present—is increasingly available to new audiences. However, an unresolved challenge is the provision of access to those outside the academy (although the American Folklore Society has made great strides in addressing this for its members) while accounting for the fact that journal publishing is costly. As university budgets are repeatedly cut, the precarity of university presses should be of great concern to all.

Journal editing is a challenging and rewarding job. Balancing the day-to-day tasks with producing a journal that satisfies members of a diverse field is not easy work, but it is important work. It is also work that involves many people beyond the journal editor, so please submit your good work, agree to review manuscripts, write reviews of new work, and support university presses.

Publishing Scholarly Books:
Amber Rose Cederström

Amber Rose Cederström earned her PhD in Scandinavian studies at the University of Wisconsin–Madison and is Acquisitions Editor at the University of Wisconsin Press.

When I was an undergraduate studying folklore, my professor mentioned once that a prominent member of the field (Tristram Potter Coffin) had described it as "the bastard anthropology begot upon English." The ribald description stuck with me, not only because I find it crudely accurate but because it captures something that remains true: the study of folklore occupies a liminal space in the academy and is often pushed to the margins or found, often thriving, in the cracks left by the artificial separation of disciplines. "Stealth folklorists" can be found in a variety of departments: not just English and anthropology, but also area studies, sociology, religious studies, theater, and many more. And, as this book demonstrates, they also are found in many other places besides and outside the academy. I returned to get my PhD after starting a career in publishing and fully intending to return to it, and I am fortunate I was able to swiftly find a place at a university press, which offers exposure to the academic's pursuit of the mind without the pressures incumbent upon the lucky few able to find tenure-track opportunities.

As an acquisitions editor, I also occupy something of a liminal space, although, in this case, the job is central to the business of academic publishing. Acquisitions editors must represent their press to authors and the field and simultaneously must represent authors and the field to their press. And yet our dual roles must be united in purpose if we are to be effective; after all, it is to everyone's benefit to produce the best books possible. My training as a folklorist taught me to look for hidden patterns, to listen carefully and allow silences, to read carefully, and—perhaps most important—to recognize that I can learn from every person and every source. These skills are applicable to my work as an editor in a variety of ways. Finding the patterns that underlie an author's work can help me guide a manuscript's development from disparate pieces into a unified whole; allowing authors space to talk through their research has yielded clearer and more thoughtful conclusions; attending to the shape of the field—for example, where its senior scholars are focusing and where its incoming graduate students are advancing—allows me not just to map the current landscape but also to anticipate its changing forms. The ability to learn from anyone is, frankly, a skill that serves all of us, no matter what career we pursue or life choices we make.

My days are spent corresponding with authors, potential authors, and experts in the fields for which I acquire titles; receiving and evaluating, and sometimes soliciting, proposals; conducting market research; planning the shape of my lists (that is, the academic disciplines we publish in and that I acquire, including—in my case—folklore, Nordic studies, and classics); negotiating contracts; coordinating with other departments of our press, like sales and marketing, editorial, and production; and, of course, reading and commenting on likely manuscripts. I also try, in both more and less formal contexts, to help educate authors and younger scholars on the processes of academic publishing. Like any industry, academic publishing uses its own jargon, makes its own assessments as to successes and opportunities, and changes over time. Academic publishing operates differently today than it did thirty or even ten years ago. For instance, academic presses no longer blithely accept lightly edited dissertations; for those currently writing their dissertations who wish to subsequently publish them as books, I suggest utilizing helpful resources (like William Germano's *From Dissertation to Book*, 2nd edition), waiting a full year between finishing the dissertation and starting revisions, and embargoing their dissertations for as long as possible if forced to deposit them in online repositories.

I am lucky to have found a job at a press that already maintained a list in folklore studies, and I'm eager to develop it further. To that end, in addition to my daily duties, I attend the American Folklore Society annual conference, pore over its program, and communicate with its members; I read journals like the *Journal of American Folklore, Western Folklore*, and the *Journal of Folklore Research*; and I do my best to keep up with the folklore publications from fellow presses. I also try to consider what future books might serve the field and reach out to potential authors and editors to discuss them.

From a publishing perspective, the field of folklore presents several challenges. Because of the interdisciplinary nature of the field, it is somewhat disingenuous of me to say we have a list in "folklore studies," which might include publications about folktales, legends, labor culture, humor, vernacular material culture, folklore theory, and so on. Successful lists typically have some specialties within the sprawling vibrancy of a field that in part flourishes in the cracks between other disciplines, and yet the field as a whole remains fairly small, and each piece of it is commensurately smaller. The market for most folklore books is therefore limited. More, as departments across the university shrink, merge, or vanish, there are fewer scholars with the time and resources to write such books; many scholars with "day jobs" like mine are hard-pressed to find the time for research and writing. Sadly, as tenure-track jobs disappear, younger scholars are also less likely to write books.

Nevertheless, publishing remains a crucial way we communicate with each other about our research, discoveries, theories, and conclusions. It is also an important signal to the rest of the academy, and to the public at large, that the field is present and vigorous and able to contribute to the inexhaustible wealth of human creativity and knowledge. I cherish my small role in driving the field forward, and if I wish—as Judith McCulloh did in 1989 in this book's forerunner, *Time and Temperature*—that I could publish more folklore books, still I am proud of those we have recently published and those now in the works. Our particular strengths in contemporary ethnography and folklore of the Upper Midwest have produced gems like *Packy Jim: Folklore and Worldview on the Irish Border*, by Ray Cashman; *If You Don't Laugh You'll Cry: The Occupational Humor of White Wisconsin Prison Workers*, by

Claire Schmidt; and the Grammy-nominated *Folksongs of Another America: Field Recordings from the Upper Midwest, 1937–1946*, by James P. Leary, among many others too numerous to mention.

I've often thought that being an acquisitions editor is like being a farmer: we help plant seeds, cultivate those that grow, and joyously harvest the results. We also explore the landscape to find promising areas for further exploration and development, lending a supporting stake here and taking a cutting there. Publishing in any academic field is a push-and-pull endeavor. We try to help drive the field forward in fruitful directions and respond to its currents; we must listen and respond to authors as well as seek them out. Acquisitions editors must be somewhat jealous of their areas but also aware that particular projects might be better placed elsewhere, for the good of both the author and the field. My hope is that, in my role as acquiring editor in folklore studies, I can continue to help the field develop and grow.

Producing Festivals: Maribel Alvarez

Maribel Alvarez earned her PhD in anthropology at the University of Arizona, where she serves as Associate Research Social Scientist and Associate Research Professor and as the Jim Griffith Chair in Public Folklore.

I walked into the crammed storage room that doubled as festival office and breathed a deep sigh. The small, dimly lit room boomed with laughter and exhortations. Close to a dozen community volunteers gathered around a collapsible plastic table carrying on sideline conversations. Someone offered me a donut. Except for a few people who turned around to greet me with kind, muted smiles, no one took notice of my presence. Unfazed by external interferences, the group was absorbed in what I would later come to recognize as the frenzy of "festival planning mode." Any large event requires focus, endless hours of work, and attention to details, but for those who labor in folk and folklife festivals, there is an added secret sauce in the whole affair—conviviality. People commit time and effort for the greater cause of art, culture, and traditions, certainly, but they choose to go the extra mile of devotion for the rewards of social lubrication that yield the pleasure of knowing one another and the community's needs with astounding degrees of specificity. As a newcomer who lacked the history and intimacy of social relations in Tucson, I felt anxious and out of place.

But all good things come to those who wait (or are willing to invest time learning). It wasn't long before I became skilled in discerning where the Ukrainian elders prefer to be located to avoid direct sunlight, what time on

Saturday night the Scottish pipers must be scheduled and where they would stage their grand entrance, or why the Mexican lady who sells eggshells filled with confetti on the edge of the festival grounds must not be pressured to join the Folk Arts Demos tent. In the beginning of my journey, as the newly arrived folklorist who replaced the iconic founder of the Tucson Meet Yourself Folklife Festival (TMY), I relied heavily on my academic training to reassure myself I would figure things out.

But that was never the whole story. Undoubtedly, my growth as the festival program director was aided by the training I had received as an anthropologist and folklorist in graduate school. Anthropology instructed me in participant observation, a reliable method to gain the trust of strangers. It was a method aligned with values I cherished: it meant rolling up my sleeves and helping where I could be most useful. Through the process of helping, friendships warm up, and it becomes possible to notice patterns of thought and behavior that make you competent enough to ask questions that do not embarrass your collaborators. When least expected, you may even possibly laugh at insider jokes that otherwise would be off-limits for an intruder. "I got this," I used to tell myself, masking with academic bravado my insecurities in those early festival meetings when I didn't yet recognize the difference between the magnificent translucent flour tortillas from the state of Sonora, Mexico, and the fluffy and bready *tortillas de harina* sold at chain supermarkets. As a folklorist working in a folklife festival, I found reassurance in my understanding of the debates of the day about the politics of festival representations (for example: Can we ever truly escape stereotypes? Are we merely preaching to the choir?).

Luckily for me, the division of labor among the festival's volunteers spared me from the dreadful details of production. My role as folklorist (or at least the one I had conveniently assigned to myself) seemed more symbolic than practical, leaving the heavy lifting of operations and infrastructure to others. My intellectual goals included studying the festival as an anthropological occurrence. Of course, I was also willing to attend meetings and offer my sage advice as a professional folklorist, form stubborn opinions about the way things were done, and volunteer my share of reasonable festival planning and execution hours. In those days, never did a Porta Potty cross my mind, and I did not feel compelled to inquire about food health inspections, electrical power distribution, or garbage roll-offs, or to suffer the anguish of budget woes. This is not to say I did not care deeply about the outcome of the planning efforts that engaged volunteers throughout the year. Folklife festivals are love affairs: they seduce you with their sheer sincerity and raw beauty. I was hooked on TMY from the start, but the burden of its logistical execution did not rest on my shoulders. And then, it did.

Little did I know that within a few years of my arrival in Tucson, financial events on a national scale would shake the foundation of how the festival had been planned and produced for the previous thirty-five years and would confront me with a reckoning that no graduate school seminar on social theory could have anticipated. The financial crisis that swept Wall Street in 2008 caused all municipal financial and in-kind (donated services, etc.) support for the event to cease. The cost of producing the festival quadrupled overnight. People's bottom lines were hurting, and donations were harder to come by. Everyone involved agreed that without a major restructuring of the event—moving to a smaller niche folk gathering or a larger and more visible and compelling public offering (as some of the most dynamic community volunteers in the team were advocating)—Tucson Meet Yourself might not survive another year. All eyes turned to me: the responsibility of carrying on the legacy of the beloved festival founder and folklorist, "Big Jim" Griffith, was at my doorstep. By then I was also fully aware that this annual cultural ritual celebration had become entangled into the dynamics Charley Camp and Tim Lloyd once called the "metabolism" of social relations in the community. I knew I had to decide whether to go big or go under. Going big would be exciting: add more artists and traditional food options, improve the quality of the sound systems, invest in marketing, add paid seasonal staff, raise money from corporate sponsors, and enhance the visibility of the brand.

In spirit and disposition, I embraced the challenge: we went big. We formed a team that painstakingly overhauled every aspect of the festival, except its mission and long-held relationships with the ethnic and traditional arts communities of Southern Arizona. But my learning curve was steep, painful, and humbling; going from folklorist-writ-large to take-charge festival producer demanded I acquire new skills and knowledge in areas of operations I knew little to nothing about. Among them was overseeing volunteer recruitment and deployment on a mass scale (over eight hundred volunteers are needed to produce TMY every year) since volunteering is perhaps the most crucial element affecting whether a particular festival is deemed successful or not, its wonderful artistic gifts forever clouded by laments about overflowing trash bins.

Once stripped of the academic-folklorist distance I had so carefully wrought, the planning of mundane event-production details (such as water and soda sales and adequate lighting) began to meld into the substantive curatorial decisions about artist and program themes that were the folklorist's prerogative. I came to see the festival's production as a whole cloth of educational challenges, and while staff and volunteers looked at me kindly as their teacher and leader, the fact was that I was their student in more ways than they knew. From electricians I learned the magic of voltage lore, from traffic controllers I learned the patience of directing the public to comply with rules, and from the festival operations director I learned why banning Styrofoam products mattered if we aspired to produce a "green" event. Through this personal and institutional metamorphosis, one question loomed large: had my academic training as folklorist-ethnographer given me any transferable skills or instilled any aptitudes to accomplish the expanded role of festival producer? Yes, but not in any textbook sort of way. My training in anthropology and folklore had taught me values that became lifelines when the proverbial rubber met the road: accept that anyone and anything (especially the most ordinary) can be a source of knowledge; that our job is one of service, not stardom (I learned never to protect my feelings at the expense of the transparency and rigor of sound, friendly critiques); and, perhaps the most important lesson of all drawn from a folklorist's heart, that generosity will always trump efficiency. Today, I produce Tucson Meet Yourself from A to Z, with the help of an incredible group of content creators, logistics team members, and volunteers. More than 150,000 people attend the three-day event, and each year we put back into the pockets of traditional artists, clubs, churches, and small-ethnic-business owners nearly $500,000 in earnings. I raise the money, set the large vision, and talk to the press (still my bailiwick). But you'd be surprised how much things have changed: I can now tell a Phillips screwdriver from a hex key. My festival team has become almost family, and as families do, every once in a while, someone might see me struggling with a festival logistical conundrum and ask me, tongue in cheek: How many folklorists does it take to change a lightbulb?

Leading Cultural Tours: Joan L. Saverino

Joan L. Saverino earned her PhD in folklore and folklife at the University of Pennsylvania and is a visiting scholar at that institution.

"It was a stinkin' neighborhood"—this colorful line comes from an interview with an elderly woman reminiscing about her childhood in the Philadelphia Northern Liberties neighborhood, when smelly tanneries and other factories were interspersed with row homes. The quotation was included in tours of that now comparatively pristine-looking area that we developed as part of the PhilaPlace.org project at the Historical Society of Pennsylvania (HSP). As folklorists we are trained to recognize and use evocative descriptions that convey meaning from interviews we've conducted. This usage is an example of how a folklorist's repertoire of skills is well suited to plan and lead travel experiences. Although tour guide was never my primary identity as a professional folklorist, it is a hat I have donned at different points in my career. This essay outlines my own experience to foreground ways that folklore studies training gives us tools to organize and lead unique cultural tours.

I have led various excursions with university students and adult academics as well as ones for a more general public. With any audience, my goal has been to facilitate: to promote self-learning, encourage critical-thinking skills, and challenge long-held assumptions through unobtrusive assistance and guidance. I develop tours around specific themes. I often incorporate anecdotes and stories from those I've interviewed, and, whenever possible, I foreground local people—who, after all, are the best at representing their own communities. My intent is that these tours will stimulate attendees to begin to think in new ways about their experiences, the sites they've encountered, and the diverse people they've met.

Through our training in ethnographic methodology, we tend to develop deep relationships and broad networks of people with specialized knowledge in places most people wouldn't know about or have access to. We conduct in-depth interviews that result in a repertoire of key stories that aren't documented anywhere else and can be fruitfully incorporated in tours to illustrate points that can adhere to the thematic message to be conveyed.

For instance, I documented Italian American communities in Northwest Philadelphia as part of a grant project at the Germantown Historical Society. Two of the deliverables were a bus tour and a printed self-guided brochure. I incorporated input from Italian Americans who had grown up in the area when planning the tour itself. This thematic tour followed a general theme of settlement and ethnic identity, but through the stories people shared, I was able to create a cohesive story illustrating the unique character and history of the Italian communities. Historic tensions existed between the elite and the immigrants. I heard the story of Luigi Serianni from his grandson. Luigi was a stonecutter from Calabria who bought land and built four houses with his own hands in tony Chestnut Hill. George Woodward, a local philanthropist living during the Progressive Era, was buying up property. He wanted to build a public park on land owned by Serianni and African Americans. After a heated court battle, Luigi lost his property and had to move to a nearby street, where he lived out his years devastated by the loss. The park is enjoyed by the neighborhood today with no marker revealing its origins. It is a story of the loss and displacement of ethnic and Black minorities at a particular point in historical time that would not be known without oral documentation. Through interviews I also learned about the historic tensions between the southern and northern Italians in Chestnut

Hill, owing to differences in language and local opportunities too complicated to explain here. What is important to note briefly is that these tensions resulted in southern and northern Italians opting to live on separate streets in the neighborhood. Although the demographics have changed, the built landscape still illustrates the boundaries and tensions that once existed. The tour was developed around a narrative that could be visually evidenced by the landscape.

At the Historical Society of Pennsylvania, I was the project director of a grant that focused on heritage tourism. The outcome was two neighborhood trolley tours of Northern Liberties and South Philadelphia, Philadelphia's oldest immigrant neighborhoods, both of which are rapidly gentrifying. We examined change over time by looking through the lens of landscape and place. This led to a larger grant project I conceived—PhilaPlace.org—that carried forward the theme of change over time through mapping technology. Launched in December 2009, it was a digital place-based history and cultural collaborative with multiple large institutional and community-based partners. Featuring a variety of content, it included the itineraries of those trolley tours. Clips of video interviews were included, which allowed visitors to enjoy the tours vicariously online or follow the actual routes in their own cars. My point here is that tours can stand alone to be enjoyed by armchair tourists or can be ancillary to on-the-ground tours.

For the actual tour of South Philadelphia, the trolley stopped at the corner of Washington Avenue and 9th Street, the heart of the legendary 9th Street Market, in front of Giordano's produce store, and Paul Giordano climbed on. The youngest son, now in his late seventies (from a family of twelve), of the legendary vegetable vendor family, he regaled the attendees with tales of his childhood. With confirmation from other interviewees, we asked him to include the story of how his mother became the driving powerhouse at the Market and mention that his parents spoke Yiddish, Italian, and English to their customers. With his colorful stories, we could convey historical facts, counter stereotypical notions about Italian women, and demonstrate that South Philadelphia was never solely Italian but has always been a diverse area by illustrating his parents' multilingualism.

For years, friends had asked me to lead a tour to southern Italy, where I do research, but I did not want to tackle arranging a multiweek excursion alone. As a folklorist, I also realized I didn't have the specific knowledge of a professional guide who plans such tours. Due to a serendipitous meeting a few years ago with a woman who has a small company that arranges Sicilian tours, we carried out our first tour together. This collaboration allowed me to focus on sharing my content knowledge while leaving the logistical planning and the resolution of problems that arise to a professional guide. When a problem presents itself—one couple's plane is delayed or someone couldn't manage the walking required—my tour-manager partner is experienced in finding solutions.

As a folklorist, sometimes my narrow scope of research feels self-serving. But I find arranging small group tours a personally satisfying way to introduce people to places and people they wouldn't discover themselves. One aspect of folkloristic training reinforces our goal to present local guides and artisans who can explain their own culture and traditions. When we greet Pierfilippo, who has returned to his small hometown in the Sicani Hills to help its faltering economy through tourism, I feel I am doing something worthwhile for everyone involved. In 2019, Pierfilippo led our group through Sant'Angleo Muxaro and presented fundamental aspects of Sicilian culture so that, in his words, tourists can "touch the heart of Sicily." He introduced us to Maria, who had returned to open a bakery after decades in England—she served us pizza hot from her ovens. The cheese maker demonstrated the cheese-making process, which included a tasting. We toured Pierfilippo's uncle's storefront, which he had transformed into a *presepio* nativity scene complete with moving figures performing daily activities. Pierfilippo then took us up the mountain to meet an elderly healer, who was consulted regularly by biologists from two local universities and had built a small house filled with shelves lined with folk remedies. In his garden, the healer served us lunch composed mostly of herbs and vegetables he'd grown; later, he was kind enough to consult gratis with any of those on the tour who had a health complaint. By facilitating interpersonal contacts with keepers of cultural traditions and seeing them at their work, I can help visitors feel less like voyeurs and more like participants in local life.

During this Sicilian trip, I learned it is even possible to reverse the stereotypes people hold. A well-traveled and introspective friend revealed that she held negative views of Italy after reading articles about nefarious olive oil importation practices. She decided to take the trip hoping to dispel those beliefs. After the tour she thanked me because her bad feelings were replaced with a positive impression merely through the warm, generous, and honest interactions she'd had with Sicilians.

In summary, folklorists already possess the basic tool kit to develop tours that satisfy interactive and experiential learning. With thoughtful planning, careful attention to outcomes, and ethical considerations in mind, folklorists can plan immersive cultural tours that in the best circumstances stimulate greater intercultural and cross-cultural understanding while people enjoy themselves.

Performing Music and Theater: Kay Turner

Kay Turner earned her PhD in folklore at the University of Texas, teaches performance studies at New York University, and is a past president of the American Folklore Society.

My folklore career intersects my art as a performer, and both are integrated into a forty-year commitment to feminist, lesbian, and queer history and politics. This makes for a heady brew! But I have drunk it long and gladly. It has allowed me to explore women's lives on many fronts, but with a twist: bringing folklore's simultaneous interests in tradition and change, community and marginality, into play. I am concerned with rethinking and re-presenting women's legacies, especially uplifting those that resist dominance and refuse normative assimilation. Certainly I have done what's academically usual in pursuing my concerns: study, fieldwork, writing, teaching, curating, and public folklore projects. But I have also performed them in music, song, theater, community ritual, and the occasional spontaneous eruption. The folklore field provided both ground and seed for my artistic aspirations. I offer here a nosegay made of flowers picked from that field.

In 1972, at least intuitively, I began connecting my folklore and performance careers when I happened upon a copy of Jan Vansina's 1961 study, *Oral Tradition*, and decided to give that name to my protopunk, gender-upending, acapella quartet, Risk-Kay and the Oral Tradition. Performing rewrites of pop standards such as "Heard It Through the Grapevine," "California Girls," and "Testify," we gave the oral tradition new meaning as a lesbian feminist code for action. Not that I knew what the oral tradition really is—such knowledge came later.

In that same year, my girlfriend, Nancy, convinced me to vacation with her in Mexico City, where she had spent her childhood. I had no idea what to expect, but at age twenty-three, I was game to go anywhere. That trip changed the course of my life. Within two vacation weeks, I was sold: Mexico, Mexicans, and Mexican arts awakened me to what I would later learn was folklore, the expressive culture of a people. Now it was me who asked Nancy to return. After a yearlong trip back to Mexico and on to Guatemala and Honduras in 1974–1975, my interests coalesced around the folk Catholicism I observed in the dances, music, and rituals enacted at patronal fiestas. In October 1974, while living in Quetzaltenango, Guatemala, I was introduced to the women's home altar tradition by a Quiche Maya butcher named Virginia, whom we regularly greeted at her marketplace stall. One day she invited us to her hacienda for dinner, but before partaking, she ushered us into a bright-pink room that contained her private devotional altar, which she defined for me as a "beautiful necessity."

The rest, as they say, is her-story. Mexican American women's home altars, a site of personal religious performance, became my dissertation topic at University of Texas, and that interest evolved into study of the broader implications of performed devotion—icons, shrines, processions—which, in turn, led to exhibitions, installations, and publications and then to documentation and interpretation of ephemeral memorials created in response to September 11. Since April 2020, I have been involved with other New York artists to create memorial sites that recognize the loss of more than 150,000 Americans (as of this writing) in the COVID-19 pandemic. And as I write this in June 2020, the people's memorials to George Floyd swell daily to hold the tragedy of his death. In home altars and homemade memorials, performance and performativity meet in meeting needs that cannot or will not be served by office or institution.

I was lucky to be educated at UT-Austin during the 1970s—the height of the performance-centered approach to folklore taught by Richard Bauman, Joel Sherzer, Américo Paredes, and Roger Abrahams, following the leads of sociologist Irving Goffman and anthropologist Victor Turner. We learned to key and frame folklore performances as highlighted, marked events. I knew what the performance of gender looked like long before reading Judith Butler. Although the romance between folklore and performance of that era didn't make a lasting marriage, I and others of that generation—Nick Spitzer, Meg Brady, Beverly Stoeltje, Manuel Peña, Pat Jasper, Debora Kodish, Alicia Gonzalez, and Suzanne Seriff—came away with a performance-oriented mindset that, I daresay, providentially governed our professional careers. I managed to live in the best of both work worlds folklore offers: academic and public. Each provided rich opportunities for researching, teaching, and presenting performance. After moving back to New York in 1998, I spent many years directing the Folk Arts Program at Brooklyn Arts Council and teaching in performance studies at New York University.

As a performer, music is the central source of my expression. I am reminded that the urge to make music and the desire to think as a folklorist intertwine in the lives of numerous colleagues. Roger Abrahams, Richard Bauman, Ralph Rinzler, Joe Hickerson, and Alan Jabbour were dedicated folkies in the 1960s, as was I. (My public music career began circa 1965 in Detroit's hootenanny cafés.) That connection to music has continued—for example, in late-night sessions at American Folklore Society conferences, where Lucy Long, Erica Brady, Karen Canning, Steve Winick, and many before them have aired their talents. In a certain sense, the academic pursuit and public folklore presentation of traditional music defines us in the public eye, but we are also a folklore nation of dancers and storytellers, practitioners as well as scholars of narrative and movement, including dancers Eric Morales, Nicole Macotsis, Olga Nájera- Ramírez, and Jeanna Jorgensen and storytellers Kay Stone, Jo Radner, Milbre Burch, Kathryn Morgan, and Joseph Sobel. Perhaps our study and enjoyment of small-group, face-to-face artistic expression nurtures a desire to be in the face of our own audiences. Folklore studies gives ample evidence of performer professors, and I am certainly among them.

My distinction lies in the queer leanings of my practice, combining folklore, feminist, and lesbian agendas in performances meant to raise consciousness and raise the roof. In the mid-1980s, I founded Girls in the Nose (GITN, active from 1985 to 1996), a rock punk band, with folklorist Betsy Peterson and local Austin musician Gretchen Phillips. I had long wanted to challenge the stereotype of the pleading, yet ever-hopeful, lesbian singer-songwriter genre with some electric guitar–driven transgression. Betsy and I were also cofounders, with Pat Jasper, of the public folklore organization Texas Folklife Resources. While traveling the state from Beaumont to El Paso doing fieldwork, she and I found ourselves too often too alone in dingy budget hotels. But she had her guitar, I had my voice, and we both had our impending PhDs. The first songs I wrote or cowrote for the band ("Where Girls Go," "Menstrual Hut," "Meat," "Medusa," and "Two Altars" among them) embedded my enthusiasm for feminist folklore combined with lesbian politics. GITN went on to tour nationally, release two records, and continue integrating folklore into the mix of our gay madness.

Folklore-inflected songs spilled into other projects of a more "theatrical" nature. I must remark further on the hospitality to performance provided at American Folklore Society (AFS) conferences. Not just the folkies but the feminists have had our day, taking liberties with the profession in "The Croning," a triennial ritual induction of postmenopausal folklorists into a sisterhood of wisdom and "no regrets." I invented the ceremony ad hoc at the request of Rosan Jordan to do something to honor older female colleagues during the society's centennial celebration in 1989. What was little more than a feminist skit aimed at telling the "true life" story of Carl von Sydow's daughters (in reality, this famous Swedish folklorist had sons) morphed into an AFS tradition. With an endless supply of songs, costumes, amulets, and other "she-nanigans" provided by Crones, Cronees, and Cronettes in the AFS Women's Section and my rewrites of the folklore canon, such as "Little Menstrual Redcap" and the "Demise of Fertility Symbols," our rites summoned a perverse air of outrage and hilarity. All hail the hag!

After a transformative guest professorship at the University of Winnipeg in 1998, my academic interests shifted center from women's altars to fairy-tale witches. Again, folklore and performance found a source of inspiration. In 2012, following publication of *Transgressive Tales: Queering the Grimms* (coedited by me and Pauline Greenhill), I initiated an academic book project and an accompanying lecture-performance series, "What a Witch." The book investigates traditional witch stories while my performances explore the witch figure, deconstructing her attributes and powers in participatory story rituals that also feature music and movement. These "pedagogical performances," given in galleries, museums, and festivals from New York City to Tarxien, Malta, attempt to unlearn age-old prejudices and revise simplistic interpretations with queer folkloristic insight into what ethnographic filmmaker Maya Daren called the "successful deviance" of witches.

Performance was in my bones from an early age. I likely would have become a performer of some sort even if I had never found folklore. But the performer I became and am to this day is indebted heavily to our discipline—that special corner of the humanities where performance is viewed as an essential part of being human.

PERFORMING STAND-UP COMEDY: IAN BRODIE

Ian Brodie earned his PhD in folklore at the Memorial University of Newfoundland and is Associate Professor of Folklore at Cape Breton University.

I am funny. Although I am sure there are a host of psychological reasons that can be proposed to suggest why I developed this skill set or why it was encouraged, if only tacitly and reluctantly, by others, let us not have this personal essay start off *too* personal. But it has allowed me entry into all sorts of situations because what I lack in actual charm and value and talent and insight is seemingly offset by my somewhat memorably imaginative waffling.

Before I entered into academia, I was drawn both to opportunities to apply this facility in the limited contexts of Canadian adolescence (high school improv teams, speech and debate, school assemblies) and to the examples that popular culture provided, first to imitate and then to emulate. A serious fandom developed, and as I rambled through various disciplines—philosophy, theology, religious studies, and finally folklore—inevitably comedy, and particularly stand-up comedy, would intercede. As I'm only realizing now, in lieu of much "actual" oral tradition in my life (which, of course, I *did* have, only invisible to me, as people of privilege presume the esoteric is the sole preserve of others), the broad repertoire of stand-up became my default personal and lived example for verbal art.

It is too simple to make a direct correlation between folk talk and popular talk, just as it is too simple to make a direct correlation between the American folk music the folklorist studies and American country music. Mediation, markets, capitalism, standards and practices, and the inertia of them being their own thing with their own distinct sets of aesthetics, influencers, and canon mean the latter terms of these two parallels are different beasts from the former, and yet the ethos of the latter terms feels virtually indistinguishable in intent, if not in form or scale, from the former. One can use the approaches developed in folklore scholarship to speak of the latter terms, but as a guide, not a cudgel: not forcing them to conform to your models (which is what I presume cudgels are for).

When I am asked to distinguish ethnomusicology, which is also taught at my university, from folklore, I tend to suggest that ethnomusicologists project themselves into the person on the stage—what it is to be a tradition bearer or artist—and that folklorists project themselves into a person in the audience—what it is to be a passive tradition bearer. It is the latter for whom the performance is intended, and they are the person who knows (or is learning) what that performance means, who evaluates the relative strengths and weaknesses and relevance of that performance, and who may or may not choose to attempt assuming the performer role themselves. Like any member of that community, the ability to understand a piece of music or a meal or a ritual or a cudgel is not dependent on the folklorist's own ability to play it or cook it or enact it or wield it because they are all part of the collective understanding of being a member of that community, not simply atomized specialties.

Nevertheless, taking a cue from ethnomusicology (but also for funsies, so I have plausible deniability of influence), long, long after I established my credentials for analyzing stand-up and was safely tenured lest an ad lib get away from me, I tried my hand at it, and I am passable. I do not feel quite worthy of the honorific "stand-up comedian," in part because the occupational folklife of working comedians would disdain my dilettantism. But I have stood on a stage, and, without much characterization, props, musical accompaniment, or choreography, I have made a room of strangers laugh— and made a few dollars doing so.

In addition to being funny, I am also cool, so, of course, the other day I was pondering over the quaint and curious *The Critics and the Ballad* (edited by MacEdward Leach and Tristram Potter Coffin in 1949), particularly Charles L. Seeger's "Professionalism and Amateurism in the Study of Folk Music":

> The love of the physical or natural scientist for the data he deals with would seem to be a more abstract nature, be these spiral nebulae, electrons, snakes, or nerve ganglia. It may be integrated with the precision, comprehensiveness, and orderliness of his methods of work in a mystical love of a cosmic whole. The social scientist or humanist may find the same generalized experience in his study but has in addition the love of particular things such as works of art, where personalized expression is highly emphasized. It is upon these grounds that some would withhold the designation "scientific" from the studies of the arts. (152)

Folklorists are familiar with the argument, but it is always good to remind ourselves: the things we study are shaped in part by aesthetics, by the group's sense of something more than the merely instrumental. Nerve ganglia may be beautiful, but their beauty is not there to delight or signal a continuity with a past and a future. But even the humblest of folk objects, like—and I'm spitballing here—a cudgel, is formed through processes that are situated in the messiness of human interaction. And as we move across the spectrum of the inventory of things from the instrumental to the almost pure delightful, their appeal is so self-evident that somehow their serious study is called into question.

Stand-up is entertainment, engineered to evoke laughter as the prime response: clubs called Laugh Factory or Comedy Store attest to the capitalist and market-driven equation of mirth as a product. It is also frequently profane and vulgar, and while we can cite Joyce and Bakhtin and Abrahams and all those who rightly celebrate the corporeal and the carnivalesque as a corrective to the otherwise inoffensive presentation of culture that the powerful choose to cultivate, sometimes there is perhaps one dick joke too many. So scholars of stand-up scramble to justify its study as legitimate, in a way not dissimilar from folklorists in general, defending their discipline and their object of inquiry in the face of challenges from those who think instrumentally.

In my work I have spent a long time trying to dismantle the tendency to write "The Stand-up as [X]" articles: as cultural critic, as anthropologist, as moralist. The stand-up comedian *is*, just as the folklorist *is*, and I do not need to explain it in others' terms. What I can do is suggest what happens when that orientation is brought to another role, but I aim to do so not by circumscribing how the skill set of my training is sort of, kind of, surprisingly, if you take a few steps back, applicable to this different arena, but how a way of seeing the world folkloristically brings greater depth. I live in Unama'ki, unceded territory of the Mi'kmaw people, who have developed the idea of "two-eyed seeing" as a means of integrating traditional and contemporary ways of knowing. The metaphor is stereoscopic, with neither eye having precedence but both required to orient oneself in the world.

Ultimately, however, as I reflect on how my folklorist role and my (putative) stand-up comedian role intersect and intertwine, I consider what happens on stage, which is not dissimilar from what happens in the classroom or at an American Folklore Society conference or on the front stoop. When it is going well, all the ways the people present at that performance self-categorize are suspended, and I am neither folklorist nor stand-up comedian, and they are neither teacher nor administrator nor cudgelsmith, and we are present to each other in delight.

PRACTICING THE ACT OF WRITING:
MICHAEL DYLAN FOSTER

Michael Dylan Foster earned his PhD in Japanese at Stanford University and is Professor in the Department of East Asian Languages and Cultures at the University of California, Davis.

When I graduated from college, I wrote a letter offering my services to Lands' End, the clothing retailer known (in those days) for its lively mail-order catalog. I had no interest in clothing, but I made them a brilliant proposition: I would walk across the United Kingdom, from John o' Groats in northeast Scotland all the way to Land's End in southwest Cornwall. Along the way I would interview farmers and craftspeople and dispatch short, sparkling essays for each catalog. What better way to advertise the authenticity of Lands' End products! And all I asked in return was a tent, a rucksack, some sturdy clothes, and food for the journey.

Not surprisingly, they didn't hire me. They explained politely that, as charming as the idea was, they were not presently in need of an itinerant correspondent. (In retrospect this was an exceedingly generous reply considering I hadn't even realized the company was based in Wisconsin.) Now I realize, of course, that I was essentially trying to be a folklorist—although at the time I had no idea such an occupation existed. The occupation I did know about—and dreamed of pursuing—was that of novelist. My heroes were people who had traveled the world creating stories from the raw material of their own and other peoples' experiences.

So even without a rucksack from Lands' End, I went off to Britain. I worked as a dishwasher, a bartender, a carpenter's assistant, and a house painter. I hitchhiked through Scotland, England, Wales, and Ireland discussing livelihoods, legends, traditions, beliefs, and the meaning of life with anybody generous enough to give me a lift. Every night I recorded my experiences and observations in a journal.

While traveling through the Ring of Kerry in Ireland, I told the proprietor of a fish-and-chips shop that I planned to be a novelist. His face lit up. It just so happened, he explained, that he was in the market for a novelist! He made me fish and chips and related a spooky and oddly moving experience that had occurred a few months earlier. I listened intently, and late into the night, with my sleeping bag unfurled in a tiny shed behind his restaurant, I painstakingly shaped his tale into a handwritten seventeen-page story. The five-pound note he handed me the next morning was the first money I had ever received for my writing. Perhaps, I thought, I am a professional author now.

It wasn't until years later—after publishing a few short stories (with many more rejected) and writing a dreadful unpublished novel featuring people I had met on my travels—that I discovered folkloristics and realized that so much of what interested me about the world could be understood through its lens. At that point, I had also spent almost four years working in Japan, an experience that not only informed my research interests but also reminded me every day of the importance of getting language right and how words shape our interpretations.

Fiction writing for me was an experiment in empathy, an attempt to see through another's eyes and feel with somebody else's heart. Like an actor inhabiting a role, I would fall into a particular voice for each story: an old man on the Lower East Side of Manhattan, a waitress in a pizza restaurant, a young boy meeting his doppelgänger on a snowy night. When I began to study folklore in graduate school, I made the conscious decision to write my academic essays in the voice of a scholar. I based this voice on professors I admired and articles and books I was reading. Of course, writing about folklore is different from writing fiction, but for me it uses the same muscles and emerges from the same desire to imagine the world through another's eyes.

My research concerns Japan, and although I have written several essays in Japanese, I am most comfortable writing in English. This can be frustrating: many of my Japanese teachers, friends, and interlocutors cannot understand what I write, so I resort to orally summarizing for them or even just circling their names in the text. A few years ago, a Japanese graduate student translated one of my books into Japanese. This student had excellent English reading skills and a brilliant grasp of the subject matter, and his initial translation was thorough and precise. And yet it had a two-dimensional quality. Only as we reviewed each sentence together did I gradually realize that writing is also a form of *play*. What was lost in his translation was the fun made possible by the particular rhetorical affordances of English: alliteration, parallel structure, extended metaphor, metonymy, plays on words, irony, allusion, and irreverent idioms. (This is not to say that Japanese cannot be playful, just that directly translating such qualities is all but impossible.) Only when I reread my own book with slow deliberation, and an accompanying sense of defamiliarization, did I realize that, at least for me, writing is playful: the pleasure, the feeling, the meaning—they come not from the words alone but from the play between them.

As I develop as an author and folklorist, I find myself increasingly conscious of my own voice and the voices of my interlocutors, but I also want to attend to my readers—their concerns, their backgrounds, and their ways of apprehending the words on the page. Such attention is especially pertinent for folklorists because, in distinction to many other disciplines, our work is often closer (and I dare say more meaningful) to the people we write about. The stuff of folklore interests a diverse audience who don't care about the lingo of professional folkloristics. So I was thrilled when an editor asked me to write a book about Japanese monsters as a "crossover" publication—based on scholarly research but accessible to a broad public. I had plenty of material and naively thought it would be simple. But it turned out to be the most difficult writing project I had ever undertaken because it forced me to keep in mind an imagined readership—intelligent and curious undergraduate students who spent a lot of time with video games and other forms of Japanese popular culture. Writing for this constituency was both frightening and enlightening; "translating" years of academic research into digestible morsels taught me to see my author-self-text through the eyes of readers very different from me.

Despite what I have written here about the published product, I also want to stress that for folklorists—at least for me—authorship is not just about creating a polished piece of prose that crystallizes thoughts and sentiments in a package transferrable to others. Rather, the process of writing is a mode of discovery in itself; to poach the now clichéd phrase from Claude Lévi-Strauss, writing is "good to think [with]." Even as I type these words, I am thinking with them: deleting, rewriting, interacting emotionally, never sure what the next sentence will bring. Writing communicates but also, through struggle, creates.

For me, this interactive process is especially apparent in ethnographic fieldwork. For years I have researched rituals on a rural island in the south of Japan. I carry a notebook, jotting down reminders, questions, comments, and observations. And every evening I handwrite a narrative of the day's occurrences—just like the journals I kept while hitchhiking so many years earlier. Often, after a long day of interviews, followed (as is common in Japan) by a long evening of eating and drinking, I am too exhausted to chronicle everything, so I just make a quick list of points to expand later. And during every free moment over the next few weeks, I catch up with my narrative, writing down what happened the day before or the day before that. It feels as if I am living two lives simultaneously—the present of the world around me and the very recent past as I (re)construct and (re)interpret it in my notebook. These worlds intersect productively: I look up from my notebook to confirm with a friend something that happened a few days earlier, even while noting what is happening right then and there.

More important, the act of writing itself becomes a working through of experiences, as if I am authoring my life; the words emerging from my pen narrate the past even as they create the future, redirecting my inquiry and informing what I do next. These field notes are always unfinished and certainly not meant for anybody else to read. But the writing—the alchemical encoding of experience, memory, feeling, and ideation—is itself an act of exploration, interpretation, and creation. I have yet to make that walk from John o' Groats to Land's End, but as a folklorist, I know there will be people to meet and stories to hear. That journey, like all journeys, is an open book waiting for an author.

USING FOLKLORE IN FICTION AND POETRY: NORMA ELIA CANTÚ

Norma Elia Cantú earned her PhD in English at the University of Nebraska and is the Norine R. and T. Frank Murchison Professor in the Humanities at Trinity University and the 2020–2021 president of the American Folklore Society.

Brinca la tablita/ Yo ya la brinque / Brincala de vuelta / Yo ya me cansé / Dos y dos son cuatro / Cuatro y dos son seis / Seis y dos son ocho / Y ocho, dieciseis

Jump over the little board / I already jumped it / Jump it again / I am already tired / Two and two are four / Four and two are six / Six and two are eight / And eight, sixteen

As a poet and a fiction writer, I rely on the folklife and folklore of my community to inform my creative work in significant ways. As in the aforementioned rhyme from the children's game La Tablita, which requires children to jump over two sticks placed parallel on the ground, as I jump over the two fields of creative writing and folklore, I must negotiate, as many of us do, among folklore studies and other disciplines—in my case literature and Chicanx studies. Over twenty-five years ago, when I published *Canícula: Snapshots of a Girlhood en la Frontera* (1995), I coined a term for the hybrid text I had written, which relied heavily on the customs, traditions, and cultural and linguistic expressions of the US-Mexico borderlands. The work included photographs and didn't fit neatly into any one genre; I was working with fiction and ethnography at once. The term *creative autobioethnography* occurred to me as one that described my novel perfectly. I was not the first to write ethnographic work in a literary style, and I was not the first to fictionalize the story of doing fieldwork. But the former works tend to be more creative nonfiction or memoir, like Claude Levi-Strauss's *Tristes Tropiques*, and the latter do not use photographs. I have continued to write stories, another novel, and poetry using this hybrid fusing of folklore research and creative storytelling. I'd like to divide this essay into two parts addressing unifying themes in my use of folklore in my poetry and in my fiction.

I do not resort to folklore as an add-on to lend "color" or verisimilitude to my work; I rely on folklore to deepen insight into who we are as human beings; the lore of the people is an integral part of my fiction and seeps into most of my poems, too. My stories rely on folklife but also on the gamut of lore: the wisdom, traditions, customs, knowledge, and linguistic and cultural expressions of my community. By using a children's hand-clapping or jump rope rhyme or the tale of La Llorona—the wailing woman ubiquitous in Mexican folklore whether in Mexico or Greater Mexico—in my academic and creative work, I seek answers to questions about why we do what we do as human beings alone and in groups. Why does Laredo, Texas, celebrate George Washington's birthday? Why do people in a small town in Spain religiously trudge up a hill to visit a hermitage every May 3? Why do religious dancers in Laredo dance before the holy cross on that same day? Why do folktales captivate our imagination and dwell in our subconscious? Why do so many families hold lavish and expensive birthday parties for their fifteen-year-old daughters? Sometimes, the questions are more *what* or *how* and merely set the scene for a conflict that is often internal in my characters. Or not. These bits of folk wisdom, in which lie the answers to my questions, are sprinkled throughout the narrative *como probaditas*—as small tidbits to entice and whet the appetite.

As a folklorist, I tell stories, relying on the tools of the creative writer to develop plots and descriptions as a writer would. Because I write about the border, my work is often deemed regional. In fact, as a folklorist, I claim that title with pride. My latest novel, *Cabañuelas*, takes place in Spain, albeit with strong ties to the culture and life on the border. I begin *Cabañuelas* with a cultural scene heavy with meaning—a *tamalada*, the Christmastime Mexican ritual gathering of family and friends to make tamales. I situate the scene in Laredo as a preface to the action of the narrative so it allows for foreshadowing and provides the reader a first glimpse of the protagonist in her South

Texas cultural milieu. The aforementioned creative autobioethnography, *Canícula*, fills in the details about Nena, short for Azucena, a complex and often contradictory—some would say unreliable—narrator whose world is upended when she moves to Spain to study fiestas. In *Canícula*, Nena is a child between two cultures (Texas and Mexico) growing up with two languages (Spanish and English), two ways of measuring the world (metric and imperial), and two identities (school and home, public and private). Her world is bicultural, bilingual, and bifurcated in ways she doesn't even know. At school she speaks English and is forced to acculturate to the dominant culture, acquiring ways of being in the world that are anathema to her life at home, where she retains the Mexican working-class culture of the border.

As a creative autobioethnographic text, *Canícula* allows readers into a world rich with the traditions, customs, artifacts, and linguistic and cultural expressions—in short, the folklore—of the people who live on the border, whose Spanish and indigenous ancestors bequeathed a way of life that is ever changing and yet remains the same. The traditions of those native to the borderland, such as eating the fruit of the mesquite and the nopal, joined with the Spanish traditions that had previously mixed with the Arabic during the Moorish occupation of Spain, including folk Catholic traditions. Thus, Nena lives in a border culture where hybridity and liminality are the norm; in *Canícula*, the structure and the style are also hybrid as the book includes photographs for certain short vignettes.

In *Cabañuelas*, Nena is still in that in-between space, but she is now a professor at the university, a scholar researching celebrations. True, the ethnographic research and the analysis that would be fitting in an academic book are only hinted at in the narrative. Moreover, because Nena is a scholar—a folklorist—she often interrupts the narrative with information about fiestas, legends, linguistic play, and such. One reader commented to me, "*Aprendí mucho*" (I learned a lot). "Oh," I answered, ready to chastise him for confusing the protagonist with the author, "about me?" "No," he answered, "about Spain and the fiestas."

In my poetry, folklore appears seemingly serendipitously. Even while relying on the same traditions, customs, artifacts, and linguistic and cultural expressions, my poetry carries more than a story and often pokes into an affect that cannot be conveyed otherwise. A poem is a shimmer of a deeper truth. In my view, that is at the center of folkloristics as well: the study of human essence—a deeper truth that lies in the lessons learned weaving a basket, dancing a ceremonial dance, retelling a folktale, repeating *dichos* folk sayings, carving a wooden duck decoy, or creating a quilt. In a novel the folklore can be the backdrop, but there is no such luxury in poetry. Every single word, every single space on the page has meaning. In *Meditación Fronteriza: Poems of Love, Life, and Labor,* my recent poetry collection, a reader may find descriptions of folk Catholic traditions alongside the occupational folklore of a *cartonero* (a person who collects and sells cardboard) in the streets of Laredo. The poem "Miel de mesquite" is about kids harvesting and sucking on the juicy fruit of the mesquite, but the deeper truth is the mother's Alzheimer's. The poems about Catholic rituals for Easter or Christmas push the reader to consider the function of empty ritual.

From the particular idiosyncrasies of a particular character to the plot-relevant traditions practiced by groups of characters, the creative project remains one of integrating ties between cultural life and fictional life; they are one and the same. Whether in poetic form or in spinning stories that tell of people's lives, I use the folklorist's tools to create my work.

WRITING TEXTBOOKS: LYNNE S. MCNEILL

Lynne S. McNeill earned her PhD in folklore at the Memorial University of Newfoundland and is Associate Professor in the Department of English at Utah State University.

Inspiration is a strange thing. Picture it: I was sitting in a small, cramped hotel meeting room in San Diego, California, listening to a terribly dull statistical analysis of interpersonal crime at the 2010 annual meeting of the American Criminal Justice Society. I am not a criminologist. I am not a statistician. I was in the audience for my criminologist friends (none of whom was the boring presenter, by the way), and because I was sitting in the front row, I was doing my best to follow the very important (I assume) point being made about Pearson's r or chi-squared or collapsed ordinal variables or whatever it was. It was hard to focus. That's when it hit me, literally out of the blue: I should write an introductory folklore textbook, it should be really, really short, and it should be called *Folklore Rules*. I began writing madly, mapping out in my notebook the initial draft of what would remain the overall content and structure of the book through to its publication three years later. My friend at the presenters' table sought me out at the reception afterward to let me know how impressed she was: "You were taking more notes than anyone else in the room!"

For as much as I enjoy studying different specific instances of folklore—a legend here, a meme there—I knew from quite early on as a folklorist that one of my strongest drives was to talk not about the stuff of folklore but about the discipline itself. My discovery of the field of folklore studies was marked by an awareness that I'd finally found a discipline that appeared to match my own boundless (and erratic) enthusiasm. As an undergraduate I loved fairy tales; as an MA student, my attention turned to legends; and as a doctoral student, the world of digital traditions drew me in. I've written about foodways and memes, cat ladies and fairy tales. The golden threads that run through this diverse range of interests, however, are the basics of folklore as an intellectual approach. The roots of my role as a textbook author can be found in the ways this discipline works so well to help us understand and appreciate so many diverse things.

From my first year as a folklore student, I was obsessed with the discipline's descriptions of itself. I would often have the sense that a clear-cut, easily articulable disciplinary or generic definition was floating very near me, just out of sight. With degrees from three different folklore programs, I felt well positioned to try to distill the various ways different experts explained the field into a straightforward message of relevance and significance. The utility of the popular sticker-based phrase "folklore rules" to communicate two points at once—that folklore studies is awesome and also has some basic guiding principles—came to me embarrassingly late in the writing process. I mainly wanted a reason to bring the stickers back.

The joy of writing an introductory-level textbook (or teaching an introductory-level course, for that matter) is that you get to really sink deep into the basic ideas of the discipline: its definitions, differentiations, and applications. Folklore studies, as we know, has its finger on the pulse of social groups, whether families, occupations, or regions. Even the initial insight that supposedly trivial communication can carry real cultural weight can be a transformative experience for readers and students. I have never gotten tired of the "Wait a sec, is *this* folklore?" conversations I have with my Introduction to Folklore students each semester, and while a part of me knows I should be equally relishing the deeper critical analysis in which my graduate students engage (which I also love), I can't shake the inherent joy of watching a new student realize the inspirational power of the folkloristic perspective. Their majors don't matter, and their future careers don't matter; folklore adds obvious value to their worldviews.

As you can perhaps imagine, when I was writing *Folklore Rules*, I could feel the already fine line between teaching and proselytizing fading fast. And it's true; I see myself largely as a disciplinary ambassador. I want other people to love folklore and its study the way I do. My own experience with the way folklore studies helps us see the minutiae of everyday life—the way it shows us the power and significance of the small and familiar—makes me feel more an evangelist than a teacher. *Folklore Rules* is unabashedly profolklore; why hedge the fact that I genuinely believe folklore studies is the best discipline from which to launch any intellectual pursuit? And I'm not exaggerating (well, not much): I think one of the most significant things writing for an introductory-level audience has shown me about my discipline is how it can be used in so many other professional and personal contexts. My students share with me their own individual revelations: discoveries of occupational folklore in their chosen career paths, a better appreciation for family folklore at the holidays, a deeper understanding of the importance of the games the noisy kids down the street are playing, the unexpectedly personal meanings of another's religious practices.

The opportunity to share these discoveries with an even broader audience through a widely used textbook has been humbling. Representing a diverse discipline—in which so many people have found deep personal connections—in under a hundred pages will undoubtedly leave some subjects wanting. Critics have quite rightly called me out for overlooked topics, key concepts too easily glossed over, too conversational a tone. To these critics I say yes! If those weaknesses make for deeper and better discussions of folklore, if they push readers to be more serious and engage more critically with the concepts of the discipline, then I'm calling it a win.

The field of folklore studies needs more ambassadors. The volume this essay appears in is a major leap forward, highlighting the many manifestations of a discipline too few people even know exists. In a way, though, every folklorist is (or at least should be) a kind of textbook author. Every exhibit, every meeting, every publication, every consultation, every tweet, every performance is an opportunity to share the basics of folklore with a new audience—one that may contain members of the next generation of folklorists. Every in-depth analysis of a particular expressive tradition within a specific, even idiosyncratic cultural context can still speak to the broad issues at hand: that folklore studies opens the world for us, lets us touch the most mundane-yet-revealing essence of a people, and guides us to a greater appreciation of the human experience. Praise be!

WRITING FOR EDUCATION AND ADVOCACY:
STEPHEN WINICK

Stephen Winick earned his PhD in folklore and folklife at the University of Pennsylvania and is the writer-editor in the American Folklife Center of the Library of Congress.

In 2007, US senator Bob Menendez of New Jersey wanted to honor the African American spiritual with a Senate resolution. His staff contacted the

Library of Congress for help. The task was referred to the Library's American Folklife Center (AFC), and as the center's writer-editor, I was largely responsible for writing the text. I began with Menendez's notes and crafted a resolution, which was introduced by Menendez in the Senate and Representative Rosa DeLauro in the House. It passed in both houses, and the African American spiritual was declared a national treasure in February 2007. Behind the scenes, the identical resolutions were largely devised and written by a folklorist in the role of a government writer-editor.

My name doesn't appear in the resolution, but the text carries traces of my biography. I had been a regional folklorist for the state of New Jersey, and I quoted the New Jersey Historical Commission, much to Senator Menendez's delight. I had recently read Frederick Douglass's writings, and I quoted his observations about spirituals. And, of course, I had recently been hired by the American Folklife Center (AFC), which was brought into being by an inspiring law; I quoted that law in the resolution. I even managed to mention proverbs, the topic of my doctoral dissertation! Despite the resolution's legislative writing style, with its string of *whereas* clauses, I like to think that other folklorists, on seeing it, would say, "A folklorist must have written this!" While the resolution didn't have far-reaching material consequences, it's satisfying to know I helped the US government—and, by extension, the American people—officially declare that the genius of African Americans as expressed through folklore is a national treasure.

Since I work for the government, the goal of my efforts is to support folklife with government resources. Specifically, I use writing to advocate for folklore (the discipline, the field, and the subject matter itself), within the bounds of the law that created the AFC. As a writer and independent creator, I craft new text, which ranges from in-depth research to website blurbs. That's the more solitary part of the job. But as an editor, much of my job is teamwork: blending and harmonizing words written by more than one colleague, deciding on overall strategies or schedules for our written products, or simply helping colleagues express themselves.

This work has changed over the years, and I've produced a wide variety of texts. I edited a quarterly magazine and wrote most of the content for about eight years. I've written about AFC for other press outlets, including the *Library of Congress Magazine*, *Dirty Linen*, the *Huffington Post*, and *No Depression*. I've been a contact for the press about materials in my areas of expertise; I have been quoted in the *New York Times* and have appeared on *CBS Sunday Morning*. I rewrote AFC's classic fieldwork manual, *Folklife and Fieldwork*, and then oversaw its translation into Spanish and Chinese. I've written and edited many promotional and outreach items, from brochures and bookmarks to a traveling exhibit of folding vinyl banners. I've edited internal government reports about AFC's activities. I've written and edited copious amounts of text for the Library of Congress website, including biographies of musicians who play in our concert series, biographies of scholars who speak in our lectures and symposia and abstracts of their talks, essays for online collections of folklore and folklife documentation, and entries in the Library's *Performing Arts Encyclopedia*. I've edited and touched up all manner of library tools, from research guides to collection-finding aids.

I'm increasingly a social media strategist as well. I helped found the AFC Facebook page in 2009 and pulled the trigger on our very first post in January 2010. The page is still going strong, and I estimate I've made between three thousand or four thousand posts. These are generally bite-sized articles: a paragraph or so of text about folklife with an image and a link to a collection item. In 2012, we decided to discontinue our *Folklife Center News* magazine, and I proposed the blog *Folklife Today* as a replacement. I'm the blog's general editor (or lead responsible content author, in government jargon), as well as the most frequent contributor. We also have a team of regular contributors and solicit guest posts. I made the debut post on Halloween 2013 and the 730th post in June 2020.

Writing for social media has advantages over paper. The magazine was sometimes influential; an article I wrote about the history of the song "Kumbaya," detailing my rediscovery of the first sound recording of the song on a 1926 wax cylinder, has been widely read and used extensively in folklore classes. It inspired cultural activists in Georgia to get their state senate to name "Kumbaya" the state's first state historical song, and it was ultimately covered in both the *Atlanta Journal-Constitution* and the *New York Times*. More often, though, the impact of *Folklife Center News* was hard to assess. Most of its twelve thousand subscribers were libraries. Was it actually being read? Where and by whom? With the blog, we get useful metrics on our readership. Also, much of our archive consists of audio and video recordings, which we can embed directly in the blog when we write about them; in the blog version of my "Kumbaya" article, you can hear the cylinder itself.

Probably most important, blogs are native to the environment where people look for information. People only buy books or look in journals once they've done an internet search. Blogs put information where the readers already are, allowing writers to reach more and different audiences. Our most popular blog post is a research article I wrote about "Ring Around the Rosie" and the plague. Google makes it a top hit for people searching for that topic, so in the month of May 2020, it was read by over thirty-five thousand people—much more than our old paper magazine or most journal articles.

Unlike most independent bloggers, government writer-editors must coordinate blogs with other social media channels and produce them as nonpolitical government officials within the context of larger agencies. For example, I'm not free to express my personal political beliefs, and information I present is generally supported by evidence from Library sources or links to unique archival collections. I coordinate the blog with the *Folklife Today* podcast, which we began in 2019; I write most of the scripts and cohost with fellow AFC folklorist John Fenn. We tell different versions of similar stories in blog and podcast form and promote the blog and podcast on the Facebook page. We produce these social media channels in coordination with the Library of Congress Office of Communications as elements of a unified communications strategy.

When this works, it can have a powerful, personal impact. In a 2018 blog post, I told the story of two singers, Becky Elzy and Alberta Bradford, who were born in slavery in Louisiana. Alan Lomax recorded them in 1934 singing ten spirituals, including "Free at Last," the song extensively quoted by Martin Luther King Jr. in his "I Have a Dream" speech. Lomax's notes did not list a date for the recordings, but in my research, I came across a letter in John Lomax's papers at the University of Texas. It revealed that Alan had driven off to make these recordings late in the day on June 17 and was expected back "in two or three days." Given that Alan did not know the address of the woman he was seeking, the roads were treacherously muddy, and recording African American singers in the Jim Crow South frequently involved interference from white gatekeepers, the most likely date Alan made these recordings was June 19. In other words, I discovered that Lomax had recorded two women who had been born in slavery singing "Free at Last" on Juneteenth, a traditional African American holiday celebrating emancipation.

In the blog I was able to put the recordings of Elzy and Bradford online where people could hear them, along with the extraordinary story of the session. In June 2020, in the context of a new and broader awareness of Juneteenth stemming from widespread social activism, the Library of Congress sent a special bulletin by email and on Facebook, bringing together Juneteenth stories from around the Library, including my blog post.

On Juneteenth 2020, we received the following comment on the blog: "Becky Elzy was my great-great-great grandmother! What a wonderful find on this Freedom Day! Before today, my living family was unaware of these recordings. . . . It was passed down through the generations that 'Maw Becca' was a singer but to hear her voice is such a blessing! Thank you for preserving her story and sharing her voice with the world."

On a good day, that's what a folklorist can achieve as an advocate.

CHAPTER 4
Advocating and Partnering

Advocating for Community: Howard L. Sacks

Howard L. Sacks earned his PhD in sociology at the University of North Carolina and is National Endowment for the Humanities Distinguished Teaching Professor Emeritus at Kenyon College, where he has also served as Provost and Senior Advisor to the President.

When I first arrived in rural central Ohio in 1975 as a founding member of Kenyon College's Department of Anthropology and Sociology, I still had Tommy Jarrell's fiddling in my head and a boxful of Seagrove pottery awaiting placement in my new office. My wife, Judy, and I had relocated north after four years in Chapel Hill, North Carolina, where I'd pursued a sociology doctorate and developed my interest in the subjects and methods of folklore. In those North Carolina days, with nearly no cash but a functioning Toyota, we used our free time to drive around the Piedmont, absorbing a rich world of fiddle tunes, pottery making, storytelling, and blues harmonica that managed to stay vital amid the pressures of mass culture. Understanding folklife in community was, I confess, incidental to my PhD dissertation topic, but it immeasurably shaped what I've subsequently done as a teacher, scholar, and citizen.

I see academic and public-sector work as two moments of a single process: public life inspires my teaching and scholarship, which in turn inform my activity in the community. The intellectual foundation for my efforts lies in American philosophical pragmatism, based at the University of Chicago in the early twentieth century. Of particular note is its settlement school model, which underpinned the folk schools that emerged in the southeastern

181

United States ostensibly to "uplift" native communities by documenting and marketing traditional crafts. But for my own projects, I've reworked this approach considerably to be inclusive rather than prescriptive; the aim is collaboration for community enhancement.

My initial challenge was to gain acceptance in a place where people know one another over generations. Judy and I had a lucky card in that we're old-time musicians, and acoustic country music has always had a thriving audience here. Before long there were invitations to grange hall gatherings and town picnics. But the larger problem lay in linking Kenyon College—which prided itself as a haven for contemplation, isolated by design—to its rural surroundings. An early opportunity emerged for me as the new director of the Gambier Folklore Society and its signature event—the Gambier Folk Festival.

Originally suggested by folklorist Archie Green on a visit to campus, the festival grew into a highly regarded showcase of regional and national traditional arts. Intimate in scale, the event mirrored the compactness and pace of local life. Residents strolled the college's middle path, chatting with artists making their way across campus. Invited performers stayed in nearby homes; we assigned the blues piano player to a household with a baby grand at his disposal and the Nashville master fiddler to the farmhouse of a young violin student. Artists and volunteers alike treasured these unscripted opportunities, the "festival within the festival."

Each year's programming featured three nationally recognized artists—most were National Heritage Fellowship recipients—and one from Ohio. Evening concerts paired the familiar with a type of performance or culture local folks might not have encountered previously. A farmer once stopped me after a concert to convey his delight: "Howard, I came to see that bluegrass band, but I think I liked those *tamburitzans* even better." Audiences explored these connections in daytime workshops and a Sunday crafts demonstration and sale. The festival soon became the largest annual event on the college calendar, eclipsing football games in bringing people to campus. In late August someone would invariably stop me at the gas pump to say, "It just wouldn't be fall without the folk festival."

Continuing this focus on community arts, I collaborated with local officials on an area heritage festival to be held in Mount Vernon, our county seat, as well as on numerous projects with my colleagues. When an art professor who worked in local schools discovered the county had a significant quilting tradition, we arranged funding for and directed a countywide documentation project and instituted an annual quilt exhibition. I heard stories about an antebellum theater, Woodward Hall, that had featured a variety of local and national entertainments until 1900. I found the current owner, swept out a half century of dust and dirt, and offered tours; Mount Vernon townspeople lined up around the block to get a look.

The Rural Life Center, which I founded in the 1990s, expanded this partnership between college and community. Over the past twenty-five years, the center's projects have addressed rural diversity, sustainability, agriculture, and public spaces. Many of these efforts arise in direct response to community statements of interest. The Family Farm Project offers a case in point. Our conversations with farmers, equipment dealers, meat processors, and auctioneers impressed upon us the difficulties farm families faced in continuing a way of life they dearly hoped to pass on to their children. University-based agricultural programs addressed their problems from a big-ag perspective, with a biological fix to increase yield or an economic innovation to build global markets. We took a more holistic approach, considering the interconnections among environment, economy, society, and culture— in short, putting the "culture" back into agriculture.

Drawing on their extensive fieldwork, my students produced a radio series, school curriculum, and newspaper articles to stimulate a public conversation about the importance of family farming to rural life. Interestingly, this dialogue coincided with growing community concern about exurban sprawl from nearby Columbus and long-range planning to address the issue. In public meetings about these plans, residents overwhelmingly prioritized the need to preserve rural character.

To advance this goal, the Rural Life Center proposed an ambitious initiative to establish a countywide local food system that would create a new market for local farm products, boost the area's economy, and provide fresh food for families. We created a local food council—composed of producers, processors, distributors, and consumers—to guide our efforts. Together we published a guide to local food products, established a weekly farmer's market in Mount Vernon's Public Square, and developed a wholesale produce auction in a nearby Amish village. We provided products to the local food bank, and a retired gourmet chef prepared recipes for each new delivery. To build consumer interest, Kenyon students produced *Where Does Our Food Come From?*—a massive exhibit tracing food from farm to table. "Foodways," a thirteen-part newspaper series, explored topics including ritual foods, trapping, and feeding the hungry.

These efforts, in turn, changed life at Kenyon. Courses throughout the curriculum—from Practical Issues in Ethics to Italian Cinema—incorporated local food themes and trips into the community, and students conducted paid summer internships on sustainable farms. To foster large-scale institutional buying, Kenyon built a new dining hall designed to maximize the use of local foods. Within a few years, half of our food purchases were sourced from area farmers.

Going local soon attracted national interest. Universities visited our food service to consider how they might adapt our techniques. The producers of Farm Aid held a national conference at Kenyon on the emerging farm-to-table movement, with field trips into surrounding farm country. Numerous Ohio counties and municipalities have now created their own local food councils. The governor invited me to join his Ohio Food Policy Council to launch a statewide local foods initiative.

Over the course of my forty-year career, I've enjoyed regular opportunities to make contributions at the state and national levels: serving on National Endowment for the Arts folk arts grant-review panels, producing countless festivals and folk arts tours at the National Council for the Traditional Arts, evaluating state humanities programs, and consulting with communities and organizations across the country. I recently joined fellow folklorists in the American Folklore Society (AFS)'s international collaboration on the efforts of China and the United States to preserve intangible cultural heritage. I've learned much from this work and appreciate its significance, but contributing to my own community has always felt more meaningful. I have a greater impact in my own backyard and a direct stake in where I live. I'm pleased that some of what we've accomplished has offered a model for others to follow.

Today, looking south on Main Street from Mount Vernon's Public Square, I see tangible indications that this work has made a difference. The farmer's market continues to pack the square each Saturday morning, and the music and arts festival we started is now celebrating its fortieth anniversary. A block south, the Woodward just completed a $25 million historic renovation. The building houses a local food store at street level and a commercial kitchen in the basement for farmers to produce value-added goods. When the theater upstairs recently hosted a performance of *A Raisin in the Sun*, theatergoers were greeted in the foyer by *The Community Within*, a Rural Life Center exhibit, on loan from the county historical society's museum, documenting two centuries of local African American life. And a restored nineteenth-century warehouse on the next block houses Kenyon's new Center for Community Engagement. Grassroots advocacy doesn't mean thinking small; it means living a grounded and engaged life.

Advocating for Communities and Their Environments: Mary Hufford

Mary Hufford earned her PhD in folklore and folklife at the University of Pennsylvania and is Associate Director of the Livelihoods Knowledge Exchange Network (LiKEN).

On a clear, crisp fall day in 1995, photographer Lyntha Scott Eiler and I took a helicopter ride from Charleston, West Virginia, to the headwaters of the Big Coal River in Raleigh County, courtesy of the state's Division of Environmental Protection. Across the rumpled terrain, seen through the helicopter's glass bottom, autumnal colors were peaking: the deep yellow of hickories, vibrant red of sourwood, and blazing orange of maples. As we began following Route 3 on its parallel course with the Big Coal River, the patches of fall color gave way to a vast denuded flatland of rock and rubble, pocked with flashing black impoundments of coal waste, electric yellow and green effluent sediment in catchment basins, and chevrons of riprap wedged between flattened mountains.

Although Lyntha and I had been reading and hearing about this form of mining for months, this overview was a shock. We had spent nearly a year documenting customary uses of forest species and landscapes in what ecologists consider to be a world hot spot of biodiversity. Through many conversations with people living in the hills and hollows, we had witnessed extraordinarily rich and complex social worlds shaped by generations of interactions with the cove-forest species and landscapes of the Allegheny Plateau. We had learned by now that every wrinkle in this unglaciated terrain was named and that its species and spaces were deeply entangled with the histories of communities sharing life in the Big Coal River Valley. We were there because the West Virginia Division of Environmental Protection, fully believing it was acting in the best interest of coalfield communities, had invited us to see for ourselves how mining corporations were improving the quality of life for West Virginians, but what we saw from the air was the wholesale destruction of dozens of square miles of storied environments filled with common-pool resources that had sustained human and more-than-human communities since prehistoric times.

By the time we took that helicopter ride, I had been working as a folklife specialist at the American Folklife Center (AFC) at the Library of Congress for more than a decade. Since 1982 my work at the AFC had focused on the environmental dimensions of cultural planning, testing what was then the new rubric of "cultural conservation." In the 1980s the field of public folklore was coming of age against the exciting and visionary backdrop of the National Environmental Policy Act (NEPA) and the related suite of laws, including the American Folklife Preservation Act, passed by the "preservation Congresses" of the 1960s and 1970s. Hailed when passed in 1969 as the "environmental Magna Carta," the NEPA prescribed the collaboration of multiple sectors and disciplines in environmental review ahead of any development project requiring federal oversight. In step with the nation's bicentennial, when landscapes, historic properties, and even folklife became objects of federal protection, cultural workers plunged into daunting work toward more holistic approaches to environmental assessment.

However, as a research object, folklife is not equivalent to an ecosystem. An important effect of environmental folklife is to engage communities that are invisible stakeholders in environmental decision-making. This was anticipated by advocates for the American Folklife Preservation Act of 1976, who reasoned that support for folklife would "amplify voices in a democratic polity." Ahead of their time, the AFC's team field surveys of the 1980s engaged communities in public conversations that included environmental topics and documented stylized, collective ways of knowing and being in particular places in relation to particular environments.

Our public fieldwork in the 1980s followed a government-sanctioned research paradigm that separated an environmental research phase from the outcome (or application) of environmental management. This expert-driven paradigm privileged expertise and placed decision-making in the hands of government agencies. I led two team field projects for the AFC that created folklife archives that could be consulted by managers of the Pinelands National Reserve in southern New Jersey and the New River Gorge National River in southern West Virginia. Chipping away at the expert-driven paradigm—hoping to amplify, in a democratic polity, the voices we had recorded—we formally recommended that our partners, the Pinelands Commission and the National Park Service, create processes for ongoing consultation with communities on ways to address "community life and values" (our translation of *folklife*).

By the early 1990s, a crucial paradigm shift was underway, normalizing community-based participatory research and management and marked by President Clinton's signing of the environmental justice memorandum, which signaled the confluence of the environmental and civil rights movements and directed federal agencies to consider undue environmental burdens on vulnerable populations imposed by any federal action. Its interest in subsistence-based reliance on environmental resources (fishing, hunting, gathering, and so forth) recognized that communities are connected to their environments through the practices studied by folklorists.

Environmental justice supported a trend toward the practice of citizen science, the framework for the AFC's project in the Coal River Valley. Working on such projects, first in the West Virginia coalfields and then in Ohio's "Chemical Valley" during the 1990s and 2000s, I witnessed the power of shared inquiry to shape new public spaces. In such spaces, the always eloquent voices of frontline communities, previously muted by corporate players that had captured state environmental agencies, started to be heard. To nurture this public, these projects structured shared inquiry in ways that paused the undue influence of such powerful players. Experts from the academy and government assembled with members of frontline communities as they, instead of industrial polluters, became the clients for scientific expertise.

Ecologists designed the Appalachian Forest Action Project in response to concerns about the decline of forest species as voiced by the elders in a coalfield community. That project carved out a space in which local knowledge of forest species and ecosystems, initially shared within the community through the forms studied by folklorists—stories, phenological observations, vernacular names for species, forest practices, and agricultural technologies—was verified and accredited by evidence-based science. As an environmental folklorist, my job was not simply to document and archive folklore but to explore with community members something the science could not provide on its own: the significance of the findings for the community. What would it mean if forest species decline resulted in a far less diverse forest? This question marks the head of the trail to an understanding that people whose lives are entangled on a daily basis with a given environment must be leaders in research about that environment, a principle codified in the participatory action research slogan "No research about us without us." Modeling with community members the times and spaces enabled by this particular ecosystem made it clear that the forested hills and waterways foundational to their ways of life were being eviscerated not only by pollution from fossil fuel combustion upwind of the region but by upcoming decades of mountaintop removal mining. As an environmental folklorist, I worked with interested community members and Library of Congress staff to present the social and cultural values of the mixed mesophytic forest and watersheds. This resulted in a Library of Congress American Memory presentation, "Tending the Commons: Folklife and Land Use in Southern West Virginia." But how, I wondered, could we be doing more to amplify voices in a democratic polity?

Over the next two decades, the framework of environmental justice opened new doors for my work in government (the American Folklife Center), academia (the University of Pennsylvania), and the nonprofit sector (the Livelihoods Knowledge Exchange Network). While directing Penn's

Center for Folklore and Ethnography, I served as a social science evaluator on a citizen science project in Washington County, Ohio. Representatives of the polluting corporation, DuPont, were excluded from monthly meetings of the community advisory group, and we noticed that participants from the Little Hocking River water district began openly sharing stories about cancer, a topic that was never addressed publicly for fear that even to speak about cancer would drive away a major employer in the region. It was clear that the shared inquiry of citizens and experts into the conditions of their water had generated safe spaces for saying what was unsayable under ordinary circumstances. Such spaces can become emergent incubators for democratic environmental decision-making.

Abruptly severed from their environments, human communities may experience trauma triggered by the loss of familiar settings. Folklorists who have worked with the elderly and refugees are well acquainted with the power of storytelling to precipitate lost environments in ways that are collectively therapeutic. During the exchange of African dilemma stories and animal tales shared by elderly Liberian refugees in Philadelphia and documented by graduate students in folklore at Penn, the sights and sounds of West Africa flooded into the spare, fluorescent-lit room of the senior center. In the stories told by an elderly evacuee from the Coal River, miniature vehicles constructed from cereal boxes re-member once-familiar sights in a hollow now submerged under billions of gallons of coal slurry. In a time of growing unpredictability and nearly routinized environmental catastrophe, recognizing and providing time-spaces for communities to lead their own healing from the pain of dislocation are the work of environmental folklore. Equipped with performance theory and steeped in the understanding of how performances of genres of communication structure social relationships, folklorists can bring worlds of expertise and experience anchored in the same species and materials into public conversation.

USING ETHNOGRAPHY FOR COMMUNITY ADVOCACY: MIGUEL GANDERT

Miguel Gandert earned his MA in photography at the University of New Mexico, where he is Distinguished Professor of Communication and Journalism and Director of the Interdisciplinary Film and Digital Media Program.

Although I am known as a professor and a documentary photographer, I was extremely fortunate to have been trained as a folklorist as well. I received the finest instruction possible when I was asked to teach the photography component for a field school cosponsored by the Library of Congress American Folklore Center, the University of New Mexico, and Colorado College and led by faculty from these institutions. My education was developed and broadened by some of the best in the field. The experience of being a folklorist has, without a doubt, informed my work for the last twenty-five years.

While teaching photography for the field school, I developed a strategy for working in the field and viewing images that I call "The Three P's: People, Place, and Process." In the first, we reflect on *who* we are photographing and our responsibility to be aware of how we represent them and then our audience. The second mandate involves *place*—how the environment informs the context of place and what kind of data can be gained by simple observation. Finally, there is *process*—the sense of what understanding we gain by interpreting the interactions within the frame.

Hotel Mariachi: Urban Space and Cultural Heritage in Los Angeles is a model for why folklore is important and how it can affect a community in a positive way. Like so many of my projects, it began in the classroom. Teaching ethnography for the historic preservation program in the University of New Mexico's School of Architecture and Planning, I supervised a student named Catherine Kurland. Cathy described the nineteenth-century Boyle Hotel in the East Los Angeles community of Boyle Heights: part of the Cummings Block building, built by her great-grandfather George Cummings and her great-grandmother Sacramenta Lopez. She expanded on the history of Mariachi Plaza across from the hotel based on her research on the family history of the 1889 Queen Anne–style building, now home to over one hundred mariachi musicians. She was confident the musicians would respond well to our tentative efforts to document their art form, the historic building, and the vibrant culture surrounding both. She had also contacted the East Los Angeles Community Corporation (ELACC), a low-income housing organization, and we were introduced to an impressive array of Angelenos who generously shared their knowledge of the community with us.

The beauty of doing photography and fieldwork is that one must show up in person. Outfitted with cameras and an audio recorder, Cathy and I arrived in Boyle Heights and drove to the venerable old building at the corner of Boyle Avenue, First Street, and Pleasant Avenue, now known to most as the Mariachi Hotel. My first interview was on the plaza itself, where I talked with Luisito Garcia. The octogenarian musician told me he had spent almost a half century living in a four-room apartment at the Boyle Hotel and was feeling worried about his future and that of his fellow mariachis. I talked to several people in the community, thinking someone in LA would have already initiated the fieldwork to document what appeared to be an urgent situation. To my surprise, no one had.

Cathy and I decided this was a project worth doing, especially when we found out the hotel was on the market to be sold. City planners had their eye on the property and were planning to either convert the elegant Boyle Hotel into luxury condos or level the building and replace it altogether. These potential changes made it urgent to work quickly to get what we could before construction changed the community. As we worked, we began to integrate a better understanding of the complexity of the Mariachi Plaza and why the space had become a touchstone for the musicians, both as a community and as a reliable source for finding work. When a mariachi band is hired to play an event, the plaza is where the hiring happens. Each musician represents a group and uses a cell phone to call an appropriate number of musicians for a gig. The mariachi men and women all wear black embroidered *charro* outfits, sometimes with matching ties for each newly formed group of players. While exploring the neighborhood, we found a school for instructing young entertainers, a tailor shop providing *chaquetilla* jackets, a print broker specializing in business cards, and a music store dealing in the *vihuelas* and *guitarrónes* used by the mariachi musicians.

With support from ELACC and the newly created Boyle Heights Historical Society, Cathy prepared a nomination to list the hotel as a Los Angeles City Historical Monument. In the meantime, we had come to the realization that this would not be a short-term project. The listing process took over a year, and when it was finally granted, we felt a renewed sense of satisfaction. Cathy was at work on the historic designation, which would help save the building and preserve the integrity of its past. At this point, as if by magic, ELACC signed an agreement to purchase the hotel, committing to the preservation of the building's historic character and to its maintenance as a low-income residential hotel for the mariachis. We gave ELACC access to our archives, and they were able to use our material to raise the money to repair the hotel while maintaining its cultural integrity. Eventually, more than $25 million completed both the work and the cause.

Around the same time, Cathy explored the possibility of a web domain; after discovering that mariachiplazalosangeles.com was available, she grabbed it. We began sharing our work there, although it was our intention to eventually hand off the domain to the mariachis.

One of our LA trips coincided with the celebration of Cinco de Mayo, normally a time when hundreds of musicians find work. We did run into a few who hadn't, which they blamed on a shortage of trumpets. We were also there on the plaza in November during the feast day of Santa Cecelia, the patron saint of musicians.

That first year we attended the public concert at the plaza put on by the city of Los Angeles, although we realized this aspect of the work would not be complete until we returned a year later to photograph the mariachi celebration with a Catholic mass and a huge procession around Boyle Heights. It was quite an experience to see over four hundred musicians playing at once as they paraded through the neighborhood. I made two short videos and a satisfying number of dramatic images with 35mm film cameras and a panoramic camera.

We realized that the importance of the music was central to the project; at this point, I asked my University of New Mexico colleague Dr. Enrique Lamadrid, a well-known folklorist with whom I've worked for over thirty years and who taught at the American Folklife Center (AFC) field schools in Colorado, to join us. Enrique provided the project with a framework to examine the importance of Los Angeles in the history of mariachi music and the surrounding community. With Enrique on board, we decided we now had the raw material for a book.

The decision to publish involves analyzing the best way to frame a story about a particular community and culture. Evangeline Ordaz-Molina, one of the founders of ELACC and an instrumental figure in saving the hotel, provided the introduction to the book and summarized the issues in her essay. Because of Cathy's family connections, we decided her personal story linked with the history would be the first chapter and Enrique's research on the role of Los Angeles in the preservation of the city's mariachi music and culture would be the second. Emphasizing the contributions of women to the historical art form was also an important consideration. A statue of Lucha Reyes, a popular singer during the 1930s and 1940s, stands just south of the hotel in the center of the plaza and offers recognition and encouragement to the new generation of mariachi musicians who pass through the plaza.

In addition to the book, we produced a CD of music recorded during the mass and the feast day. There is an oral history and photographic archive, and we have done several exhibitions that included the photographs, audio, and video. For me, the most exciting of these was in Boyle Heights, where a group from the Mariachi Union performed at the opening and closing of the exhibit. Fortuitously, the Mariachi Union and ELACC were able to get a donation to purchase the exhibit, and it will soon become a permanent exhibit in the Mariachi Culture Center, which now includes new low-income housing being built by ELACC on the only open piece of land left on the plaza. This project shows the potential to be found in a good work. I hope our images and hard work contributed to the saving of the Mariachi Hotel and the creation of low-income housing in Boyle Heights.

Community Organizing: Jacqueline L. McGrath

Jacqueline L. McGrath earned her PhD in English at the University of Missouri and is Professor in the English Department at the College of DuPage.

When I was a kid, my dad was a teacher in the Chicago Public Schools. If you know anything about the Chicago Teachers Union, you know we went on strike, as a family, at regular intervals throughout the 1970s and 1980s. At eight years old, I was already a veteran of several strikes, so I knew the routine. My dad drove to school to walk the picket line each day and returned home to work on his draft of the great American novel while we waited for the school board to come to their senses and settle.

A few days into one strike, my dad took my older brother and me to the picket line on a cold January morning. We bundled up in our snowsuits with mittens on strings, scarves tied around our faces, and feet wrapped first in plastic grocery bags to stay dry and insulated, followed by a layer of wool socks and boots. The final accessory was a sign duct-taped to my chest and back: "Please Pay My Daddy So I Can Eat." We drove to his school building on the southeast side of the city, parked, and walked the picket line with other families for what felt like hours. Then we stopped by the strike office to check in and ended with a single White Castle hot chocolate, split three ways. My dad made the experience fun, so we didn't feel scared. And we knew it was the right thing to do—for the students and for the city.

As a family, we took certain things for granted: You walked the picket line for a strike. You wrote letters to the editor. You spoke up when a family member or friend used a racist slur. You fought back when the bullies jumped you on the way home from school. You cared about fairness and justice and using your voice to fight for those values. We knew being an activist meant showing up in some form as individuals. But we also understood that building power meant doing it within a community: becoming part of a coalition, showing up with a group, and leveraging its collective voice and power to move the dial. Maybe growing up in a union family makes that the most obvious truth in the world.

So showing up with a group was as natural to me as breathing as I made my way through school. In high school, I volunteered to campaign with classmates for the school referendum before I could vote. In college, I rallied with classmates for racial unity and against the campus bookstore's sale of products that relied on sweatshop labor, and I was often part of the committee organizing it all. In graduate school, I participated in teach-ins about the Iraq War, and I tried to organize a graduate student labor union.

But "other people do more," I said, when my professors praised my efforts. I demurred because I wasn't doing anything special when I started holding meetings with graduate teaching assistants at my large land-grant Midwestern university in the early 2000s. I'd met union organizers and labor rights activists before, and I knew that holding meetings here and there in basements and bars over a period of several years didn't really count, especially because our work teaching undergraduate students and working in campus office buildings editing journals or tutoring during summer programs wasn't oppressive. After all, as I often joked, we weren't keeling over at our desks from work-induced heart attacks. I'd read folklorist Archie Green's *Torching the Fink Books and Other Essays on Vernacular Culture,* and I knew the story of Joe Hill; our labor injustices were material but minor compared to the fights that came before.

Throughout graduate school I kept showing up as I learned to be a professional folklorist and conducted fieldwork. I started to understand how the skills I'd gained from organizing and campaigning and protesting might apply to work in the field. I'd learned to watch an audience react during a speech—nodding agreement or calling out a response—rather than focusing only on the stage. I'd learned to listen for stories and sayings so I could tell them, too. I'd learned to befriend true believers so I would be included if not always welcomed. And I'd learned to fit into a living room or a kitchen or a car ride or a church pew, to be an observer rather than in the spotlight. It turns out being an organizer and activist is good practice for being a folklorist in the field, and vice versa, in all the ways that can't be taught in a methods class.

So no one was surprised when I decided to focus my dissertation research on the narratives and beliefs of a Catholic Worker community (a charity and justice movement founded by Dorothy Day in the 1930s) in the college town where I lived. I spent time with them in shelters and after-school programs, and I interviewed people whose beliefs compelled them to act for fairness, justice, and the Golden Rule. I was not a true believer, and I never joined the community myself, but I had sympathy, empathy, and enough skill by then to make it work. I learned a lot from these passionate people about how to proselytize effectively, what makes a good protest performance (effigies and mock funeral processions, for example, are tremendous visual aids), and how to conduct yourself with dignity while being arrested: valuable skills I tucked away in my memory for when I might need them myself.

In my professional life today, I serve as a leader on many boards and committees, and my default mode is to deploy my community-organizing tools to see just about any project through. For example, in 2005, I worked with fellow AFS Folklore and Social Justice Section members Sue Eleuterio and Bill

Westerman to program a series of panels on folklore and the Iraq War at the annual conference of the American Folklore Society in Milwaukee, Wisconsin. It seemed necessary to highlight—and pay a small stipend to—Iraqi oud artist Rahim AlHaj and Iraqi novelist and refugee Mahmoud Saeed. Both men were keen to explain their art for an audience of scholars, and I enjoyed watching AlHaj challenge individuals with advanced degrees to name all the countries with oud traditions. We could not do it. If any audience could, you'd think it would be folklorists, but we missed a few. He admonished the crowd and educated us, a small act of cultural assertion. Another panel featured recent Iraq War documentaries, and in the discussion afterward, I marveled at the responses from fellow folklorists: "I didn't know it was like that," someone at the panel said after we watched a documentary filmed in 2004 in the aftermath of the US invasion. Creating dialogue within a community of scholars may not be a radical act of resistance, but it meant something at the time. Later, some members (including me) urged the AFS Executive Board to make a statement against the Iraq War. Moving the dial, organizing support, one step at a time.

In my own community, I sometimes work with an Industrial Areas Foundation (IAF) group. It is, as community activist Saul Alinsky wanted it to be, "an organization of organizations," and its tactics combine fieldwork and community organizing. In my capacity as a unionist and an English professor, I have helped research several community issues: financial concerns about the Forest Preserve District, the need for noncredit English as a second language classes at our community college, and the ways municipal police departments in our region work with individuals suffering mental health crises. The IAF model is to get the facts, get leaders on the record, and hold them accountable for what they say. It sounds so simple.

So how is a folklorist a community activist? Well, you show up. You show up, in your community, and you don't have to lead the picket line or organize the meeting, although sometimes you do because you know how. You watch, listen, and learn the idioms. You volunteer your technical skills for the cause, whether that's recording an event or editing a press release or fact-checking the talking points or creating the questions for the community forum. And then you listen to the stories. You learn them. You learn the patterns to them and the values expressed in them, and you serve as part of the audience for them. We are born into some of our communities and choose others; as folklorists, we also observe them. The reality is it's just a hop, skip, and a jump from there to playing a role in organizing them. I could never accept the notion that folklorists should observe but not participate because of ethical or scientific concerns. If you're not with them, why are you there at all?

CONNECTING UNIVERSITY AND COMMUNITY:
KATHERINE BORLAND

Katherine Borland earned her PhD in folklore at Indiana University and is Associate Professor of Comparative Studies and Director of the Center for Folklore Studies at The Ohio State University.

My early career experience outside a university setting profoundly shaped my perspective on university-community engagement. In April of 1994, with a newly minted folklore PhD from Indiana University, I cast around for work, and in May, I landed an interview for a position as the executive director of Delaware Futures, a fledgling college-access program in Wilmington. During my interview, I somewhat naively explained to the hiring committee that my ethnographic training made me an ideal candidate to build the program. One member immediately demanded that I define this method called ethnography. I launched into an explanation of the importance of cultural context, learning from the people we wanted to "serve" with our program, and identifying our target audience as not just the teens but their parents and neighbors and teachers. I talked about the importance of meeting people in their own spaces, interviewing kids at their homes, visiting teachers at their schools, and hanging out at partner organizations' community centers and events, rather than sitting in the office waiting for people to find you. I pitched the idea that Delaware Futures, which at that moment consisted of a room with a desk, a committee, and a start-up grant sufficient to hire an executive director, should understand itself as part of a larger web of people and programs working to provide opportunities to underserved youth in order to build a more equitable society. With their help, its ethnographer–executive director would learn about and contribute to that web.

The pitch worked: I got the job. Within two months I had recruited my first class of eleven rising eighth graders and convinced their parents to let me take them on a five-day wilderness trip. (I had never worked with eighth graders or led a wilderness trip, but I was open to learning and lucky, I guess.) Within a year, by leaning on my board and accessing the community web, I had set up the six components of the program: weekly programming for group meetings, paid internships with local businesses, college scholarships for successful graduates, tutoring (by Delta Sigma Theta sorority members), regular one-on-one advising, and summer team-building trips. I had also written and won enough grants to hire an adviser—the incredible Stan Mifflin, whose good humor allowed us to weather all setbacks—who immediately set to work recruiting a second class of rising eighth graders. By the time

I left Delaware Futures in 1998, my staff had grown to two full-time advisers and an AmeriCorps volunteer serving fifty students. Today, Delaware Futures remains a vital Wilmington program that has helped produce close to three hundred first-generation college graduates.

In 1999, I joined the faculty of a regional campus of The Ohio State University and began the teaching, research, and service necessary to achieve tenure. But my years dedicated to constructing educational experiences rooted in the world carried over into my college classes. Soon I was folding Paolo Freire, Wangari Maathai, and Elías Sanchez into my syllabi and developing OSU's first international service-learning experience, a class I taught every other year from 2002 to 2013. This course took students, many of whom had never left Ohio, to communities in Nicaragua to learn about grassroots development efforts and obstacles. It also gave students a direct experience of global inequities that we interpreted through the lens of politics and policy.

Shortly after receiving tenure, I wrote my own job description and became the first assistant dean of the Newark campus, responsible for building educational enrichment (honors, service learning, and study abroad) and university-community engagements. In this way I moved from creating what are now called high-impact educational experiences to mentoring and encouraging other faculty to construct these courses. Additionally, in partnership with Central Ohio Technical College and Denison University, I embarked on a university-community initiative to strengthen our local all-volunteer college-access program, A Call to College, by building a program promoting early college awareness targeted at middle school students. Like my earlier work at Delaware Futures, this project required collaborative visioning, grant writing and reporting, program building, and, most important, hiring and training the staff to execute the plan and providing them with the ongoing support and development they needed to sustain it.

When I moved to Ohio State's main Columbus campus and transitioned back to faculty in 2011, I continued to build my own practice-based course offerings, serve on review committees for service-learning courses, and explore collaborative opportunities for university-community engagement. In 2014, for example, when I became the director of the Center for Folklore Studies (CFS), I designed my ethnographic methods class to contribute directly to the center's folklore archives by constructing a team-based research project. My students and I digitized the collections of a local grassroots solidarity group that had been active in the 1980s and interviewed its members about their memories of that work. Shortly after, an opportunity arose to imagine a new direction for the archive when the Center for Folklore Studies was awarded $100,000 from an anonymous donor to establish the Ohio Field School, a multiyear collaborative ethnography project in Appalachian Ohio. This initiative allowed us to adapt our team-based methods course to the needs and aspirations of community partners, who function as our teachers and advisers in the ongoing work. Once again, through grant writing, hiring, and training, we are working to concretize the engagement in a way that allows new hands and minds to take up the work as the initiators—the assistant director of CFS, Cassie Patterson, and I—move on to other projects.

Another recent community-engagement initiative, Be the Street, works to train students to facilitate improvisation with community groups, on the one hand, and to build performance ensembles among residents of the Hilltop neighborhood of Columbus, Ohio, on the other. Residents learn and practice a variety of techniques to craft their own stories of place and place making against the prevalent outsider depictions of decay and decline. Exciting as this work has been, over the past three years, our university team has shrunk by attrition to two, making the work as it is currently constituted unsustainable. As a consequence, I am currently working with the project's artistic director, Moriah Flagler, to develop an ethical exit strategy, which will involve transitioning leadership and training from university students and faculty to community partners. We are fortunate that two enthusiastic community partners have joined our planning team to imagine the form the work might take in an environment of minimal financial resources. In fact, as our planning meetings have moved out of university conference rooms and into the coffee shops our partners use as their offices, the negative connotation of "exiting" has yielded to a richer experience of collaboration and community grounding.

I would be remiss if I didn't point out that university-community engagements have received well-deserved criticism due to the unequal distribution of benefits, despite good intentions on both sides. I am also acutely aware of the ways university structures often prevent the sort of exploratory research necessary for truly collaborative project planning, forcing faculty teams to pitch an already-developed idea or program to their potential partners. And yet, if we stick with our partners, over time we can address that imbalance and shape our work to more closely address community-defined goals. My training as a folklorist has allowed me, I think, to at least recognize what communities are already doing, value community expertise, and listen for the places where university resources and expertise might further their projects. At the very least, as ethnographers and university partners, we aspire to be appreciative learners and documenters of community-based creativity and problem-solving. Understanding cultural contexts remains an important foundation for building anything new. And building with an eye toward extracting oneself eventually from the process mitigates the formation of fiefdoms and dependencies, allowing university-community engagements to evolve as processes that grow and change over time.

Exploring Home: Langston Collin Wilkins

Langston Collin Wilkins earned his PhD in folklore at Indiana University and is Director of the Center for Washington Cultural Traditions.

In the world of folklore studies, whether public or academic, some could argue that my focus has been narrow in scope. Many folklorists spend their careers exploring various spaces that are disparate in nature and far from "the familiar." "Outsider" is a preferred standpoint, and it generates a supposed objectiveness to the work. I am not here to quarrel with that. But my career has taken a different trajectory up to this point. The majority of my work has been focused on a single locality: Houston, Texas—the city that raised me for eighteen years and that I consider to be my hometown.

To be more precise, I've been researching the traditions and heritage of what I call "Black Houston": the practices, traditions, and general way of life of African Americans in the city. Historically, the majority of Houston's Black population has lived in two areas: a group of neighborhoods north of downtown that locals call the Northside and a similar interconnected group south of downtown called the Southside. Both these areas have housed African Americans across several generations and have been the sites of rich cultural activity. Local styles of gospel, jazz, blues, and hip-hop were born there and have gone on to have international impacts. Strong pockets of Louisiana Creoles have developed a unique Black Catholic tradition in the area and generated an indelible part of the city's foodways. It is a community where you will see a young Black guy in a souped-up Cadillac and a young woman on horseback travel the streets together. The slow and muddy rumble of local hip-hop music provides a fitting soundtrack for both.

My journey as a folklorist has been haphazard. I entered Indiana University in the fall of 2006 with a singular focus on studying hip-hop culture. I had no idea of the particular aspect of hip-hop I wanted to examine or the particular region where I wanted to work—especially important since hip-hop is so rooted in place. At some point, however, I began to feel a pull to explore home—specifically the hip-hop culture of Houston's Black neighborhoods. It could have been a bit of homesickness, or it could have been a need to explore the self. No matter the reason, I ended up moving back to my parents' house and made the Southside of Houston my "field."

I have now spent several years researching, writing about, and publicly celebrating Black Houston, mostly through the lens of hip-hop culture. My doctoral dissertation and eventual book examine the ways attachments to neighborhood, and a sense of local heritage, inform music making among local hip-hop artists. My study showed the ways Houston's social history and contemporary communal life has produced a strong pride of place among Black residents and how this pride of place has led to the establishment of a distinctly local hip-hop style and identity. As an ethnographic work, the study was based on information gained from living in the Southside, attending events, building relationships with artists, and also interviewing them, as well as thorough historical and archival research.

Slab culture has been the true hallmark of my community research. Slabs are vernacular cars created by modifying older model American luxury cars by adding enhanced stereo systems, explosive wet-looking paint jobs, chrome front grills and bumpers, and cone-shaped rims called *swangas* that can extend up to two feet from the car. Slabs and their surrounding culture were born in Houston's Black neighborhoods in the early 1980s. There are also subpractices attached to slab traditions—most namely swangin', a form of competitive play. While some like to associate slab with vernacular car cultures in other American regions, it is a distinctly Houston-based practice. It first emerged within the illegal drug underworld of the 1980s but moved away from that and has been closely associated with the local hip-hop scene since the 1990s. In terms of my work, slab began as a subset of my larger dissertation study on the local hip-hop scene. However, I quickly realized that the culture was worthy of a more focused examination, and my slab work soon occupied a distinct space within my research. In 2013, I worked with several local institutions to organize the Houston Slab Parade and Family Festival, an event that celebrated slab and the larger hip-hop culture of the city. Held in the heart of the Southside, the event featured a parade, a car show, music performances, and more. A truly diverse crowd of over forty thousand came to celebrate this unique and underappreciated local tradition.

The slab parade bore fruits I could never have imagined. It immediately helped reposition slab and hip-hop cultures within the Houston cultural landscape. Almost overnight, slab went from being a deeply insular practice to one of the most recognizable parts of city heritage, both within and outside the city. Several mayors have cruised in slabs during the city's historic Art Car Parade. It has been featured in national publications and broadcast on the Travel Channel and CNN and is even depicted on a Nike T-shirt in honor of Houston. (See, for instance, the *Business Insider* article "The history behind 'slabs,' the custom cars with an important place in Houston's hip-hop community.")

My work with slab cultures reflects a community researcher's multiple modes of engagement. We can play several different roles within a community and for a tradition. At the most foundational level, I was a researcher, and the genesis of the slab parade was rooted in my research. As I learned more about the tradition through observation and interviews, I felt a strong need to help bring it more visibility, and a parade was the most compelling option. Second, I was an organizer and convener, the middleman between many disparate groups: the slab community, the arts and heritage sector, and the general public. But the slab parade was not an easy sell to the wider Houston public: remember, the tradition was born within street culture and is commonly associated with criminal activity. Many residents felt it was not worth celebrating at the very least or was a dangerous endeavor at most. In response, I became a slab ambassador of sorts by helping spread awareness and understanding through lectures, panels, and meetings with city officials. Finally, in the wake of the slab parade, I have moved more firmly into the roles of historian and documentarian.

My work as a community researcher has been to highlight the complex nature and cultural vibrancy of my home community, which has faced multiple forces of marginalization. Houston's Black residents have dealt with punishing racism, segregation, and economic oppression. Despite this, we have managed to be resilient and have created practices that have affirmed, sustained, and progressed us. This is the beautiful culture that raised me. Unfortunately, systemic oppression can blind such communities to the depths and power of their culture. In this light, I am absolutely proud of my research into Black Houston, which I believe has helped the community discover, celebrate, and cultivate its heritage. Folklore training has given me (and the other folklorists doing similar work in communities all over the United States) the understanding and skills to pursue this opportunity to affirm a remarkably irrepressible community. It is incredibly fulfilling and impactful work.

Advocating for Labor: James P. Leary

James P. Leary earned his PhD in folklore at Indiana University and is affiliated with the Center for the Study of Upper Midwestern Cultures at the University of Wisconsin–Madison, where he is an emeritus professor of folklore and Scandinavian studies.

My efforts as a folklorist advocating for labor are diffuse and sporadic yet rooted and persistent. The second of seven children, I grew up on two rural acres in northwestern Wisconsin. My older brother and I handled conventional outdoor seasonal jobs: shoveling snow, cultivating gardens, cutting grass, and raking leaves. I also helped with weekly domestic chores: folding laundry, grocery shopping, scrubbing floors, cleaning bathrooms, and occasionally changing diapers. Around 1964, when a high school pal derided the latter tasks as "woman's work," I was startled briefly before countering with my mother's imparted wisdom: "Any work that needs doing has dignity and worth." As I write this essay amid the COVID-19 pandemic, I expect that many share my mom's appreciation of "essential" yet low-status work, but that teenage recognition of and opposition to gender and class biases undergirding hierarchical conceptions of toil and toilers was an "aha" moment for me.

Another came in the summer of 1970, following my sophomore year in college. Working at the Blue Hills Foundry, I led the queue for our weekly "pour": transferring fiery liquid steel into molds that, once cooled, yielded cast sewer steps and barn stanchion plates. It was thirty years before Aziz and Chandra published "Impact, Recoil, and Splashing of Molten Metal Droplets" in the *International Journal of Heat Mass Transfer*, yet I knew through veterans in the trade that our mud-lined hand ladles should have been warmed. A fellow summer worker unfortunately forgot this critical task. When our foreman pulled the drop-bottom cupola furnace's tap-hole plug, molten metal spewed down the spout, bouncing off my cold ladle's bottom to settle in a splat, searing and sealing my right eyelid. My left eye also closed, watering sympathetically. An unexpectedly blinded undergraduate English major who had just discovered the field of folklore, I wondered for several anxious days if or when I would be able to see and, especially, read again. (I would.)

My summer lunch-hour reading—Woody Guthrie's *Bound for Glory*, Samuel Charters's *The Country Blues*, liner notes for *Folk Music from Wisconsin*—took on new meanings. Striking images, fervent dreams, and exuberant and fraught realities suffusing folk/roots sayings, stories, songs, and tunes by seasonal harvest hands, itinerant musicians, and lumberjacks all suddenly, vividly, viscerally conjoined with my own experiences. I realized that foundry labor—like my other summer and part-time menial yet necessary jobs: haymaking, bark peeling, press tending and collating sections for a weekly newspaper's print run, processing warehouse stock, and janitorial cleaning—not only offered invaluable short courses in the school of hard knocks but also united culturally diverse folks along class lines.

My fellow foundry workers, for example, were of mixed English, Irish, German, Czech, Polish, and Swedish heritage. Acknowledged and sometimes figuring in playful joking, our differences were diminished on the shop floor by a common purpose; by insider knowledge, terminology, and technology;

by workplace rhythms, teamwork, successes, and dangers; by memorialization in symbols, objects, songs, and stories; and by intrinsic contributions to a full understanding of the human experience. I came to recognize that my jobs and those of all workers merited documentation, appreciation, and advocacy.

This recognition deepened in 1976 throughout the Smithsonian Institution's twelve-week bicentennial Festival of American Folklife. Hired by the Working Americans program—launched by visionary folklorist, union carpenter, shipwright, and labor-lore champion Archie Green—I apprenticed with veteran occupational folklorists Bob Byington and Bob McCarl. Sometimes aided by organized labor, I helped conduct field research across a broad span of occupations, plan public programming in cooperation with participants, and produce two-week festival segments featuring skills demonstrations and narrative sessions focused on Workers Who Build, Workers Who Feed Us, Workers Who Clothe Us, Health Care and Service Workers, Workers in the Arts, and more. Ever since, I've striven to expand my understanding of the lives, lore, and worth of workers and advocate for greater public awareness by adapting strategically to shifting contexts.

Some advocacy has been embedded in ongoing professional activities. As a scholar, I've published and edited essays, special issues of journals, and books illuminating workers' stories and songs. As a teacher, I've devoted units, assignments, and entire courses to occupational folklore/laborlore. As a public folklorist engaged with the documentation and creation of media productions, events, and exhibits, I've included erstwhile employment information in biographies of traditional artisans, musicians, and raconteurs. Far from existing in romanticized folk communities, most made gritty livings like the musicians with whom I collaborated on a double LP/booklet, *Accordions in the Cutover* (1984): farmer, commercial fisher, trapper, logger, miner, ore puncher, cat skinner (heavy equipment operator), carpenter, factory hand, teacher, librarian, house cleaner, clerk, secretary, bartender, hairdresser, and more. Sometimes occupations have intertwined with folk artistry, as exemplified by Carl Vogt, a former threshing crew hand who, as a machinist and cabinetmaker, made farm machinery miniatures on the side; Inga Hermansen, a Danish immigrant cross-stitch embroiderer and seamstress who ran a drapery business; Xao Yang Lee, whose facility with Hmong needlework aided second-shift handwork for a woolen mill; and Potawatomi cradleboard fashioner Ned Daniels, successively a logger and a welder in the ironworkers union.

Regularly crediting labor's implicit presence in projects with other emphases, I've also practiced explicit advocacy. I joined and presently maintain retiree membership in the American Federation of Teachers, as well as in the Industrial Workers of the World, whose direct-action tactics I'd learned the hard way. In 1986 Janet Gilmore and I were independent folklorists conducting a yearlong state folk arts survey for a nonprofit organization that insisted on paying us for piecework rather than at a daily rate, set an impossibly high monthly quota for artists documented, and vastly underestimated the time required to discover, contact, visit, interview and photograph, create archival records for, and write a report about each artist. When friendly persuasion failed, we went on a two-person strike that won fair working conditions. In the aftermath, assisted by other independent folklorists, I drafted a policy, "Professional Standards and Rights for Contract Folklorists," for the American Folklore Society's State of the Profession Committee. Published in the *AFS Newsletter* and website and in *Folk Arts Programming in New York State: A Handbook and Resource Guide* (1990), it contributed to improved conditions for independent folklorists.

Like a handful of other folklorists, I've embraced periodic chances to work directly with union members. Recruited in 1978 for a folklore field survey on Minnesota's Iron Range, I partnered with members of Steelworkers Local 1938 to document the lives and laborlore of underground and open-pit iron ore miners. My aforementioned fieldwork with Ned Daniels, done in 1994 for exhibits on Woodland Indian traditional artists, figured in a Wisconsin Workers Memorial in Milwaukee's Zeidler Park, sponsored by the state AFL-CIO, the Milwaukee County Labor Council, and the Wisconsin Labor History Society. As a consultant, I assisted with images and quotations for a series of plaques, one of which featured Ned's experience with fellow indigenous ironworkers: "I worked with Chippewa, Menominee, Winnebago [Ho-Chunk]. They were good welders too. Structural steel. I roomed with [Wisconsin Ho-Chunk ironworker] Robert Funmaker. Every morning we'd sing a religious song from the Grand Medicine Lodge."

An eventual faculty position at University of Wisconsin–Madison furthered collective efforts with union members, immigrant and workers' rights activists, public folklorists, and academicians. In 2004, heeding Archie Green's call, I joined union members, artists, scholars, and documentarians in Oakland, California's Pile Drivers Hall for the first Laborlore Conversation. Five years later, at Archie's request, I organized the sixth Laborlore Conversation, which occurred in Chicago two months after his death as a joint event with the Labor and Working-Class History Association. Similar town/gown and labor/scholar coalitions emerged in Madison, where I was fortunate to assist first-generation and low-income members of the nation's first Working Class Student Union in creating a "cultural showcase" modeled after folklife festivals; to produce a film, *The Art of Ironworking*, with members of Ironworkers Local 383 that has had more than 190,000 YouTube views; to help organize and participate in *Fighting Forward 2013: A Labor and Working Class Summit*, in cooperation with the Working-Class Studies Association and UW's School for Workers; to recruit members of the building trades for presentations accompanying an exhibit, *Wisconsin Labor: A Contemporary Portrait*, held in the Madison cultural center they had built; and to offer presentations to public libraries statewide on "What Folksongs Tell Us about Work, Class, and Cultures in Wisconsin" as part of the Wisconsin Humanities Council's labor-oriented ShopTalk initiative.

As a longtime member of the American Folklore Society, including two stints on the AFS Executive Board, I was also lucky to join with many others in amending our "Criteria for Selecting Annual Meeting Sites" to prioritize conferences "in hotels whose labor force is unionized." Staunch commitment by AFS leadership to that tenet was crucial in October 2019 when the largely minority membership of UNITE HERE's Local 7 won their "One Job Should Be Enough" strike with our conference hotel for better pay and working conditions.

We folklorists, after all, are fellow workers alongside the people whose artistic cultural traditions compel us. Just as an injury to one is an injury to all, our advocacy for labor is advocacy for our collective worth as human beings.

ADVOCATING FOR PEOPLE WITH DISABILITIES: AMY SHUMAN

Amy Shuman earned her PhD in folklore and folklife at the University of Pennsylvania and is Professor in the Department of English at The Ohio State University.

A central focus of my folklore scholarship has been questions concerning who claims the right to tell stories about what to whom. This concern intensified when I became a disability rights advocate. I began as an advocate for my son, now thirty-three, who has intellectual disabilities that include difficulty speaking. Often he spells out long words to be understood, and often it's hard to tell whether he's talking about something that happened several years ago or yesterday. His sense of relevance is different than others might expect, so sometimes I'm a translator. I'm constantly put in the position of speaking for him, as his advocate, but I resist that assignment as much as possible and instead work for social change so my son and others with disabilities can be their own self-advocates. His stories are not mine to tell without his permission, and even then, my goal is to create conditions in which he can be heard. Better listening is good but never sufficient in the face of power differentials and injustices that prevent some people from speaking at all. Questions of who can speak, who speaks for whom, and about what invite us to address those injustices.

The disability rights movement slogan, "Nothing about us without us," is about the importance of people with disabilities making decisions about their own lives. People with disabilities are often spoken for, even when they are present. This concern serves as a useful caution for any discussion of folklore and advocacy. Folklore methodologies can help us understand the complexity of our obligations when we do speak on behalf of others, especially as culture brokers, and can keep us attentive to the potential dangers of exploitation when we venerate others, often with the idea of helping them.

Venerating others can be dangerous territory for disability rights. People with disabilities are accustomed to being celebrated for overcoming obstacles, often in charitable campaigns in which they are praised as inspirational. Disability rights advocates refer to this as inspiration porn. Inspirational accounts often make ordinary actions seem exceptional; in the crudest terms, they categorize people as less able or even tragic and then recognize their accomplishments through a lens of pity and stigma. These practices of humiliation in the name of inspiration are objectifying and exploitive. Many, if not most, examples of inspiration porn look like harmless celebrations of someone with disabilities receiving momentary acceptance and acclaim: the high school student with Down syndrome is elected prom queen or king or the ball boy suits up at a basketball game as both teams silently conspire to give him the ball repeatedly as he shoots until he makes a basket and the crowd cheers. Olivia Caldeira discussed how these inspirational practices work in her essay in the book *Diagnosing Folklore*.

My son wants to participate in everyday life as an ordinary person, not as a spectacle, and my work as an advocate is also nothing special; it's a daily practice, and at the same time, social change requires constant vigilance and extraordinary measures. As an ally, I am mindful of the pitfalls of speaking on behalf of others, promoting inspirational narratives, and participating in other forms of exploitation as I advocate for people with disabilities. "Nothing about me without me" guides my work, but at the same time, I find speaking on behalf of others and engaging in celebratory events and narratives to be unavoidable. In this essay, I outline some of the problems I've faced, without suggesting that I've surmounted them.

Like those in other activist movements, disability rights activists *do* venerate, celebrate, and find inspiration from others with disabilities.

Representations by people with disabilities, designed to promote and sustain coalitions, are necessary to social justice movements and, as statements made by insiders, do not objectify people by pointing to their exceptionality.

As a folklorist, I am similarly aware of exploitation, a concern to many folklorist advocates. But advocacy for disability falls through different cracks than calling attention to endangered spaces or addressing racial or other social injustices, as Debora Kodish describes in her American Folklore Society keynote address on folklore and activism published in the *Journal of American Folklore*. As important as the discussion has been, it fails to recognize ableism as a social injustice. Ableism (discrimination in favor of able-bodied people), a concept often disguised in terms like *competence* or *normal*, is pervasive in the field of folklore. In my work as a folklorist and an advocate, I've found the most productive intersection between disability and folklore to be the critique of the celebratory. Barbara Kirshenblatt-Gimblett's *Journal of American Folklore* essay "Mistaken Dichotomies," for example, refers to "the emancipatory potential of folklore as praxis, that is, how what we do as folklorists can be of socially redeeming value in ways that go beyond celebration." In folklore, the celebratory is recognized as part of the romantic legacy of the field; in disability discourses, the celebratory invokes the inspirational, a discussion that includes the critique of ableism. In my work, I've found that the core of both critiques is the recognition of what counts as value, as added value, as diminished value, and for whom: the celebratory is not always value-added.

As I write this, I'm in the process of creating a support group of people with intellectual disabilities and their families and care workers to advocate for postsecondary education programs leading to community employment. Building on a successful postsecondary program at The Ohio State University that I helped develop, the project brings together a variety of organizations and professionals who control the limited available resources; they control resources in part by restricting access to not only who can speak but who has command of their technical language.

Advocacy is a speaking-for situation, and even though it is necessary when, for whatever reason, people can't or don't speak for themselves, it requires attention to the political and social circumstances that constrain full participation—what some disability rights activists and advocates refer to as self-advocacy. My son's disabilities often create obstacles to his self-advocacy; at the same time, he understands the concept of self-advocacy and asserts his positions, opinions, and desires.

Many folklorists have consistently and cogently argued that advocacy is not a choice but a necessity. In his 2000 *Journal of American Folklore* essay, "I'm a Folklorist and You're Not," Steve Zeitlin argues that advocacy is central to the definition of folklore, especially through recognition of under-valued cultural expressions. Several folklorists, including Robert Baron in the *International Journal of Heritage Studies* and William Westerman in the *Journal of American Folklore*, have written about the relationship of research to advocacy, the history and significance of earlier work, and the ways the field might reconsider its responsibilities. Disability advocacy requires what Bernice Johnson Reagon described as "coalition politics," not only, as she so forcefully argues, because accomplishing social change requires getting out of our exclusive spaces where we meet only people who have shared identities and goals but also because, for people with disabilities, exclusion itself—lack of access—is the problem. Being disabled is a social construction defined by lack of access, not by biological diagnosis. Disability advocacy as coalition politics obligates us to ask about the assumptions we make about what counts as normal and how we stigmatize others as other, whether in terms of cognition, mobility, mental health, communication, or other abilities.

Folklorists serve as advocates whenever we offer the tools of our field to others to further their endeavors. I regard my position as an advocate primarily as an ally, recognizing that my role is secondary to members of the community who set their own agendas. Folklore methods can be useful for serving social justice or enhancing awareness about cultural practices. At the same time, as Susan Ritchie noted in 1993 in the pages of *Western Folklore*, "We need to be aware that enhancing awareness doesn't necessarily lead to social change."

Advocating for Poetry: Steve Zeitlin

Steve Zeitlin earned his PhD in folklore and folklife at the University of Pennsylvania and is the founding director of City Lore in New York City.

From an early age, I was aware of the beauty and power of stories, jokes, and humor in my own life, although I didn't yet know to call it folklore. As expats living in São Paulo in relative isolation, my two brothers and I grew up close. We developed our own private language and humor and, as one person put it, "refined our communication into a work of art." Once, when we lived on the first floor of a fifteen-story apartment building, Murray was passing out Chiclets, and rather than taking one, I took five. Murray responded by asking, "Why don't you just jump out the fifteenth-story window for a breeze on a hot day?" Ever since then, when I overdo anything, my brother calls it "jumping out the fifteenth-story window for a breeze on a hot day." I knew, even back then, that this artful banter was at the heart of life.

Years later, when I was studying Old English poetry in the library at the University of Pennsylvania, I took a break from my graduate studies and wandered aimlessly through the stacks. I chanced upon a few books by folklorist Benjamin Botkin, who had worked for the New Deal–era WPA Federal Writers' Project. I opened one of Botkin's books to a random page and can still recall the children's rhyme I read there: "I should worry / I should care / I should marry a millionaire / He should die / I should cry / I should marry another guy." This is the job for me, I thought: listening to people's stories, rhymes, and what Botkin called "folksay." Soon after this encounter, I discovered that the University of Pennsylvania had a Department of Folklore and Folklife. I arranged for an interview with the department chair, Dr. Kenneth S. Goldstein, who explained to me that folklore studies is a religion and folklorists are its missionaries. I promptly reported for duty.

Even before I began to study folklore, I loved writing and reading poetry, and many stories and colloquial phrases that I heard as a folklorist became inspirations for my poems. For my course called Writing New York Stories, which I taught for more than ten years at Cooper Union, I had everyone in my class write a "list poem" in which each line began "I am from . . ." The poem that spawned this wonderful assignment is by Kentucky-born poet and children's book writer George Ella Lyon. "I am from clothespins, from Clorox and carbontetrachloride," she writes, a detail that stemmed from her family's occupation of running a dry cleaners in Harlan, Kentucky. In their poems the students conveyed details of their lives. Alicia Vasquez wrote, "I am from ducking bullets by the bedroom window with Mom in 1974 where a tree grows in Crown Heights, Brooklyn / I am from controlling the flow of fire hydrant water through a can of Chef Boyardee while dreaming of swimming in a real pool one day." A teacher who worked with my wife, Amanda, in Louisiana described her rural experience: "I am from the death scent of wild rabbit, dove, and quail in my father's hunting vest." These poems, which ordinarily would not be considered folklore, served as a link between folklore and creative writing, between collecting stories and sharing one's own. I believe this convergence of poetry and folklore, this union of personal and cultural perspectives, gives birth to something new: a new way of seeing ourselves and a new way of being in the world.

My interests in creative writing and folklore come together around listening. Among the highest compliments I've received was from my friend Marc Kaminsky, who once described me as "a poetic listener." He described the way a friend, the anthropologist Barbara Myerhoff, listened as "something akin to soul-flight: a period of grace, when she was granted the gift of leaving her own life to travel in another's." Listening deeply is key to the work of both the folklorist and the poet.

In 1997, when the Lila Wallace-Reader's Digest Fund, through the leadership of program director Holly Sidford, promised support for then-emerging folklore nonprofits, I came up with the idea for a People's Poetry Gathering, bringing together my interests in folklore and poetry. A number of organizations were then dedicated to traditional music and arts, but only the Western Folklife Center, which produces the Cowboy Poetry Gathering, focused on folk poetry. Founded by City Lore and Poets House in 1999, the People's Poetry Gathering was a biennial event that brought together folk, literary, community-based, and city poets. During these festivals in 1999, 2001, 2003, and 2006, parts of Lower Manhattan were transformed into a poetry village for three days. (A documentary about the 1999 Gathering is now online.)

The Gathering combined readings with musical performances, including poetry rock concerts by singer-songwriters such as Ani DiFranco, Patti Smith, and U. Utah Phillips; panel discussions; and offbeat happenings, such as a reading of Edgar Allan Poe in the Marble Cemetery at midnight. We highlighted fisherman, farmer, hobo, Jamaican dub, African *djali*, and calypsonian poets, along with traditions of poetry recitation. We brought together blues singers and poets. I remember Sterling Plump's stunning lines of blues poetry recited at the Gathering's convening and still timely today: "I wear dirty clothes / And dodge the cops on the beat / I wear dirty clothes / And dodge the cops on the beat / I'm so poor, people, / My address is in the street."

All told, the Gathering threatened to overwhelm City Lore's tiny staff and never produced the kind of earned revenue that would have been needed to sustain it long-term. So we morphed the program into a series of People's Poetry projects. We collected the poetry inscribed on tattered paper pinned to street memorials after September 11, curated an exhibition at the New York Historical Society, and hosted Poetry Dinners, in which poets and musicians performed in appropriate ethnic restaurants.

When the Rockefeller Foundation put out a call for projects with innovative technologies in 2009, we proposed and were funded for the POEMobile. The POEMobile is a magnificent art truck with brightly painted iron wings arching above its roof and poems in two dozen languages emblazoned on its sides. Jointly sponsored by Bowery Arts + Science and City Lore, the truck projects poems onto walls and buildings in tandem with live readings and musical performances in neighborhoods throughout New York. Specially designed software enables the projected poems in their original language to dissolve into English and vice versa. The community experiences the impact of the poetry in their spoken tongue while the English-speaking visitors and neighbors are able to grasp the life experiences of the foreign-language poets they live among. When the POEMobile drove to Bridgeport, Connecticut, for an arts festival, one woman was moved to tears when she saw a line in Tlingit, her native Alaskan language, inscribed on the truck. She called her mother in Alaska to let her know. A few minutes later, an inebriated visitor saw me in the driver's seat and asked if he could purchase a hot dog.

Another outgrowth of the Gathering is *Khonsay: Poem of Many Tongues*, a documentary film I coproduced with the poet Bob Holman that can now be found online. The piece is a tribute and call to action for linguistic diversity. A fifteen-minute motion poem (poem on film), each line comes from a different treasure or minority language. Forty-eight speakers each speak in their mother tongues as, line by line, language by language, the poem is created. The textual version of the poem was featured at the 2013 Smithsonian Folklife Festival.

My favorite definition of poetry is "an intensification of language," and it is present both in poetic masterpieces and in the poetry of everyday life. In my personal life, I have always been struck by how, as we become more intimate with one another, our conversation shifts from prose toward poetry. As my friend Solomon Reuben, a therapist, puts it, "Heartful sharing becomes artful sharing." We condense our stories into brief phrases that sum up a story and will be recognizable to our friends and family. We begin to use catchwords and allusions, and much of our conversation is laden with these associations. At the same time, our talk becomes increasingly patterned and rhythmic. For me, in the beginning, there truly was, and is still, the word— and human beings are, indeed, *Homo poeticus*.

In our intro to *Khonsay*, we note that half the world's languages will vanish by the end of the century. The issues are political, cultural, and environmental, but they also reverberate through our personal lives. My friend Virginia Randall, a student in my class at Cooper Union, brought it all back home in her writing about the death of her partner, Michael, and the subsequent loss of their private world of expressions and jokes. To capture her sorrow and longing for the private language they shared, she ends her piece: "I'm the last speaker of 'us' now."

Advocating for a Region: Thomas A. McKean

Thomas A. McKean earned his PhD in Scottish studies at the University of Edinburgh and is Director of the Elphinstone Institute at the University of Aberdeen.

A regional folklorist's work is about individuals and place. We join and start conversations and focus on community and individual experience within it to learn something of wider humanity. Some might think of regions as bordered areas delimited by geography, homogeneity, or a distinctive local culture, probably rural, and often paired with terms like *development, identity,* or *needs.* For the folklorist, though, a region is a far more diverse, flexible, and interesting idea: New York City or Singapore can be considered cultural regions just as easily as some stereotypical hinterland.

Folklorists are uniquely placed to resist this human urge to compartmentalize and divide. Bringing grassroots specificity to the table, the regional folklorist can work to ensure that the multiformity of culture is recognized and valued by exploring the diverse strands that together create a region's sense of itself. So, taking a cultural region as our field of work, we can think productively about what a regional folklorist might do.

I am fortunate to work in an institution that combines academic and public folklore. The academic side gives us leeway to explore analytical and theoretical abstractions—ruminations that tell us something about a very specific art form or the wider needs, functions, and mechanisms of culture. Public folklore work is more applied; there, we are active in communities to learn and to facilitate sharing, understanding, and communication. In fact, the two are inextricably linked. Here in the North-East of Scotland, we see a regional folklorist's work in circular terms, with individuals, groups, communities, and academics cross-fertilizing each other. The circle can begin at any one of these points, with partnerships, coproduction of ideas, and research questions emerging from any of the partners. Sociocommunity aims and outcomes are built in from the start, informing the folklorist's duty of advocacy. Thus, a regionalist plays the well-known role of participant-observer across the entire arc of his or her professional life, not just in a fieldwork situation. And this means real action.

The North-East of Scotland is often thought of as fairly self-contained, with its own distinctive dialect of Scots, formerly forbidding geographical boundaries, tied-to-place industries of farming and fishing, and a world-renowned oral tradition of ballads, songs, and stories that has remained relatively stable over several centuries. Fertile ground, one might say, for a regional folklorist, as indeed it is. Over the last few decades, I have worked with extraordinary singers and storytellers exploring the meaning, techniques, and social function of our oral traditions. It is fascinating and rewarding work on both academic and personal levels.

But the folklore regionalist is also an advocate with a responsibility to exemplify and promote ethical practice. We have a duty of care for individuals and groups, as well as a campaigning platform from which to call for change. If our discipline teaches us one thing, it is that variation is central to tradition and to humanity itself. Being aware of a region's cultural diversity, and the fact that there is sometimes little communication between social groupings, we design projects that build bridges. Thus, our Home-Hame-Дом-Dom project brought together participants from some fifteen different countries to explore traditions of cooking, language, songs, knitting, and other expressions of cultural identity. The skills themselves are peripheral; the real goal is to create a space for encounters, communication, and communion; help build a sense of community; and create a feedback loop in which participants set the agenda for what they want to do and learn. Our Polish-Scottish Song Group likewise brings together different communities for shared activity, using songs from both countries as a mechanism for creating *communitas*. We're also codesigning a project with similar goals with the long marginalized and misunderstood Scottish Traveller community. By working in partnership, we hope to foster understanding and break down social barriers identified by the community themselves, rather than those determined by me, an outsider.

Working across these sometimes-isolated cultural groups is essential, but isolation is found elsewhere, too. Our Boaties Project, for example, brought skilled older model boatbuilders together with young apprentices, septuagenarians with teens, and males with females. Not only were model-making skills passed on, but new cross-generational relationships were also established. Another group vulnerable to isolation is the elderly, and none more so than those who lose their second language (English) to dementia, reverting to their native Scots, often in care-home settings where the carers do not speak the language. They thus become unable to communicate, silenced due to cultural and demographic changes well beyond their control. Through planned workshops educating carers in the local dialect of Scots, we hope to bridge that gap and help give voice to the basic needs and aspirations of these elderly people. We're working hard to break down social barriers around the Scots language (called Doric in this area), long seen as the language of home and humor and banished from school, university, and civic life. From educational programs and pioneering immersion schools to community events (such as a Doric *Messiah*), we are taking vernacular language to places it has historically been excluded.

Regionalism is perhaps at its most visible with regard to the tourist industry, a crucial factor for many economically marginal areas. The cultural tourist requires unique and preferably "authentic" experiences. As local and national regions market a certain essentialized version of themselves—the city that never sleeps; the land of tartan, haggis, and bagpipes; the town of gastronomy—often imposed by literati, colonialists, or economic powers, it is our job, with our bottom-up approach, to offer counternarratives or, at least, to nuance entrenched narratives with real-life experience. We work with local communities to identify the stories they want to tell, bringing in a fine-grained reality that helps make encounters satisfactory for both parties. Drawing on these community resources, we've worked with local and national tourism agencies to develop short films and podcasts, opening up stories long known locally to the wider world; as part of our reciprocal partnerships model, we run capacity-building workshops and hands-on training sessions on heritage work and project design, helping groups develop their communities as they wish.

Many regions are sure of their distinctive identity, while others may feel they don't have one, just as many people do not feel they themselves have an accent. Thus, they look to other places for "culture." But the discipline of folklore is reflexive; it asks us to look inside ourselves and our communities to explore the unique way each of us makes sense of the world. One of the great joys of working with students is seeing them develop this self-awareness as they study culture through new lenses, whether as locals or incomers, explicitly aware for the first time that they carry as much culture as the next person. This is the beginning of cultural confidence and a nascent basis for cross-cultural understanding.

The very idea of region is closely connected to this cultural confidence. In my experience, those cultures and subcultures with a confident sense of themselves and their own value are able to stand shoulder to shoulder with any other, sure of their own self-worth and therefore able to value others without being competitive, demeaning, or aggressive. What need have we to put another group down if we are secure in who we are? The work of the folklorist and regionalist, with our emphasis on bottom-up working, should thus be intertwined with cultural self-esteem. In some projects and contexts, this is an explicit aim when we repurpose or reintroduce local skills, traditions, and knowledge or devise new creative paradigms in partnership with individuals and groups to help enhance cultural self-esteem. At other times, such developments are unanticipated by-products of the work.

Regionalism finds its home in many national and state programs around the world, where it draws attention to the local—to distinctive practices, ideas, and worldviews that are often under the radar or sometimes under threat. Safeguarding programs and top-down heritage regimes (such as UNESCO's intangible cultural heritage lists) tend to abstraction, either describing a macro tradition in terms of frameworks of practice or focusing on one particular manifestation of a wider tradition, which has a tendency to privilege that practice over an equally valid one next door in the eyes of both insiders and outsiders. The regional folklorist is therefore a key mechanism for highlighting particularity, multiformity, and variation in local traditions.

Only by seeing the fine grain of culture can we step back and see the whole in any meaningful way. Stand too close and you may only see the brush strokes; too far away and you see a broad sweep lacking meaningful detail.

The regionalist's work, like an uncompressed digital image file, gives us the minute detail needed to allow fine-grained understanding while contributing to the overall richness of a macro view. By building nuanced understandings, the regional folklorist can help build stronger communities and stronger individuals more able to accept and, indeed, treasure diversity.

Advocating through Consultancy: Susan Eleuterio

Susan Eleuterio earned her MA in American folk culture at the Cooperstown Graduate Program of SUNY Oneonta and works as an independent contractor in Highland, Indiana.

I have often joked that my resume looks like I can't hold a job, but the truth is that I have always been and remain interested in a variety of ways to be a folklorist. These have included helping students and teachers explore their own and each other's cultures; using exhibits to document folk and traditional practices, places, and people; collaborating with artists and teachers in creating school-based residencies and curricula; and developing public programming with folklorists, community scholars, and artists. My peripatetic life as an independent contractor reflects all these interests, along with the reality of being a working mom and partner. This work has taken me to New Orleans (creating a cultural-understanding program for park district employees), North Dakota (providing professional development for artists about working in schools), and Missouri (collaborating on creating school residencies in folk arts), among other places.

At a time when many are questioning the value of an education in any humanities field, not just in folklore studies, one might wonder about the best way to prepare for life as an independent contractor. Having degrees or certificates in multiple fields certainly helps. My education began as an English major with an education minor. Completing the work to become certified as a teacher meant I was qualified to work as a consultant with school-based programs. My undergraduate education was also enriched by taking a course in folk song with Dr. Robert Bethke, Delaware's first folklorist, who encouraged us to research our own family folk culture. I interviewed my Portuguese grandmother (*Vovoa*), who sang *fados* to us and remains the inspiration for my passion for encouraging others to document, preserve, and share their own family and community heritage.

After studying American folk culture and museum studies at the Cooperstown Graduate Program of SUNY Oneonta, I was awarded a National Museum Act fellowship at Old World Wisconsin. I conducted field and archival research about social and community life in the 1800s to develop an interpretation plan for two Norwegian American farm exhibits and a related education program for school groups. I encourage anyone who contemplates independent contracting work to seize as many opportunities for experience like this as possible and to realize that what may seem a less than ideal part-time or temporary job can lead to other opportunities down the road.

My next professional position, as a folk arts program coordinator at the Illinois Arts Commission, meant that later, when my family moved to Ithaca, New York, I was able to obtain a contract with the Ithaca Public Schools to create folk arts programs for faculty and students involved in the merger of two schools (one rural, the other in town). The administration wanted to help alleviate cultural differences through workshops and residencies. We accomplished this by inviting the "town" school's cafeteria director to offer programs on soul food cuisine, asking a rural kindergarten teacher who told me he had "no culture" to offer workshops on his family's Irish stories, and collaborating with a local gospel choir.

I returned to the Midwest in the early 1980s, completed my MA thesis, and had three children in two years. I highly recommend that you complete your academic work once you start it because the degree will make you competitive when applying for independent contracts. I also recommend volunteering to serve on folk and traditional arts and humanities grant-review panels for state government agencies, where you will get to know a variety of cultural heritage specialists and artists.

In the 1980s, I was hired to develop an intercultural-understanding program for a large urban high school in Cicero, Illinois, where the population had changed from primarily White European to majority Hispanic in just a few years. The faculty and staff were, in some cases, frankly prejudiced about their new student population, and there were long-standing racial tensions in the community.

Beginning with fieldwork in the community, we developed folk arts workshops for students and teachers and an annual folk festival that took place for nearly ten years. Our projects included asking students in the English as a second language program to bring in family photographs, which were transferred to fabric squares by photography students and then made into a quilt by the home economics classes. The quilt still hangs in the school and represents the collaborative culture of Mexican and Polish immigrants crafted into a beautiful art piece by students whose parents had moved to the community many years before. We taught theater students how to conduct oral history fieldwork and had them interview senior citizens to create a play celebrating the town's centennial. The festival incorporated everything from Italian foodways to Czech and Mexican folk dance to Polish traditional singing and gave students, families, and staff the opportunity to spend time together in a positive environment. I led professional development workshops for the faculty in using folk arts and culture across the curriculum to improve writing skills and help increase intercultural understanding.

During the last twenty years, I have been hired to develop and deliver professional development programs for folk artists in Missouri and North Dakota about working in schools, and for teachers in Illinois, Iowa, and Wisconsin on learning about the culture of their students. I cocreated curricula with teaching artists and staff folklorists of the Missouri Folk Arts Program through the *Show-Me Traditions: An Educators Guide to Teaching Folk Arts and Folklife in Missouri Schools* (https://mofolkarts.missouri.edu /wp-content/uploads/2017/06/showme.pdf), which won the American Folklore Society's Dorothy Howard Prize in Folklore and Education.

In North Dakota I was privileged to follow up this professional development work with a contract to create a series of teacher's guides with North Dakota folk artists. I also was hired to complete the *Illinois Mississippi River Valley Project Teacher's Guide* based on a collaborative effort to demonstrate the influence of the Mississippi River on Western Illinois arts and culture, which resulted in lesson plans cocreated with artists and poets from the western region of the state.

In 2017 I became a consultant to the Center for Folklore Studies at The Ohio State University, collaborating with faculty and staff folklorists, students, and community members to develop public programs, evaluation, and design for a traveling exhibit, *Placemaking in Scioto County, Ohio*. Through a second contract, I am codeveloping curricula and school-based programming tied to the exhibit and the center's Scioto County archives with local educators.

All these contract opportunities came as a result of networking at regional and national meetings with fellow folklorists who not only became friends but called me when contract work in folk arts education and public programming became available.

Life as an independent contractor can be scary and hard. I've had friends who literally slept in their cars on the way to gigs, and the fluctuations in funding streams are real and likely to continue after the current pandemic ends. At the same time, independent work provides an opportunity to travel, collaborate with community members in multiple locations, work in concert with other folklorists who may not have the specific skills you bring to the table, and build on fieldwork and research others have done. I recommend that you join the American Folklore Society's Independent Folklorists' Section (https://www.afsnet.org/page/Independent); its members can create professional profiles online and apply for travel stipends to attend the AFS annual conference. AFS also has adopted an official policy about appropriate compensation for independent contractors.

Because of our interdisciplinary interests and expertise, folklorists are uniquely qualified to work in a variety of professional roles and settings. The life of an independent is never boring; it will give you the opportunity to be flexible and will enable you to meet people across the country who will become lifelong colleagues.

CREATING PUBLIC POLICY: DIANE E. GOLDSTEIN

Diane E. Goldstein earned her PhD in folklore and folklife at the University of Pennsylvania and is Professor of Folklore at Indiana University and a past president of the American Folklore Society.

The phrase "location, location, location" is a real estate cliché, but I've often argued that the same could be said of participation in public policy. Having what we have to say heard outside our own field and making it matter depends on being in the right place at the right time, and in September of 1994, I had the good fortune to be exactly there.

I was teaching in the Folklore Department at Memorial University in Newfoundland and working on a book on folklore and HIV. One afternoon I received a message from our dean, who knew of my research, asking if he could nominate me for a Health Canada committee on AIDS. I agreed, assuming the committee was likely to be like other Health Canada committees and grant panels I had sat on—narrowly focused on health promotion. I was wrong. A few months later, I was contacted by the chair of the Canadian National Planning Forum for HIV/AIDS, who announced that I had been selected to sit on his committee. And this committee had no small mandate: our task was to develop Phase II of the Canadian National AIDS Strategy. Although I hardly knew what "the table" was, in policy terms, I suddenly had a seat at one.

Thanks to a knowledgeable and activist patient constituency, HIV/AIDS governmental committees had begun to learn hard lessons about including widespread representation of stakeholders on decision-making bodies. Gone were the days when survivors would quietly sit by and allow scientists to make decisions about their health. Our group of twenty-five included researchers from a variety of disciplines, people living with HIV/AIDS, representatives of national nongovernmental AIDS organizations and research-funding agencies, federal and provincial officials, and one (only one!) representative from the pharmaceutical industry. I was not sure how I snagged a seat on this amazing committee. Later, I found out that location, location, location had served me well. The committee chair wanted a representative from the humanities and also required representation from Atlantic Canada; I fulfilled both requirements. While the scarcity of HIV/AIDS scholars in the humanities in the mid-1990s disturbed me greatly, so too did the slow attention to the virus demonstrated within Atlantic Canadian health sectors. The lack of a collegial context for my work, previously so distressing, suddenly had become a personal asset.

The humanities are crucial to developing public policy and resolving policy issues. Our insights on diversity, history, heritage, expressive culture, process, and thought are as important—arguably even more important—than the contributions of the sciences or technological fields to the development of effective public policy. We don't often associate the humanities with public policy because formal structures for humanities input into policy making are mostly nonexistent. But humanities scholars have also generally been reluctant to get involved in policy making, perhaps feeling that our role is to critique power structures rather than support them. Both can be the case. Both should be the case.

I felt that my presence on the committee was able to bring topics our discipline cares about to the fore. I worked primarily on efforts to create formal networks that would facilitate research collaboration, including facilitating participatory research with community members and recognizing the importance of sex workers, drug users, and other frontline grassroots individuals as community scholars with critical insights to contribute to the policy-making process. I also worked on the development of national ethical and legal guidelines for research, prevention, and treatment involving marginalized populations, including injection drug users, aboriginal communities, homeless communities, rural communities, and the prison population. Our final report also included a statement resulting from my advocacy concerning the importance of studying the development of public discourse and folklore around HIV/AIDS.

After the end of our committee's work, I was lucky enough to have numerous other policy opportunities come my way. Strangely, my "location, location, location" mantra always held sway. My work on epidemic narrative and rumor—the importance of which was increasingly coming to the attention of public-health decision makers—led to a number of appointments on policy committees. The most interesting of these committee appointments was to the board of a huge European Union consortium—involving experts in social and behavioral sciences, communication, media, science, and health, as well as representatives of global health agencies and governing bodies—created to develop an evidence-based behavioral and communication model for responding to major epidemic outbreaks. Through each of these appointments, I was able to establish the ethnographic, expressive, and vernacular concerns of folklore as crucial to health solutions and decision-making. And through each of these policy collaborations, I grew as a folklorist, learning where our field could and could not be heard, understanding where we provided answers and where we did not, and finding better ways of addressing the needs of policy makers and the communities they (and we) serve. I grew to be able to argue that folklore provided a way to develop cost-effective, evidence-based public-health solutions that advance population health.

If public policy is the process by which government agencies and organizations translate their vision into regulations and programs that deliver real outcomes, engaging the right players in understanding problems and their solutions is crucial. Often my most important and fulfilling role was providing access to those players—that is, providing ethnographic information that could cast new light on old problems. For example, I worked on a policy committee with the Newfoundland Law Reform Commission to adjust real estate laws to better conform with cultural attitudes toward deeds, house titles, and land surveys. The lawyers at the center of this effort were trying to understand why Newfoundlanders rarely do the paperwork to get their deeds and end up essentially squatting in their own homes, causing an endless number of difficulties for the government and potentially depriving homeowners of real property. Everything about this question was complex, tied as it was to traditional attitudes to property, land use, neighborliness, orality versus print documentation, and trust in the government or lack thereof. My role was to develop, implement, and participate in a field team created to explore attitudes toward real estate and its registration. I was able to convince lawmakers that they needed to hear from community members themselves, and I was able to link the law reform society to those voices and later to interpret that information in the creation of reform. Field research is one of the strengths of our discipline, and good research should be one of the foundations of sound public policy. Much of folklore research can inform public policy, but it must be presented in the appropriate forms and contexts to have an impact on policy work.

So if location, location, location is the key, how do we end up in the right location? The answer is that if we don't find ourselves there, we should put ourselves there. I was privileged to be nominated by my dean for the HIV/ AIDS committee, but my CV contained work I had engaged in as a volunteer: doing HIV talks on the high school circuit, becoming an AIDS buddy or companion, and serving on the HIV crisis hotline. Volunteering can place you in social arenas where you can gain experience and create networks while you are simultaneously gaining folklore or policy-making training. Working on domestic violence? Then volunteer in a shelter or in a women's center to get the background. You will still be a folklorist in that effort even if you are washing floors or stuffing envelopes, and you'll be grounding your training for later policy efforts.

Knowing that our discipline can make unique contributions to local, national, and international discussions of contemporary societal issues, in 2008 Sandy Rikoon of the University of Missouri and I designed a survey of the American Folklore Society membership to inventory the involvement of folklorists in public policy work, as well as to determine strategies for the use of AFS resources to support the policy-making interests of its membership. We found that a high percentage of folklorists have contributed to public policy in a variety of areas: intangible heritage, cultural conservation, intellectual property, health, education, labor and employment, historic preservation, arts administration, the environment, rural and urban development, immigration, poverty, violence, language rights, and land rights.

In many cases folklorists were affecting public policy not as part of their job but as part of their lives. Talking to your child's school board, for example, about cultural and religious beliefs in relation to the imposition of school dress codes involves you in issues of folklore and public policy. You might be doing that as a concerned parent rather than as a cultural scholar, but you are bringing your folklore skills to the table where they are needed. That is, if the location doesn't come to you, you go to the location. Folklorists understand the contexts, perceptions, values, and beliefs that can generate important new knowledge. We just need to get ourselves to the right place at the right time.

ANALYZING PUBLIC POLICY: LEAH LOWTHORP

Leah Lowthorp earned her PhD in folklore at the University of Pennsylvania and is Assistant Professor of Anthropology and Folklore at the University of Oregon.

In my career in folklore thus far, tracking and analyzing national and international public policy has been a major focus of my work within and outside the academy. This began with my graduate research exploring the impact of UNESCO's intangible cultural heritage (ICH) program upon Kutiyattam Sanskrit theater, inscribed as India's first UNESCO Masterpiece of the Oral and Intangible Heritage of Humanity. As part of this work, I have explored in the *Journal of Folklore Research* and *Asian Ethnology* the history of the UNESCO ICH program—which culminated in the 2003 Convention for the Safeguarding of the Intangible Cultural Heritage—as well as cultural policy in India and several other countries. As a function of identity, folklore is inherently political in both subtle and overt ways. Heritage is an explicit politicization of folklore—mobilizing expressive culture in the service of official identity formation—and related public policy intimately affects our work as folklorists and the lives of the people with whom we work. Unsurprisingly, folklorists have made important contributions in thinking about and analyzing cultural policy and actively shaping it; examples include Regina Bendix's *Culture and Value*, Michael Dylan Foster and Lisa Gilman's edited volume *UNESCO on the Ground*, Valdimar Hafstein's *Making Intangible Cultural Heritage*, and Mary Hufford's edited volume *Conserving Culture*, among others.

What I will focus on here, however, is my work in an arena that is somewhat more unexpected for a folklorist: that of public policy and advocacy in the realm of human genetic and assisted reproductive technologies. I came to this work through the Mellon/American Council of Learned Societies Public Fellows program, an opportunity for early-career humanities PhDs to gain experience in the nonprofit and governmental sectors. I was awarded a two-year position as a public fellow and program manager at the Center for Genetics and Society (CGS), a Berkeley, California, nonprofit organization that takes a social justice, human rights, and public interest approach to its work on human genetic and assisted reproductive technologies. You may ask, "But folklore and genetics?!" In addition to CGS's social justice mission, it was the unlikely combination of these two that most appealed to me. As folklorists we have learned to be extremely adaptable and to see the relevance of folklore to all realms of human existence. Narratives of human biotechnologies, both official and vernacular, are narratives like any other, and we as folklorists have the expertise to provide special insight about them. And while it appears that this topic has nothing in common with my earlier work, there is an interesting connection: UNESCO has likewise declared the human genome as part of the heritage of humanity.

When I first arrived at CGS, although I had seen the film *Gattaca*, I did not know that science had nearly caught up. My first month was spent getting up to speed on the technology, distinguishing between somatic gene therapy and heritable human genome editing, understanding how the gene-editing tool CRISPR works, and learning about related technologies. What are these technologies? In a nutshell, somatic gene therapy is the modification of body cells, generally blood or bone marrow, to treat certain genetic conditions in living patients. Heritable human genome editing, on the other hand, genetically modifies human eggs, sperm, or embryos with intent to initiate a pregnancy, thereby making changes that are inherited for generations to come. It does not treat a living person but instead creates an individual with certain desired traits. Both these technologies have been revolutionized by the gene-editing tool CRISPR, discovered in 2014, which makes editing genes faster, easier, and cheaper than ever before. Somatic gene therapy is medically promising for the treatment of previously untreatable diseases. Its main problem is accessibility, as treatments generally cost upwards of $1 million and are not covered by insurance. Heritable genome editing, on the other hand, has a host of problems. These include human experimentation—as we don't know how the process will affect the individuals created thereby, although research indicates that unintentional genetic errors are likely—and the technology's potential to create a system of genetic inequality that would exacerbate existing forms of inequality. With these concerns in mind, CGS's primary goal—in partnership with racial justice, reproductive justice, and disability rights advocates—is to pursue the outlawing of heritable human genome editing in the United States.

Against this background, my two years at CGS consisted primarily of tracking national and intergovernmental policy processes and conversations on heritable human genome editing around the world in policy documents and recommendations, media reports, technology conferences, and policy-related meetings; analyzing their implications; and translating the science and policy issues for a wider public audience. The products of this work included regular blogs, short online articles, academic articles, grant applications, webinars, talks at venues like genetics conferences and law schools, organizing an international seminar, and a collaborative statement published in a high-profile science journal with concrete policy recommendations. These included, for example, "3-person IVF and Lesbian Motherhood: A Flawed Argument for Reproductive Equality" on the Center for Genetics and Society website (https://www.geneticsandsociety.org /biopolitical-times/3-person-ivf-and-lesbian-motherhood-flawed-argument -reproductive-equality) and a coauthored article, "Reproductive gene editing imperils universal human rights," on the Global Human Rights website (https://www.openglobalrights.org/reproductive-gene-editing-imperils -universal-human-rights/?lang=English). Folklorists are particularly suited for this type of translational work, as it is a fundamental part of what we already do: translate the values and lived experiences of our interlocutors to a wider audience through written work, exhibitions, video documentation, grant writing, and public events; and translate the work of our field to the wider public, other academics, funding agencies, and government officials. We have a toolbox of skills ready to apply to a wide variety of topics—even genetic technology and science policy.

An important but perhaps somewhat overlooked area of policy analysis is the public's response to policy making. This is also an area in which the skills of folklorists are particularly useful. While at CGS, I analyzed social media narratives surrounding CRISPR technology, and that work was published in the *Journal of American Folklore* in 2018. Part of the argument in the collaborative science policy statement mentioned previously is that since heritable human genome editing is a technology that will affect humanity as a whole, it is vital to include the public in policy discussions and deliberation. Digital folklore on social media platforms is both a means to gauge wider opinion of public policy and an avenue to engage the wider public in policy discussions and deliberations.

Outside the realm of policy analysis, CGS was also interested in my ability as a folklorist to hone their organizational narrative, meaning to simplify and more effectively convey their organizational story to different stakeholders: allies, scholars, scientists, the general public, and funders. While we as folklorists know that our field is diverse, those outside our field generally associate us with storytelling. Instead of bemoaning the misconception, we folklorists should use this to our advantage. Organizational storytelling is a rising trend happening largely without the input of folklorists; Dr. Karen Dietz, the coauthor of *Business Storytelling for Dummies*, is an exception. Within the nonprofit world alone, organizations such as the Center for Story-based Strategy help activists formulate their campaigns in ways aimed at changing oppressive stories at the societal level, while the Nonprofit Storytelling Conference offers storytelling tools to help nonprofits attain greater funding. I encourage folklorists to think more strategically about the unique contribution we have the opportunity to make on a wider scale.

As for myself, working at an organization like CGS—where I was challenged with learning new material, thinking about how to employ my folklore skills in new arenas, and actively engaging in social justice advocacy—was both exciting and fulfilling. I saw my experience as a springboard for either continuing in direct public advocacy work or becoming a more socially engaged academic. My journey has taken me on the latter path, and pursuing science and technology studies with a social justice lens is now a mainstay of my work and teaching.

Becoming a Politician: Jodi McDavid

Jodi McDavid earned her PhD in folklore at the Memorial University of New-foundland and is a business owner, a university instructor at Cape Breton University, and President of the Nova Scotia New Democratic Party.

My first run at an elected position was in second grade, when I was nominated as the Valentine's Day princess. I had a paper crown, and I was both humbled and a little embarrassed to be so proud of myself.

After my mother remarried when I was five, I was raised on a farm with a thick blanket of Protestant sensibility in the foothills of the northern Appalachian Mountains in the province of New Brunswick in Canada. Service to one's community was held as next to godliness and, for women, as the absolute best thing they could do. Service to community sometimes even got you out of service to family, if you were smart about it. There was some flexibility and praise associated with "being of service." Around the same time I learned about the importance of being of service, I also learned about the importance of tradition bearers. You see, my stepfather's parents lived next door to us, and having previously accepted their grandchildren-less existence, they were pleasantly surprised to suddenly have a grandchild. I was a vessel into which to pour all knowledge, from how to bake biscuits to how cut potatoes for planting. I knew enough to know what life was like outside of this and that this was different from my previous life. I knew that this was good and important. Due to a tumultuous start to life, I had few notions of family, roots, and connections. This was when I started to grasp what folklore was, although I didn't have the words for it.

For me, these notions of culture and service developed at the same time. As a folklorist I have provided a lot of behind-the-scenes leadership. For a number of years, I held many positions in Memorial University (MUN)'s Folklore Society and the student-led journal *Culture & Tradition.* I held several roles in the Folklore Studies Association of Canada. I helped develop the folklore program at Cape Breton University by creating course proposals in folklore and gender and women's studies, although never officially, as I was not full-time faculty. In my research I practiced reciprocal ethnography. I spoke from my experience for my community when asked, even if it was uncomfortable, causing me at times to be an advocate on things from my early lived experience, like poverty and violence against women.

I describe myself as an extroverted introvert, but I have always been interested in people. Using my folklore training, I would listen to people and draw similarities from many conversations. I would consider how people couched things in conversations and the verbal nuances they used to introduce ideas. The way some things were always carefully deemphasized in a conversation but repeated incessantly across conversations led me to see that people weren't confident about my take on their issue but that it was an issue nonetheless, just one a community felt conflicted in raising. That's quite possibly one of the reasons I, as a "nuanced listener," became good at things like strategic planning. I never wanted to be a politician. But I did want to provide service to my community. When my community asked me to run for public office, I viewed it as reciprocal ethnography, believe it or not. I am hugely empathetic, but for me, empathy without action is an impossibility. That said, typically my actions are small: a food bank donation, a bag of clothes to someone struggling, arranging donations for victims of a house fire, or sitting on a nonprofit board.

As a politician, I used all the tools in the folklorist's tool chest—because I believed I was doing it for the right reasons—to help marginalized members of my community. In the fall of 2019, I ran for a legislative seat representing the New Democratic Party, which in Canada pushes for what some might consider leftist policies like guaranteed basic income, subsidized day care, free medication, and the end of environmental racism. I would have been unwilling to run for other parties because this was not a matter of seeking power but of personal belief. I knew I was unlikely to be successful due to the historic representation of that party in our region. I didn't win, but I did have incremental success by getting more votes in my electoral district than my party did previously, by keeping the people's issues in the foreground, and by forcing the more dominant parties to talk about the issues and make commitments.

As a folklorist, I have been supported by my discipline in a number of ways. I have never felt pressured to drop or change things, such as my way of expressing myself or my pronunciation (born from rurality, being an Acadienne—a female descendant of the seventeenth-century French-speaking settlers of Canada's East Coast—and being tongue-tied at birth). Showing "my roots" is a lauded quality in a "down-to-earth" politician. Essentially, I haven't betrayed my class in my acquisition of higher education because the education I pursued didn't force me to. For me, to be a working-class politician was not a huge stretch because being part of the working class was something I identified with, although my current way of life was much more comfortable than it once was. As a folklorist, I was also given a lot of opportunity and support in learning about leadership, and I had very good examples. Although it may seem far removed, as a member of the MUN folklore society, I worked closely with the various heads of the department and saw different types of leadership and service. I have been extremely well mentored in my education; a number of senior folklorists (at MUN and beyond) spent a lot of time providing me with opportunities, guidance, and feedback. At times, they saw something in me that I did not see in myself, and I suppose a huge motivation for me in graduate school was to show them their efforts were not wasted. I think this type of support happens often, although not always, in our field, and I am aware from my work and previous roles in mentoring academics that it doesn't always happen in others.

Being trained as a folklorist has given me a number of unique skills. Many of us have a curiosity about the world, and we've taken on the responsibility of being lifelong learners. We are researchers and interviewers. We understand the art of oration and telling a good story and the use of vernacular speech. We have been interviewed by the media—a lot. We remain unfazed in the homes of informants, regardless of the situation we enter (a skill I called upon a lot while canvassing). Many of us are very socially conscious. We advocate for people in the best way we can: publishing think pieces and academic articles, developing museum exhibits, documenting practices under threat, or running for office to create space to give voice to those who need amplification. From a self-serving perspective, I understood networks, and I had extensive ones in the community that I drew upon for training, honesty, and support. Essentially, I looked for tradition bearers again and found them willing to impart their knowledge, for which I am eternally grateful.

Being a folklorist also helped me understand why some people identified with me. In our indigenous communities, many of the voters who reached out to me did so because I am a woman and a mother, and they stated that quite clearly. Elderly people seemed to feel I was more open to their concerns. In general, women and youth reached out to me a lot. Understanding the perception of women as nurturers and healers helped, but it also hindered, as some people considered me a one-issue candidate. Operating in a folk culture, and knowing I was doing so, was a benefit for me at times. I could say things without being explicit because the people who were listening were speaking the same coded vernacular language. I am well aware of women's ways of talk and knowing and their coded language, and I deciphered and used a lot of it during my door-to-door canvasing, speeches, and meet and greets.

As a coda to this experience, at its convention in early 2020, the provincial New Democratic Party chose me to be their president in Nova Scotia. All the committees of the party report to the president, and the president has a role in oversight and guidance as well as interpreting the constitution of the party. The president works in partnership with the party leader, who is a member of the Legislative Assembly.

After the election, being a folklorist helped, too. It helped me understand my new and developing role in my community, where sometimes I am myself and sometimes I am a totem of something else as I take on a symbolic role or have a position in a ceremony. It helped me understand that my family would struggle in different ways with my change of status. It helped me move through a liminal state—where I embodied a belief, a dream, and an expectation—to one where I had fulfilled my purpose and new ones were imagined for me and by me.

Assisting Social Services Clients: Nelda Ault-Dyslin

Nelda Ault-Dyslin earned her MA in folk studies at Western Kentucky University and is Community Service Coordinator at Utah State University.

During my second year in the folk studies program at Western Kentucky University, I volunteered in an English class for refugees and immigrants at the International Center of Kentucky in Bowling Green. The adult students who were pursuing English as their second, third, or fourth language had roots in Mexico, Burma, South Korea, Hungary, China, Japan, and Uzbekistan and spoke basic conversational English. About half the class members had arrived in Bowling Green through the United Nations refugee resettlement program, and the rest of the class had immigrated through other channels or were accompanying spouses of international students at the university.

Between grammar exercises and role-plays, the rhythm of the class was often interrupted by a caseworker appearing in the doorway, summoning a refugee student to the office. Sometimes the students returned right away, a new Social Security card or other official document in hand. Other times they didn't return to class that day, having been whisked away to an appointment at the health department for immunizations or other medical checks.

Many of the center's caseworkers came from refugee backgrounds themselves, having been resettled in Bowling Green a few decades before my time there. As I learned more about the resettlement process, I concluded that this scenario was ideal. Who better to introduce you to a new country than someone who had also experienced resettlement?

As time went on, however, I observed the cultural gulf between these caseworkers and the students. One day, after an engaging class period in which the students presented information about their names and the meaning behind them, I winced when a caseworker stood in the doorway and made no effort to pronounce a name correctly. As I passed through the halls,

I overheard employees expressing frustrations with their clients about tasks they needed to do. Even with the help of translators, misunderstandings still took place. Although the students and their caseworkers had UN refugee status in common, the array of cultural backgrounds meant there were few points of connection in these interactions.

I wondered: how could this be improved? It would be unfair to ask caseworkers to become experts in every culture they might encounter. Their job was to usher resettled refugees through a convoluted bureaucratic process, make sure their basic needs were met, and introduce the "government culture" of their new country. It was easy to see how, in the hustle of meeting deadlines and filling out forms, cultural connection was not their top priority.

In my studies, as I learned about folklore in the classroom, issues of identity in diasporic communities, and power dynamics among groups, I saw a possible answer. The caseworkers couldn't learn about all the cultures that came through the door, but a folklorist could. In other words, a folklorist would have the skill set to navigate the cultures the refugees brought with them.

This conclusion—that a folklorist could act as a mediator in places where a lack of cultural connection could affect the health, well-being, and education of community members—has influenced my approaches to the jobs I've had since graduating at the start of the Great Recession. Whether in a refugee resettlement center, elementary school, or state social service agency—or in higher education, where I now work—my training as a folklorist has outfitted me with ways to reach out to people who want to be regarded as whole, competent, independent beings navigating new systems and re-networking themselves.

In 2011 I landed a job working for the Utah Department of Workforce Services, which houses the state's refugee programs. On paper, my task was to ascertain what refugees living in northern Utah needed in order to join the local workforce. In practice, my tasks demanded that I spend more time listening than talking, learning about the concerns of community members that weren't job related. At the request of members of the Burmese Muslim and Karen communities, a volunteer from the local English learning center and I convened informal "conversation clubs" in refugee homes. Our curriculum grew out of the requests for assistance we received: role-playing how to call an elementary school to excuse a sick child, examining a utility bill to figure out how much had been charged, or talking about the benefits and limits of our public transportation system.

My teaching partner was formally trained in English-teaching pedagogy and had many years of teaching experience. She knew the best ways to break down our subjects into understandable language and to practice the principles with a variety of activities. I brought my folklore-in-the-classroom training to the table, centering my activities on the premise that students bring their own cultural knowledge to their learning environments and that teachers should use this knowledge as a jumping-off point. Our conversation partners made personal connections to the subject matter as we compared and contrasted homes, schools, and work in the refugee camps with life in Utah. Participants in these conversation groups eventually asked for a study group aimed at passing the written driver's license exam. Years later, when I helped organize the Cache Refugee and Immigrant Connection as a non-profit organization serving the Cache County area around Logan, Utah, we added a study group to prepare for the US naturalization exam. Passing these two tests requires a vast amount of cultural knowledge that can be accessed with the assistance of a folklorist who knows her students' backgrounds and understands how to carve out a space where they can connect their prior knowledge with the subjects to be mastered.

My training in folklore also made me a more respectful caseworker. As I visited Eritrean families in their homes, I wanted to start solving problems the moment I arrived, and I would get frustrated when the family started our conversation with a relaxed, "Tell me, how is your family?" My folklore training reminded me to take a step back, recognize the home to which I had been invited, and engage on this family's terms, not my own. I encouraged other case managers to understand their clients' context when they complained their clients didn't show up for appointments (which had been scheduled on religious holidays) or didn't read the translated paperwork (when some clients weren't literate in their home languages). I later worked as a literacy program coordinator in the elementary school that many refugee children attended, and I redirected my encouragement to the teachers. For the first time, many of them learned how to interact with parents who were unfamiliar with public education in the United States.

During commencement at the conclusion of our graduate studies at Western Kentucky, my cohort unwittingly lost our place as we lined up for the procession. In the chaos of black robes and loose hoods, none of us realized we were no longer walking in step with our fellow students from the Potter College of the Arts and Letters. After the ceremony, department head Michael Ann Williams rounded us up and quipped, "You shook the wrong dean's hand!" We had marched in with graduates from the College of Health and Human Services. But considering where my folklore training has led me since that day, I'd say I wasn't wrong at all.

Collaborating with K–12 Teachers: Ruth Olson

Ruth Olson earned her PhD in folklore and folklife at the University of Pennsylvania and before retirement was Associate Director of the Center for the Study of Upper Midwestern Cultures at the University of Wisconsin–Madison.

My job as associate director for the Center for the Study of Upper Midwestern Cultures (CSUMC) encompassed broad responsibilities: teaching folklore courses, managing budgets, writing grant proposals, administering research projects, and giving outreach talks around the state. But what I most enjoyed in my career as a folklorist at CSUMC has been collaborating with K–12 teachers and their classrooms as they study everyday life in their communities.

Many folklorists have done work that benefits K–12 classrooms. They have created curriculum units, teacher guides, and teaching aids (such as traveling trunks of educational materials) that help students explore particular cultures. They have developed online texts with embedded examples of specific cultural forms selected from high-quality fieldwork. In workshops and courses, they have instructed teachers in content and methods to take back to their classrooms. Perhaps most commonly, folklorists have assisted K–12 educators with folk artist residencies, setting up artist and studio visits, and preparing students for hands-on experiences. Sometimes folklorists have worked directly with K–12 students by running short-term classroom projects as folklorists-in-the-classroom. These products and interactions cover a spectrum from more prescriptive to more collaborative. For me, the greatest satisfaction comes from the most collaborative experiences.

Collaborations begin by finding like-minded teachers: those who think rigidly structured classrooms are a poor representation of the world. Those teachers often are already passionate about creating community-minded students. They are ready to embrace folklorists' abilities to work outside the classroom—ready, that is, for unpredictable events, unexpected discoveries, and emerging patterns that allow authentic learning to take place. More than just reading a book or hearing experts lecture, students learn by going out into the community to do original research.

We aren't introducing these teachers to something totally new; teachers who see the benefits of working with folklorists likely already rely on some classwork outside the classroom. We aren't there to edify them with our vocabulary and central concepts; rather, we are offering them chances for collaboration and fieldwork skills that can enhance what they already do. By working together, teachers and folklorists create learning experiences, documentation projects, and teaching practices that go beyond what either could have created on their own.

For example, growing out of our Cultural Maps, Cultural Tours initiative, CSUMC colleagues Mark Wagler, Anne Pryor, and I began collaborating in Mark's fourth- and fifth-grade classroom by taking his students out to study local culture and having them document what they learned through extensive notes, drawings, and photos. Students traveled by bus throughout their county, spending nights in churches and other community spaces and visiting a pig farm, a fire station, a historic theater, art environments, religious sites, restaurants, and much more. In the end the students created the Dane County Cultural Tour website to present the places and themes the class explored.

We repeated this process the following school year with the Hmong Cultural Tour, ambitiously traveling across Wisconsin. This yearlong project was a collaboration with the Madison Children's Museum, which was developing the national touring exhibit *Hmong at Heart*. Students observed and talked with Hmong Americans in seven cities about a wide range of experiences, from shamanism and religion to business, family, and community issues. Students strongly appreciated their access to aspects of Hmong culture unavailable to most people. What they learned also helped them understand the ubiquity and depth of their own cultures. Those of us who led these classroom projects saw so much value in this approach that we met with other educators in the state to create Wisconsin Teachers of Local Culture (WTLC).

Finding like-minded teachers and developing mutually beneficial projects is not easy. Teachers, like almost everyone folklorists encounter outside our discipline, may not have a good understanding of the field of folklore. As a way to help more teachers grasp the interfaces within our frame of "everyday life," WTLC developed the Here at Home cultural tours for teachers. This multiday tour, offered each summer in a different Wisconsin region, was subsidized through grants and thus affordable for participants, who could also choose to earn university credit. Instead of depending on public places anyone could access, such as museums, we emphasized meeting people in their homes and workplaces. Teachers regularly took part in activities that anchored them in the places we were studying. Each tour accentuated the different overlying elements that make up community. Teachers spent time in distinct situations: talking with staff at a Hmong Mutual Assistance Association, spending time in the workshop of a skilled wood-carver, carrying out a health audit of a neighborhood with a city planner, visiting a family dairy farm, touring factories and businesses to interview workers, and visiting mosques with Somali residents in the small town of Barron. Teachers became excited to see how much learning could be generated through a simple visit to a local hardware store, for example, and began to envision how they could create such experiences for their own students. For these teachers the revelation of the methods and concerns of folklore reinvigorated their teaching and their curriculum.

The basic model of a cultural tour has been adapted by numerous teachers and enacted as a single event, as extended projects, and even as multiyear investigations. In north-central Wisconsin, for example, students created a community tour, taking visiting teachers to meet a local theater owner, a potato farmer, a Sikh family, and other people and places they determined important to their town.

Without arranging field trips outside the school, a team of teachers in Augusta, Wisconsin, organized a project for their seventh-grade students to explore the textures and dynamics of community life by selecting and displaying artifacts that represented them and their families. To initiate the project, another folklorist and I presented our own cultural objects and the categories useful for unpacking those objects, interviewed students about their artifacts, and then helped them interview community elders who brought artifacts to show the classrooms. The students also contributed objects to create a mosaic in the school's dining area, building a visual record interpreting Augusta's identity.

The success of such projects relies on giving priority to what the teacher wants the students to learn and then reflecting on how the folklorist might assist that learning. A project that incorporates the inspiration of both teacher and folklorist is usually unique but time-consuming. This is where public folklorists' experience in working in teams is especially useful. Folklorists often multiply resources by involving additional community partners. We are accustomed to the mundane but necessary work of organizing details: finding or designing field trip stops with engaging speakers surrounded by rich visual content, knowing how much time to spend at each stop, preparing students for the trip by brainstorming what to look for, and knowing how to begin an interview before turning students loose to ask their own questions. For example, for a second-grade class studying local foodways and agriculture, I helped make connections with a spinach grower; we talked through a series of learning stations on the farm so the students could more fully absorb the steps necessary to grow, harvest, clean, and market the spinach. In this instance, interviewing the spinach grower was less important than keeping the students engaged through hands-on activities.

In all these collaborations, culminating events such as exhibitions and celebrations help teachers, students, and folklorists reach out to the community.

Teachers and folklorists share the goal of presenting what they've learned through the generosity of the public, and teachers and students acquire extra appreciation and value from parents and community members who have a chance to see what has been produced during a community-based project.

This impact continues long after final programs conclude. Typical of the value community partners see in these projects is this comment from a parent who helped plan and carry out our Hmong Cultural Tour:

> It was gratifying for me to see Dylan confidently conduct interviews for his paper on Shamanism and form his own opinions on the information he had collected. When Dylan started the fourth grade, one of the early assignments was to describe family culture. His response was, "We don't have a unique culture, we are just like everybody else." Studying Hmong culture has given him a greater appreciation of his own. . . . Involvement with the Hmong Cultural Tour has been a peak experience for Dylan and me. We have discussed religion, life and death, and examined our own family values. . . . I feel so lucky and honored to have been allowed to experience this unique educational opportunity with Dylan. I have received more than I have given and will always be grateful for how my family has benefited.

This is the richness of collaborative learning.

PARTNERING WITH K–12 EDUCATION: LISA RATHJE

Lisa Rathje earned her PhD in English at the University of Missouri and is Executive Director of Local Learning: The National Network for Folk Arts in Education.

One of my first projects after I moved to the Chicago region in 2011 was to plan and direct a small traveling exhibition featuring the significant folk and traditional arts of Illinois. Flexibility was built into the design so the exhibition could easily travel to diverse hosts throughout the state, including art galleries, community organizations, schools, and even a pub! Engagement was a core goal, and we secured funds for programming that brought featured artists together with the public throughout the state. I also brought the artists into Chicago schools: in one school the program took on the form of a master class in Mexican *ballet folklorico* with its already established after-school dance group. As I observed the teaching on stage, the middle school principal shared her recognition of the importance of connecting youth with their cultural community. She pointed out that almost all the students in the *ballet folklorico* group were also on the honor roll and commented, "It is not just that honor roll students enroll in *ballet folklorico*. What I see is that participating in *ballet folklorico* creates honor roll students." She recognized that in her school, students learning about their culture and heritage has a positive impact on school learning.

In a more recent public forum, I interviewed a teacher and artists who had participated in a Local Learning professional development workshop in Rochester, New York. The teacher taught fourth grade in a school she described as predominately White. The artists were from a local gospel choir and shared with students both their love of song and the stories of why gospel music was an important tradition in their African American community. The teacher outlined the preteaching she did to set up the visit: looking at the history of slavery in the United States and making sure students knew about the Civil Rights Movement. One of the artists shared as she listened to the teacher, "I was very moved when I considered at their age the knowledge that I did not possess of my own history and my ancestry." The teacher responded, "Well, as you know my school is very homogenous. . . . And I know Donna and Rita [the artists] were disappointed at first to be paired with me, thinking 'Oh, this isn't our ideal group,' and I was like, 'No, this is the ideal group.'" (The artists laugh and nod heads, responding, "Oh, yes, absolutely.") The teacher continued, "These are the kids who need to know your story. . . . And I think the thing that was so compelling for me at the end of it, because the kids made a book of your history [titled 'Singing for Freedom'] with the stories that resonated with them after we processed their interview and thought about what we would want in a history book about Donna and Rita. It was a lot of the stories that showed our common humanity." She concluded, "Teaching the kids about what folklore is . . . we dissected the word, 'folk' and 'lore,' 'people' and 'stories.' And it was Columbus Day when we were working on this, so we started to ask, 'Whose stories are saved?' And so I pointed out [to my students], 'You've saved Donna and Rita's story, which has often been left out.' So it was a great connection to history, and it was really powerful for them. Now I intend on them being folklorists all the time!"

K–12 education is a specialized field that places many demands on those who want to engage with it. There are many barriers to participation by community members in the schools: student safety and privacy, state and federal testing and standards evaluation, funding formulas and policies beholden to special interests, and curricula designed in a cramped marketplace with narrow cultural windows. My experience suggests that these same barriers also often create classrooms inequitable for full participation by all students. Using my skills as a folklorist trained in ethnography, I am finding that there are important ways of asking significant questions that can help individual actors within challenging systems create new opportunities for growth, both for learning about oneself and exploring difference in meaningful ways.

What are some of the questions that we turn to most often at Local Learning? The following list encourages learners to grow in their knowledge of why it's important to pay attention to culture in their classroom:

"Tell me about a time when you learned something informally": Accessing information about what we learn in informal, often cultural ways makes our own cultural expertise and informal teachers a little clearer.

"What would be an example of a folk group in which you are an active member?": Identifying the groups that we associate with can invite a closer examination of folklife unique to our groups, including dress, foodways, special language, and beliefs. Many educators who take our professional development workshops come to learn *about* culture, not realizing that they, too, enjoy cultural memberships in many parts of their life.

"Describe some important people, jobs, and places in your community": In mapping our communities, we begin to see how multiple perceptions of the same space may exist. Taking this further to understand what makes some spaces "safer" or "more desirable" than others begins to help us understand our own subject positions within that map.

"What would be the cultural map of your school building?": This is a loaded question that is never the lead question but instead one that may sneak up on a cohort of teachers in a new way.

Folklore is often the visible expressions of culture that is acting invisibly. This matters in K–12 education. This matters for any student who hasn't seen her stories represented in the curriculum. This matters for any parent or grandparent who doesn't see his expertise having a stake in formal education. This matters for the artist or musician whose aesthetics or credentials are not recognized as "excellent" within the Western-defined canon. This matters for social justice and educational sovereignty. It matters when teachers realize that their curricula and classrooms are not neutral after meeting an artist who shares a deeply meaningful, relevant art form—one that has a context significant to histories that weren't in the class texts—and has taken years of learning, rather than an academic degree, to master the tradition.

I now edit the *Journal of Folklore and Education*. This peer-reviewed, digital journal of Local Learning publishes case studies and best practices and deepens cross-disciplinary understanding among folklorists, educators, and artists. We can demonstrate that the study of traditional arts and their creators contributes not only to students' understanding of culture and community but also to their ability to think critically, gather and analyze evidence, learn key social-emotional skills, and express their ideas and interpretations through personal creativity: all Common Core education standards. But beyond meeting standards, folk arts education helps students better understand multiple points of view in their communities and schools. This core value is a goal of Local Learning. Educators call such learning "soft skills," which also include empathy, tolerance of difference, and connectedness between home and school.

What will the future hold for K–12 education specialists with training and knowledge in folklore and its sister fields? After 2020, K–12 education will be forever changed. The acute disruptions due to COVID-19 and the larger movement of Black Lives Matter present immense opportunities that will require partnership, a reckoning with educational structures, and a need for expanding notions of whose expertise and history counts in our formal learning spaces. As I write today, for the first time since I assumed the executive director position at Local Learning, all our workshops are oversubscribed and have extensive waitlists. Teachers are seeking out knowledge about culture, the communities that are home to their students, and the ways to address the needs of today's world in their pedagogy and curricula. The tool kit of folklore and education can be used to build multicultural understanding, strengthen communities, and transform learning. It is an exciting time to be working with teachers in K–12 classrooms.

Expanding Definitions of Regional Cultural Heritage: Nicole Musgrave

Nicole Musgrave earned her MA in folk studies at Western Kentucky University and is an independent folklorist based in Whitesburg, Kentucky.

I came to work with Hindman Settlement School's cultural heritage program fresh out of graduate school, with David Whisnant's critical and cautionary tale from *All That Is Native and Fine: The Politics of Culture in an American Region* echoing in my head. The problematic history of the Hindman School that Whisnant presents—in which outsider cultural workers, primarily interested in the White, Anglo traditions that reflected their own upper-middle-class backgrounds and values, were catalysts for altering the culture they had set out to conserve—was not a history I wanted to repeat. But I worried that the use of the term *cultural heritage* to define the work would limit the kinds of expressive cultures and communities I could engage. However, as I settled into my work in eastern Kentucky, I found I was able to use my insight as a folklorist to expand conceptions around terms like *cultural heritage* and *traditional* to critically engage emergent traditions and groups historically underrepresented within Appalachia.

My work mostly entailed coordinating programming with local schools: in-school artist residencies, after-school traditional arts classes, and classroom projects that incorporated oral history. I also assisted with planning public programming around topics related to foodways and traditional arts, and I produced a radio show based on oral history interviews for our local community station. As I became more familiar with how these tasks had been approached in the past, I learned the emphasis was on canonical Appalachian traditional arts such as square dancing, old-time music, basket weaving, and quilting. During my time at the Settlement School, I found that the work I did could continue to value these forms of cultural heritage and also bring new forms into the fold.

While the early cultural heritage workers Whisnant chronicles largely ignored the interplay between mass culture and traditional culture in eastern Kentucky, in public programming I often highlighted the dialectical relationship between the two. One radio show I produced featured an interview with musician Shane Terry, who talked at length about the vibrant punk music tradition of eastern Kentucky and the DIY culture that has grown out of the network of young people who book and promote their own shows across the region. While punk is a music genre historically associated with cities like New York, Los Angeles, and London, musicians in eastern Kentucky have put their own mark on it, and they often note the similarity between punk rock and Appalachian protest music as vehicles for expressing dissent. I also worked with screen printer and musician Mike Slone to offer an after-school screen-printing course. During classes, Mike shared with students that he became interested in screen printing when he decided to start making T-shirts and other merchandise for his punk band to sell at local shows, as was the case for other screen printers in the area. We talked with students about the history of textile production in eastern Kentucky (specifically weaving and quilting) and how practices like screen printing can be seen as an extension of that history.

Along with advocating for the inclusion of emergent art forms within the category of Appalachian cultural heritage, I also advocated for the inclusion of traditions practiced by newcomer communities living in eastern Kentucky. In traditional art classes that focused on forms less often recognized as Appalachian cultural heritage, I engaged the teaching artists in informal narrative sessions to help students better understand the cultural context of what they were learning. For example, during an Appalachian heritage cooking course taught by Melanie Turner and Charlotte Case, we invited Mexican American Paulina Vazquez to a class to teach the students to make salsa. While the students were chopping ingredients, Paulina shared how she learned to make salsa from her grandmother and how her family used it. Paulina also talked about her family's history of immigrating to the United States from Mexico and how she came to live in eastern Kentucky. Melanie and Charlotte—both White—shared their memories of when they first ate Mexican food and when they first noticed Mexican restaurants opening in eastern Kentucky. We also talked about how making salsa ties into community practices of raising gardens and canning, and students shared about people in their families and communities who make salsa. Through this conversational mediation, I was able to create an environment where students and teaching artists shared their experiences and expertise with one another. Not only did this generate opportunities for deeper personal connection among students and instructors, but it also served as an entry point into discussing the political, social, and economic forces that lead to the cross-pollination between traditional expressive cultures.

In my work assisting with planning public events at the Settlement School, I advocated for the inclusion of local experts in programming. In recent history, the Settlement School's model for hosting events has often meant inviting more high-profile performers, chefs, writers, and scholars—those with name recognition in the region—to participate in programming as a way to drum up more interest. However, attendance tended to be limited to the same group of enthusiastic Settlement School devotees. With the goal of reaching a new and broader audience, I coordinated a narrative stage with two local seed savers for our inaugural "Seeds & Stories" event. The narrative stage centered the experiences of community experts and sparked a group conversation during which audience members shared their memories around seed saving and gardening. Since this event, the Settlement School has begun incorporating narrative stages into other activities.

The desire to better integrate local experts into Settlement School programming also guided the oral history projects I coordinated with teachers. In one project, I partnered with a high school arts and humanities teacher and an oral historian to explain to students the importance of oral history and show them examples of eastern Kentucky–based oral history projects such as Country Queers and the Eastern Kentucky African American Migration Project. In teams, students interviewed community members about a keepsake that was important to them and then used the documentation to create an online exhibition. Through the interviews, students learned about local traditions such as seed saving, weaving, blacksmithing, and bluegrass music. Like much folk-arts-in-education work, the project illuminated for students the significance of vernacular culture and the importance of the wisdom of tradition bearers while also equipping students with skills in documentation, writing, media production, and interpersonal interactions. In nearly all their project reflections, students noted the value of interviewing community members and hearing their stories.

While Whisnant depicts the early Hindman School workers (rightfully or not) as romantic cultural revivalists who were detached from the political, economic, and social realities of eastern Kentuckians, a goal of mine while at the school was to create more meaningful interactions with community members by using cultural heritage forms to address community issues. For example, the school collaborated with Culture of Recovery (CoR), a program of the Appalachian Artisan Center in Hindman, Kentucky, that partners with local recovery programs to offer art and craft classes in media such as blacksmithing, instrument making, and pottery, drawing on the region's craft traditions to promote creative expression, skill building, and economic opportunities for those in recovery from substance use disorder. I served as a documentarian for CoR for over a year, during which I learned how engagement in craft traditions was a valuable part of participants' recovery processes. Participants often expressed how important it was to partake in activities that allowed them to have fun and build relationships while sober. After hearing this sentiment several times and knowing that CoR values utilizing regionally important art forms, I partnered CoR with the Settlement School to host a square dance at an all-male residential recovery center. Family and community members were invited to share in the festivities. Not only did the men at the center dance with their children, partners, and mothers, but they also danced with each other, subverting gender expectations that are often barriers to recovery. It was gratifying to witness the joy and be able to expand the Settlement School's cultural heritage work to connect with a new community.

In my time working as a cultural heritage specialist in eastern Kentucky, I've been able to leverage my training and experience in folklore to diversify the practices, artists, and communities that receive institutional recognition and support, and I've been able to help highlight the ways cultural heritage forms can be used to address current issues. While Whisnant and I are both writing about cultural work within Appalachia, folklorists in every region must be careful not to uncritically reproduce the same cultural forms that have always received attention and should take intentional steps to ensure their work is actively engaged with the social, economic, and political realities of the individuals and communities they serve.

MENTORING: WANDA G. ADDISON

Wanda G. Addison earned her PhD in English at the University of Louisiana and is Professor of English at National University.

I am always a folklorist. Regardless of what I am writing or teaching, folklore studies has laid my fundamental course. Not because I write only about folklore or teach only folklore classes; I do not. My folklore work is that of connection, of exploring home and place, along with widening perspectives and possibilities. Mentoring is similarly positioned; like folklore, mentoring speaks directly to the connection of one person to another, and it is the practice of humanity.

Mentor, counselor, advisor, teacher, or guide: regardless of the title, the role is similar—one of lighting a path. I cannot say with certainty when I became interested in mentoring, but my road here has been paved with good mentors. In thinking about who mentors, oftentimes we consider it something we do outside our normal jobs or expectations. However, when I reflect on my earliest memories of mentoring experiences, it seems clear that mentoring is interlocked with whatever activity we are doing. I recall the mentorship of my mother and a high school guidance counselor, although I did not understand either to be mentoring at the time. Seemingly, the former was doing what was expected of parents and the latter what was required by the position. My mother's steadfast, loving, and supportive hand was not only parenting, it was preparing and laying a foundation for me to envision a broader path, and it continued into my adulthood, urging contemplation and offering guidance. The mentoring I received from the guidance counselor ultimately expanded upon what I had received at home by addressing everything from effective test-taking strategies and preparatory high school classes to discussions of college and other opportunities after high school. So, while his job was to counsel, in this mentoring situation, he offered direction for a scarcely considered path.

In the years that followed, I gravitated toward opportunities to offer guidance to others. Such occasions frequently came via opportunities to serve as a workplace trainer and facilitator. Whether through classroom instruction or as an on-the-job trainer or coach, mentoring meshed seamlessly as I worked with adult learners focusing on their futures.

During my prefolklore career, working as instructor and facilitator was greatly rewarding, especially helping those new or struggling in their assignments to thrive. This points to what is at the heart of my dedication to mentoring: I do not want anyone to feel like she is floundering or without direction and left behind. I want everyone to experience success in their own terms. If mentoring or facilitating a mentoring connection achieves this goal, I am wholeheartedly onboard. I am passionate about mentoring. Investing in others through time, effort, and attention—knowing the impact it may have—is gratifying. Mentoring is a lifeline, and it brings me joy to reach out and uplift others on their journey. It is about giving back; it is an act of service, of sharing and helping.

Once I began pursuing folklore studies as an adult learner, I was reminded of the importance of good mentors; I was fortunate to have had several of them. Becoming a member of the American Folklore Society (AFS) reinforced the significance of mentoring for all who are navigating new spaces. I began my tenure on the AFS Mentoring Committee in 2017. Committee members, in part, were charged with seeking out AFS members interested in becoming mentors to early-career folklorists who wanted a mentor. This seemingly simple act of mentoring fulfilled the needs of many early-career professionals. Mentoring helped those unsure—about where to begin, how to proceed, who to ask, how to shift gears, or what happens next—find connections. The work of the committee helped create a larger footprint for formalized mentoring throughout AFS. The act of mentoring offers a bit of light on a path, with mentors extending insight and guidance on navigating a path they have previously trod. The foundation for my work on the committee was forged many years prior.

When I mentor, I am building a bridge from a past to a future. The past and future are mine as I share my lived experiences and knowledge as well as that of my ancestors with someone who is likewise sharing those things from her life with me. Mentoring—not the act but the aftermath—is reciprocal. As a mentor, I am enriched by what is shared with me and the hoped-for benefit of what I have been able to give.

Three of my recent mentoring opportunities offer examples of the expanding need for diverse approaches to mentoring. First, I served as mentor for an international doctoral student whose work in African American literature and the cultural history and literary tradition of a marginalized group of women in her community intersected with my work in folklore and literary studies. She primarily wanted guidance on her research, so we discussed theoretical frameworks and research availability. Such a highly focused mentoring encounter speaks to meeting the needs of the person being mentored. After completing her doctorate, the student recently contacted me to share additional goals and ask questions. I will continue to follow up with her, giving whatever guidance and light I can impart for her path.

A second opportunity was the inaugural mentoring breakout sessions hosted at the American Folklore Society's 2019 annual conference.

Recognizing that mentors are needed at various stages in professional lives, our mentoring committee group created mentoring opportunities around varied positions and topics in the profession, from new professional, to mid-career, to mentoring and men. While I served as the facilitator of the event, each group session was led by an expert in the mentoring area of focus, creating collaborative mentoring conversations. In this dynamic space, participants could move from one conversation to another based on their needs while also allowing later one-on-one conversations to evolve.

Third is my work with students for my institution's Black History Month program in 2020. These students were performing a short play they had written that pondered the challenges of the past and present for Black Americans. I was asked to play the role of a wise ancestor responding to their fears, frustrations, and dreams. Speaking of thought process, vision, motivation, resilience, and action, I was able to mentor the students in the play as well as those in the audience through this short performance. In addition, my presence as an African American woman in that professional space served as a powerful visual reminder reinforcing the words I shared in the role.

The same empathy, attentiveness, and foresight honed during my folklore studies and brought to my folklore work are integral to what I am able to provide when mentoring. Mentoring is a vibrant act taking place in formal and informal ways. Every opportunity holds a potential for mentoring. Mentoring centers those who are on the periphery of their fields, careers, or studies: those who may be wondering where to turn. The power of mentoring lies in the ability to help someone turn another page, open a new door, or bring clarity to their current direction. Mentoring offers opportunities for deeper self-reflection and strategic planning. Instead of a telescopic view, it offers a broader lens and a big-picture perspective. My training as a folklorist is a critical foundation for my approach to mentoring.

Preserving Historic Buildings and Environments: Laurie Kay Sommers

Laurie Kay Sommers earned her PhD in folklore at Indiana University and works as an independent consultant in folklore and historic preservation.

If you had told me thirty years ago that I would be asked to write about employment in folklore and historic preservation, I would have laughed. When I was beginning my career in the 1970s and 1980s, the two fields often occupied parallel universes. I was an undergraduate music major, but my love of history and the environmental movement led me to electives in historic preservation, volunteering with the Michigan State Historic Preservation Office (SHPO), and working on a SHPO contract. When it came time for graduate school, I was torn between music and historic preservation but decided to pursue ethnomusicology at Indiana University's folklore department; since I was already working in preservation, I thought I could always return. That proved to be true, but not in the way I envisioned.

I pursued my graduate work in ethnomusicology and folklore while funding my tuition with contract work in historic preservation. I soon realized that while I could infuse my required historic context statements with folklore content, I would lose time and money by doing so. Preservation work at the time meant archival research on historic and architectural significance. As a young folklorist fresh from the Michigan SHPO, I imagined a people-centric, rather than building-centric, approach to place and preservation. I wanted to know how buildings were used and what they meant to people. I wouldn't have the opportunity to realize that vision until much later in my career.

After completing my PhD, I considered employment in historic preservation, but the Michigan Civil Service application automatically disqualified persons with a folklore degree. It didn't matter that I had been a preferred contractor with the SHPO while completing my doctorate! This dichotomy between folklore and historic preservation shaped my career—and the two fields—for the next three decades. Although I felt I had the tools and expertise to craft an integrative model of folklore and historic preservation that (in the lingo of historic preservation) included both tangible and intangible cultural resources, that door seemed closed. For most of my professional life, I worked as a public-sector folklorist and ethnomusicologist and pursued projects in traditional music. Periodically, however, I've had the opportunity to use my folklore skills in preservation-related projects. I'll highlight three examples as illustrations of what folklorists do.

In 1989, a team of folklorists at the Michigan State University Museum assessed the cultural impact of siting a low-level radioactive waste disposal facility as part of a larger environmental assessment study, which we reported on in an essay in the 1994 book *Conserving Culture: A New Discourse on Heritage*. Inclusion of folklife into a project of this kind was groundbreaking. With my background in historic preservation and folklore, I developed methodology to survey folklife and historic resources based on criteria in the National Register of Historic Places, in particular the National Park Service's Bulletin 38, *Guidelines for Evaluating and Documenting Traditional Cultural Properties*, then in draft form. This was the first bulletin to address folklife and intangible cultural resources within the National Register process.

Creating methodology was the easy part. The difficulty was that many local people viewed us as the "enemy" (even the "Devil Himself" in a widely distributed poison-pen letter). I have done a lot of contract fieldwork; based on that experience, most people are pleased to share their traditional culture. I'd never worked in a community so hostile both to researchers and to the very idea of documenting folklife, which they viewed as an insignificant and ineffective strategy for protecting their families and farms from a perceived threat. In the face of these obstacles, we turned to something folklorists have always done well: we used the report to amplify their voices. We came to understand that one of our primary responsibilities was to reflect the beliefs and values of area residents, despite their distrust.

In 2010, I was part of a team hired to complete a Historic Structures Report (HSR) for Fishtown, a historic but still active working waterfront in Leland, Michigan, that combines a National Register Historic District with a distinctive cultural landscape. HSRs are important preservation planning tools; they provide an overview of a site's historic character, an assessment of the physical condition of the structures and landscape, and proposed treatment alternatives. The client, Fishtown Preservation, was a rare organization with both a folklorist and a preservation professional at the helm. They chose me because I could help them realize their vision for integrating folklore into the preservation and interpretation of Fishtown: they wanted to discover more about the uses of the buildings and the many fishermen and their families who worked in them, not about just historic changes to Fishtown's weathered wood shanties and icehouses. I used archival sources and oral interviews to recreate Fishtown's historic footprint over time and my ethnographic skills as a folklorist to bring to life the stories, sights, smells, and traditions of the working waterfront. Our publication, *The River Runs Through It: Report on Historic Structures and Site Design in the Fishtown Cultural Landscape*, reenvisioned Fishtown not as a static historic district (with a period of significance fixed in the past) but rather as a dynamic cultural landscape that evokes a rich sense of place today.

My final example involves the Preserving Nordic American Heritage Churches Project, for which I served as project manager from 2018 to 2020. We focused on Danish, Finnish, Icelandic, Norwegian, and Swedish heritage churches in six Upper Midwest states. The project is an initiative of Partners for Sacred Places (PSP). Although PSP is well-known for its historic preservation work, the Nordic churches project was their first engagement with folk arts. Again, I was hired because I had expertise in both folklore and historic preservation and—as a Michigander—knowledge of the Upper Midwest. Like many of our nation's sacred places, churches built by Nordic American communities are increasingly at risk due to shrinking populations, leading to fewer resources to care for buildings and the decorative arts (including folk arts) they contain. The Nordic American Churches Project addressed these concerns with two strategies: a searchable online inventory to build awareness and encourage study of Nordic American heritage churches, and support for sixteen churches to help them preserve their buildings and sustain their presence in their communities.

Unlike my other examples, this project was internet based rather than field based. We emphasized the historic folk art and craft preserved in these churches. As project manager and folklorist, I infused a folklore perspective wherever I could. Churches invited to apply to the project have both folklore and preservation attributes: historic and architectural integrity, (folk) artistry in decorative arts, and continuity of ethnic traditions. The online inventory we created, the Nordic American Churches Database (http://www .nordicamericanchurches.org), likewise includes information about arts and traditions in addition to facts about location, ethnicity, denomination, and historic and architectural features. To highlight folklore content on the project website, I selected images for the home page that combined folk art and customs with architectural features and created a Folk Arts and Traditions tab that links illustrated essays on various topics: Woodwork and Carvers; Painting and Painters; Traditional Textiles; and Food, Festival, and Recipes. It was more challenging to integrate folklore directly into the project-support component, since participating churches often chose restoration or repair projects for things like leaky roofs rather than refurbishing historic folk carvings. And although the sixteen churches continue an array of calendar customs, smorgasbords, lutefisk and meatball suppers, and aebleskiver breakfasts, the project funder wanted grants to support historic preservation, not preservation of traditions. In the end, folk culture received indirect support since participating churches received training in fundraising and community engagement designed to ensure that churches (and their folk heritage) remain viable.

These examples illustrate a folklorist's approach to preservation of place. We need more models and more cross-disciplinary collaboration and conversation. Places matter because they are meaningful to the people who use them, and meaning derives from tradition, memory, and story. In my experience, this is what folklorists can and should do.

ABOUT THE EDITOR

TIMOTHY LLOYD is the Senior Advisor for Partnerships of the American Folklore Society and was the society's executive director from 2001 to 2018. Before coming to AFS, he spent his career at the Library of Congress and the Smithsonian Institution, in the state governments of Maryland and Ohio, and in the nonprofit sector. He also served as AFS executive secretary-treasurer from 1986 to 1991. He is affiliated with the Center for Folklore Studies at The Ohio State University and the Department of Folklore and Ethnomusicology at Indiana University.

Dr. Lloyd earned his BA in comparative literature and anthropology and his MA in design at The Ohio State University, studied folklore at UCLA, and earned his PhD in American studies and folklore at The George Washington University. His research interests include cultural heritage policy, foodways, occupational culture, and the history of folklore studies.

He has taught and lectured in the United States and internationally, has published articles and reviews in the major American folklore journals, is a Fellow of the American Folklore Society, has served as a board and committee member or consultant for organizations and government agencies in the United States and abroad, and is the coauthor (with Patrick B. Mullen) of *Lake Erie Fishermen: Work, Identity, and Tradition*. He is also a professional drummer and percussionist.

www.ingramcontent.com/pod-product-compliance
Lightning Source LLC
Chambersburg PA
CBHW020242290326
41929CB00045B/1486